**Discrimination in
Rural Housing**

Discrimination in Rural Housing

Economic and Social Analysis of Six Selected Markets

Janet K. Marantz
Karl E. Case II
Herman B. Leonard

Urban Systems Research and
Engineering, Inc.

Lexington Books

D.C. Heath and Company
Lexington, Massachusetts
Toronto   London

Library of Congress Cataloging in Publication Data

Marantz, Janet.
 Discrimination in rural housing.

 Bibliography: p.
 1. Housing, Rural—United States. 2. Discrimination in housing—
United States. I. Case, Karl, joint author.
II. Leonard, Herman, joint author. III. Title.
HD7289.U6M37   301.5'4'0973   75-42911
ISBN 0-669-00557-6

Copyright © 1976 by D.C. Heath and Company

Published simultaneously in Canada

Printed in the United States of America

International Standard Book Number: 0-669-00557-6

Library of Congress Catalog Card Number: 75-42911

Contents

List of Figures

List of Tables

Table

Acknowledgments

Janet Marantz served as project director and was primarily responsible for the institutional analysis. Karl Case and Herman Leonard were primarily responsible for the economic analysis. However, this study could not have been written without the cooperation and assistance of a number of people. The work was performed under the careful supervision of E. Quinton Gordon of HUD's Office of Policy Development and Research. In addition, Cushing Dolbeare served as a consultant to the project, providing information, insights, and assistance throughout. Harrison C. White, chairman of the Department of Sociology, Harvard University, also provided thorough review and incisive commentary at several stages of the effort. The economic analysis owes much to the previous work of John F. Kain, Department of Economics, Harvard University.

Marilyn Swartz-Lloyd, whose specialty is planning and housing policy, assisted in the series of site visits on which the institutional analysis is based. Molly Beals and Linda Coventry served ably as research assistants to the project. Karen MacKenzie, Margi Robison and Jayne Neisloss were its efficient and good-humored secretaries, and Claire Nivola provided graphic design.

Finally, and perhaps most obviously, the project is indebted to some 200 housing market participants on the six sites who agreed to be interviewed, as well as county assessors and other officials who permitted access to their records. Much of this work is based on information provided by these respondents. While they must remain anonymous, their cooperation is gratefully acknowledged.

Discrimination in
Rural Housing

1 Introduction

Discrimination in urban housing markets is a much-studied phenomenon; discrimination in rural markets is not. It is clear from simple Census tabulations and from even the most cursory on-site observation that rural housing in the aggregate is inferior to urban housing, and equally clear that rural minority and female-headed households tend to live in worse housing than white male-headed households. This study is intended to determine whether and to what extent this situation is the result of discrimination.

Objectives of the Study

The study addresses two major questions, each of which can be further divided into a number of subsidiary and corollary inquiries. The two major questions are:

1. *Whether* there is unequal access to housing in rural areas for minorities and women and, if so, of what form and magnitude; and
2. *How* such inequality as may be observed is brought about and maintained.

The issue of *whether* unequal access exists encompasses a number of specific inquiries. First, is there systematic residential segregation of minorities and/or female-headed households? Secondly, where segregation exists, is there a segmented or "dual" market with price differentials for comparable housing in comparable neighborhoods, the latter differing only by racial composition? In addition, the study examines whether minorities and women are differentially excluded from homeownership, and thus from an equity base and from the tax savings which constitute the nation's major housing subsidy. Finally, the study inquires into special problems faced by women and minorities, especially the aged, in retaining ownership of housing and land.[1]

The question of *how* unequal access is brought about and maintained involves an examination of the rural housing market as an institution—i.e., a set of regularized patterns of interaction—in order to identify those mechanisms or processes by which market activities result in inequality. The emphasis throughout the study is on *institutionalized* discrimination, i.e., systematic and recurring patterns of inequality. Single, scattered and nonrecurring instances of discrimination—viz, those which are not institutionalized—are of lesser interest

1

because they do not contribute to an understanding of systematic inequality or to an attempt to account for large differentials in access to housing. The factors that may impede access to housing on a nondiscriminatory basis are of three types:

1. *Direct Discrimination:* This refers to direct denial of equal access to housing, including the ability to retain tenure, on the basis of race or sex. Examples of this factor would be refusal by homeowners to sell or rent to minorities and/or women; refusal of brokerage services or financing on an equal basis; inequalities in municipal services or zoning; and community customs ("unwritten laws") which specify segregated neighborhoods or other forms of inequality.

2. *Indirect or By-Product Discrimination:* This refers to actions which are not in themselves directly discriminatory but which, given the context in which they occur, have this effect. Examples would include some public program guidelines and resulting allocation of efforts; builders' concentration on housing which does not meet the needs of women and minorities in terms of cost, design or location, but which best serves the rational economic incentives of the builder; and conflict between town and county governments which results in stalemate on public services and thus lack of new construction and freezing of current (unequal) occupancy patterns.

3. *Internalized Discrimination:* This refers to actions, or lack of action, on the part of minority or female-headed households which result from the expectation that discrimination will be practiced against them. It would include failure to seek housing or credit, or to initiate political or legal actions to counter discrimination and intimidation.

The remainder of this introductory chapter outlines briefly the conceptual structure and the methods by which the study addresses these questions, and presents the major features of the six rural areas in which the work was performed.

Conceptual Structure of the Study

The conceptual structure underlying the study is diagrammed in figure 1-1. Market "outcomes" are those features of an area's housing occupancy which are directly observable, and whose inequality raises the question of possible discrimination. Most obviously, the outcomes of a housing market are transactions (or lack of transactions). The results of these are observable tenure patterns: ownership vs. renting, design and quality of housing occupied, and location of housing occupied. In addition, market outcomes include prices and contract rents paid for housing. Analysis of market outcomes—the "whether" of inequality—lends itself to economic and statistical methods.

The "how" of inequality is addressed through analysis of the rural housing

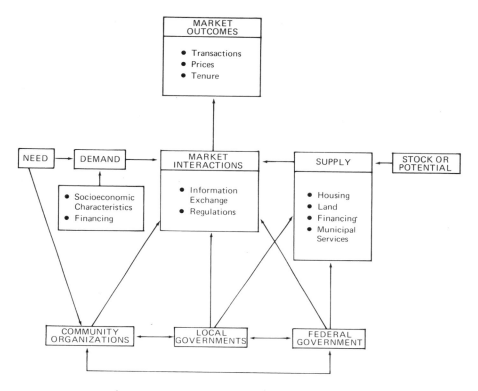

Figure 1-1. Elements of a Housing Market

market as an institution. An institution may be seen as an habitual procedure: a regular pattern of behavior among persons. It may be formalized as a corporate entity, a law, an association, etc. Many institutions, however, are not formalized: they include customs, widely-shared preconceptions (viz, "community pressure"), etc. Institutional analysis deals, therefore, *both* with the acts of individuals—housing consumers, managers of lending institutions, etc.—*and* with the supra-individual pressures by which such acts may be influenced—law, corporate policy, custom, etc. Institutional analysis is thus the construction of a "map" of the economic and social dynamics of the housing market. It begins with a functional definition of the actors comprising the market and then identifies the patterns of interaction among them.

The following is a typology of the actors whose behavior influences and is influenced by a rural housing market. In each case, examples are given to illustrate the functional category being defined. It is obvious, however, that a given type of individual or organization may play more than one role, or play on a given site a different role than the one indicated here. Such choices of roles on the part of specific actors are among the topics examined in this study.

Functional definition of actors permits analysis of unexpected or multiple choice of roles on the part of a specific actor. For instance, a broker may also function as a supplier (builder), a local government may be both a supplier and an intervener, etc. In addition, such definition *discourages the automatic identification of an organization with a function.* For instance, the function of information exchange is often identified with real estate brokers; this study found, however, that the communication function is more often performed by informal means than through brokers. As another example, an Indian Tribe was found to perform many of the functions of a community organization, although it is legally a local government.

Typology of Housing Market Actors

1. *Consumers (the "need" and "demand" elements of the market).* Consumers are those who purchase, wish to purchase, need to but choose not to purchase or otherwise acquire housing; and those who own or rent and wish to retain housing. Examples:
    a. Households (owners, purchasers, renters, sharecroppers, "squatters," etc.)
    b. Nonresidential owners, purchasers or claimants (agribusinesses, extractive industries, land speculators, etc.)
2. *Suppliers (the "supply" and "stock" elements of the market).* Suppliers are those who hold and may make available housing itself, or the requisite intermediary products and services. Examples:
    a. Sellers and lessors.
    b. Builders, developers and contractors.
    c. Lenders and loan guarantors.
    d. Suppliers of public services and utilities.
3. *Interveners (include the bottom three elements of the market diagram: community organizations, local governments, federal government).* Interveners are those who attempt to affect market activities so as to shift the distribution of social benefits. Examples:
    a. Formal and informal associations of consumers or suppliers.
    b. Publically- and privately-sponsored housing programs.
    c. Public bodies with the power to tax, regulate, zone, and/or assess value.
    d. Legislators, executives and courts at the local, state, and federal levels, i.e., those who make, enforce and interpret law, as well as those who specify, interpret and apply guidelines.
    e. The local social and political elites, and locally-effective divisions of regional or national organizations.

Housing market interactions include not only those occurring directly between suppliers and consumers, but also the interactions occurring among other elements of the market. Those occurring directly between suppliers and consumers, and labeled "market interactions" in figure 1-1, are the interactions customarily considered market activities. These are effected (and affected) by communications systems, by which consumers and suppliers learn of one another, and by the regulations which define permissible interactions. The latter may be laws and formal rules and guidelines; they may also be customs and tradition.

Other types of interactions may occur between actors in the housing market. Those most commonly encountered in this study are indicated in figure 1-1 by arrows connecting market elements. Consumers whose need cannot be translated into effective demand because of formal or informal market regulations may use community organizations to change the rules or to pressure local or federal governments to do so. Local governments may intervene directly in market interactions by setting regulations and also serve as suppliers of municipal services. The federal government may intervene in either the supply side or the regulation of the market, possibly as a result of interaction with local governments or community organizations.

Many more types of interactions are possible, of course. This discussion has attempted to outline the structure and define the terms in which the study was conducted and its findings presented. In all cases, the analysis of housing market actors and interactions focuses on identifying patterns of activity which are in intent or in effect discriminatory, and which thus serve to account for inequalities in market outcomes—prices and tenure patterns.

Study Methods

In order to address the questions of whether discrimination exists in rural housing markets and, if so, how it is effected and maintained, detailed analyses were conducted of six rural housing markets. (For purposes of this study, a "rural" market is defined as a county containing no town of over 10,000 population in 1970, and none of whose borders is within 50 miles of an SMSA.) Four of these are in the South—Arkansas, Georgia, North Carolina, and Tennessee— and have black minorities; one is in South Dakota with an American Indian minority; and the sixth is in New Mexico with a substantial Spanish-surnamed population. All selected sites have 9 percent or more female-headed households (see table 1-1).

Four major types of analysis were undertaken:

1. Analysis of market prices of housing recently sold, to test for differentials which would suggest a dual or segmented market.

Table 1-1
Minority Population and Female-Headed Households in Six Study Sites

| | ARKANSAS | | GEORGIA | | NEW MEXICO | |
	County	Town	County	Town	County	Town
1970 POPULATION:	24,976	6,191	17,858	9,091	12,170	6,962
% Minority	30%	27%	21%	29%	55%	NA
% Female-Headed Households	10%	7%	13%	18%	12%	14%

| | N.CAROLINA | | S. DAKOTA | | TENNESSEE | |
	County	Town	County	Town	County	Town
1970 POPULATION:	24,730	6,570	11,678	3,094	23,749	9,892
% Minority	45%	46%	13%	24%	13%	19%
% Female-Headed Households	13%	11%	9%	17%	10%	15%

Source: U.S. Census. Unless otherwise specified, all population, employment, income and housing figures in this Chapter are drawn from the U.S. Census of Population and Housing.

2.   An examination of detailed household data from the Census Public Use Sample to identify the characteristics of occupants of substandard housing.

3.   An analysis of statewide Census data to determine whether the likelihood of owning in lieu of renting varies systematically by race or sex, while controlling for other socioeconomic attributes.

4.   Open-ended interviews with all identifiable housing market actors to uncover forms of inequality (e.g., retention problems) not identified in the above analyses, and to identify the actors and the patterns of interaction in the housing market which contribute to unequal access.

All needed data (with the exception of Census data) were gathered on-site. For the purpose of testing for price differentials, three types of information were collected. *Market prices* of housing which had recently changed hands in an open-market transaction (excluding intrafamily transfers, wills, foreclosures, etc.) were obtained from deeds, tax records, and real estate agents. Detailed *structural characteristics* (including age and condition) of these units were obtained from county assessors' records. Finally, detailed *neighborhood characteristics*, including level of municipal services, applicable zoning regulations, general type, age and condition of housing, and neighborhood racial composition were gathered from town governments, personal observation, and interviews with local persons familiar with the housing market. Where racial segregation existed, neighborhood boundaries were drawn by knowledgeable local respondents and verified by personal observation.

Information concerning housing market actors and interactions was all obtained from open-ended interviews with local respondents. All regular actors in the housing market were interviewed: these included builders, real estate agents, commercial banks, savings & loan associations, major landowners, mobile home dealers and park owners, town and county government officials (especially those concerned with planning, zoning, building inspection, and public services), directors of local housing authorities, county supervisors of the Farmers Home Administration, and heads of housing-related community organizations.

Other interviews were conducted which attempted to characterize the level and type of need on the part of consumers: community organizations, ministers and other recognized community spokespersons, county welfare directors and administrators of social service programs, as well as selected consumers suggested by these respondents, or identified at random.[a] Finally, an overview of housing market conditions and operations was sought from such respondents as newspaper editors, staff of nearby universities or other research-oriented organizations, retired housing market actors, etc.

Information obtained from these interviews was woven into a case study of each of the six areas which details the structure, operations and output of its housing market. The case studies and individual interviews were then subjected to cross-site analysis to uncover the frequently recurring patterns of interaction, with emphasis on those which tend to result in unequal access to housing.

It need hardly be stressed that the conclusions derived from studies of six markets cannot be safely generalized to "rural America" as a whole. Site screening procedures were designed to select areas which were, if not precisely representative, at least not obviously anomalous in comparison with other rural counties in the same state. The proportion of minority population approximates that of the rural portion of the state as a whole, as does the rate of minority population change in comparison with white population trends. These site selection criteria were applied in order to avoid predictably "special" cases. One consequence of this is that none of the areas has a very low or unusually high minority population. The potentially different housing market operations of a town with, say, a black majority, were therefore not included within this study.

---

[a]A structured sample survey of consumers was beyond the scope of this study. The analysis of the social processes or mechanisms of the housing market is a qualitative study and does not require quantified need or demand data. It is more useful to characterize the types of need and demand and the reasons for which need may fail to translate into demand than it is to quantify the magnitude of need or demand. For this purpose, the insights of articulate community representatives, verified by talks with selected consumers, are more useful.

Similarly, no market with a small Spanish-surnamed minority was included, since Spanish-surnamed typically outnumber other whites in rural New Mexico.

The economic analyses present evidence which is statistically significant in the areas studied. There is some regularity of results across sites which suggests that the patterns may in fact be more generally true, but no such claim is made here. For the institutional analyses, attention was focused on recurrent patterns of interaction which underlie systematic inequality on one or more of the six sites. As with market outcomes, some of the institutional patterns were so frequently encountered across the six sites that more general applicability might in fact be the case, but this study's findings are meant to apply only to the areas visited.

Profiles of Six Selected Markets

Each site studied consists of a county located at least 50 miles from the nearest SMSA, and centered on a town of under 10,000 population. All the sites are distinctly rural, but only one is primarily agricultural. As an indication of the economic base of each area, table 1-2 presents the sectoral distribution of employment in 1970. The Georgia and Arkansas sites are primarily timber-producing, and have recently become substantially industrialized with wood-products manufacturers. The North Carolina and Tennessee sites have been traditionally agricultural, although they also have begun to industrialize recently with labor-intensive industries such as textiles and small auto parts manufacture. The New Mexico site is a ranching and mining area, which is now attempting to expand its resort sector. The South Dakota site is a farming area whose employment base is augmented by public administration in connection with the Indian tribe and the Bureau of Indian Affairs.

The areas are all comparatively poor and most show substantial net out-migration and absolute population decline. Among minorities, median income is lower, percentage of families in poverty is higher and population decline more severe than for whites. Table 1-3 shows median income and poverty status by race in 1970.[b] The relative incidence of poverty follows the pattern indicated by median incomes, and comparisons with the national incidence are somewhat more meaningful in this context because of the Census Bureau's corrections for cost-of-living differences. The percentage of families in poverty was everywhere substantially above the national proportion (11 percent), and the percentage of minority and female-headed families in poverty was consistently even higher.

---

[b]No simple comparison of incomes among areas or with the national median is intended here, since regional and urban/rural cost-of-living differences would affect real income. (National median income in 1970 was $9,586-$9,987 for white families and $6,063 for blacks.) These and other income figures are included merely to provide an order-of-magnitude description of income patterns among and within sites.

Table 1-2
Sectoral Distribution of County Employment, 1970

	AR	GA	NM	NC	SD	TN	National
Employed Civilian Labor Force:	8047	6462	3985	8449	3845	8778	76,553,599
Agriculture and Forestry	10%	8%	9%	16%	37%	7%	4%
Manufacturing	40%	34%	9%	25%	3%	32%	26%
Trade and Services	23%	27%	27%	28%	23%	30%	28%
Construction	6%	8%	10%	7%	6%	6%	6%
Education and Public Administration	8%	10%	16%	11%	15%	8%	13%
All Other	13%	13%	29%	13%	16%	17%	23%
	100%	100%	100%	100%	100%	100%	100%

Table 1-3
Family Income Status, 1970, by County

	AR	GA	NM	NC	SD	TN
Median Income:						
Total	$6,491	$6,908	$6,596	$5,711	$5,630	$5,980
White	7,752	7,741	NA	7,431	5,879	6,323
Minority	2,991	3,926	5,720	3,574	NA	4,015
Percentage in Poverty:						
Total	25%	22%	20%	29%	20%	22%
Minority	59	52	30	52	NA	41
Female-Headed	60	46	42	53	47	48

Most of the areas show the outmigration which has been characteristic of rural areas, with many people, especially the educated young, leaving the area in search of suitable employment *and*, according to local respondents, in search of acceptable housing. All the areas but Tennessee showed net outmigration ranging from -13 percent to -23 percent during the 1960s. Tennessee is an exception because the county contains a lakefront resort area which is attracting a retirement population. The inmigration to this county is accounted for largely by this elderly and entirely white population. Tennessee as well as New Mexico and the other three counties with black minorities all showed absolute decreases in minority population, ranging from -1 percent to -18 percent, while white population change showed no particular regularity among areas. South Dakota is the only area where minority population showed an absolute increase. This reflects the fact that Indians have been returning to their home area in increasing numbers in the last decade, although the small size of the increase (4 percent) indicates that outmigration is continuing concurrently.

The absolute change figures given in table 1-4 indicate that very substantial net outmigration of blacks has been occurring in the southern areas. As an indication of the natural increase against which these total change figures must be weighed, the black population of the United States increased 20 percent over the decade 1960-1970. The national increase in white population during that time was 12 percent, which suggests that all areas except Tennessee and perhaps Arkansas have shown net outmigration of whites as well.

Typically, the towns have shown less outmigration than the surrounding counties and in some cases appear to have experienced net inmigration. Population figures for the towns are not given here, since the propensity of towns to increase through annexation often makes the Census figures misleading. Local respondents report, however, that several of the towns, especially the more industrialized sites in Arkansas and Georgia, have been drawing white population in from outside the area, while black population continues to decline in both the county and the town. In addition, these two towns and the North Carolina town as well show some turnover in population as industry personnel (predominantly white professionals) are transferred into and out of the area.

Each of the towns visited contained an almost complete range of housing market actors. All had three or more real estate agencies; several large builders and numerous independent housing contractors; at least one commercial bank and one savings and loan association (and several had two of each); a local housing authority and an office of the Farmers Home Administration. (Notable by their absence were private mortgage credit companies and large-scale housing developers.) This population of actors was somewhat surprising in light of the

Table 1-4
County Population Change, 1960-1970

	AR	GA	NM	NC	SD	TN
Total Change:	756	−63	−1,636	−2,409	−1,512	1,474
Total % Change:	3%	0%	−12%	−9%	−12%	7%
White % Change:	14%	0%	−14%*	0%	−14%	9%
Non-White % Change:	−15%	−1%	−10%	−18%	4%	−6%
Net Migration:	−13%	−15%	−23%	−21%	−22%	5%

*Includes Spanish-surnamed

fact that at least half of the rural counties in the United States do not have a local housing authority, many lack S&L's, etc. It is probably accounted for by the preference given in site selection to counties with towns as close as possible to the 10,000 population limit.

A brief summary of the major features of the sites and their housing markets follows.

Arkansas. This site was, until recently, a company town, planned and built by the company, which is still the leading employer and owner of practically all developable land. Racial segregation is complete, and the black "community" is unorganized and passive. However, since company-built housing was sold to tenants on very reasonable terms, this site showed the highest levels of housing quality and of homeownership among those visited.

Georgia. This site, a timber-producing area recently industrialized, showed the lowest level of political activity and the lowest level of apparent interest in housing issues of those visited. Residential segregation of blacks is unchallenged; involvement with federal subsidy programs is limited; and very little market activity is occurring. This is a case of a remarkably stable social situation—a study in "the dynamics of nonactivity."

New Mexico. This site is a ranching, mining, and tourism area with a substantial Spanish-surnamed population. No evidence of ethnic discrimination in housing was uncovered, although the Spanish-surnamed are disproportionately poor and suffer poorer housing conditions. This situation is perpetuated by constraints on new development, which tend to freeze current occupancy patterns, especially for the low income. The Spanish-surnamed do not complain of ethnic discrimination, and have resisted appeals from the more militant Hispanic organizations in the Southwest.

North Carolina. This site, a tobacco-growing area recently industrializing, has a large black population and much severely deteriorated housing. It is the only southern site visited which has had active civil rights demonstrations, and the black population is becoming organized and vocal. While most attention is focused on employment discrimination, blacks are also protesting plans for urban renewal in a black neighborhood. Other housing-related problems (including the virtually complete segregation) have not as yet received attention.

South Dakota; This site, partially covered by a Sioux reservation, is the most economically depressed of those visited. Indians suffer extreme poverty and poor housing conditions, both exacerbated by discrimination. The town has been unsuccessful in seeking federal redevelopment monies, although the tribe has provided federally-sponsored housing and other services to members, and is currently attempting to regain some of the Indian lands which have been lost or sold over the years. Hostility among some whites and some Indians is visible and strong, and has resulted in open and occasionally violent confrontations.

Tennessee. This site, located in the rolling farm country of western Tennessee, has a long history of segregation and discrimination against blacks, and a dominant but largely invisible white "power structure." Federal housing-related programs have been resisted, though respondents are not quite sure by whom; the same is true of privately-initiated developments for blacks. Black community organization is just beginning and is currently focused on employment discrimination. Segregation in private housing is virtually complete, although this site does contain an integrated public housing project—the only one observed on the four southern sites.

It should be noted that this study was conducted at a time of uncertainty in the local housing markets. National and local mortgage rates had risen rapidly, as had building costs, with the result that very little new building and a reduced number of home purchases were occurring on the sites. In addition, the status of most federal programs has been uncertain because of the freeze in 1973 on new subsidized starts, court challenges to this which reinstated FmHA programs, and the legislative revision of HUD programs in 1974.[c] In an attempt to correct for possible biases this situation might introduce, local housing market actors were asked to relate their experience over the preceding several years, and to provide their perceptions of the likely future of the markets.

Organization of the Study

The organization of this study follows the elements of a housing market as diagrammed in figure 1-1. Chapter 2 is an analysis of market outcomes: residential segregation, housing market segmentation and price differentials, occupancy of substandard housing, and race and sex as determinants of housing tenure. This economic analysis of the results of market operations provides evidence of the forms and magnitude of inequality in rural housing.

Chapters 3, 4, and 5 are institutional analyses of the remaining market elements and their interactions, designed to uncover the processes by which inequality is brought about and maintained. Chapter 3 considers the patterns of interaction between suppliers and consumers, including the means of information exchange and the regulations which effectively govern the market. Chapter 4 focuses on the supply side of the market—supply of housing, land, financing, and municipal services—and its operations in relation to consumer

---

[c]A glossary of federal housing programs is contained in Appendix B.

demand. Chapter 5 examines the effects of housing market interventions on the part of community organizations and local and federal governments. The effects of federal housing programs and of the Federal Fair Housing Act are considered here.

Because of the relative paucity of institutional analysis in the rural housing literature, and the frequency with which the urban experience is assumed to apply to rural areas, it was judged most useful to organize the institutional discussions around a series of "assertions." These are common assumptions, myths or hypothetical "priors" about the ways in which the market *might* function. In each case, the appropriateness or inappropriateness of the assertion to the rural experience is noted and analyzed.

Following the cross-site analysis in Chapters 2 through 5, the study includes in-depth institutional analyses of two of the six areas visited. The behavior patterns which constitute a housing market become most clear when considered in the full social context in which they occur. For this reason, the generalized analysis is augmented here by site-specific analysis of the South Dakota site in Chapter 6 and the Georgia site in Chapter 7. Chapter 8 then presents the conclusions and findings from the study as a whole.

Notes

1. The inquiry into retention problems was conducted because previous literature has shown that involuntary loss of land through such means as tax and mortgage foreclosures has become a serious problem, especially for southern blacks. See Lester M. Salamon, *Black-Owned Land: Profile of a Disappearing Equity Base* (Report to U.S. Department of Commerce, 1974) and Anthony Griggs, "How Blacks Lost 9,000,000 Acres of Land," *Ebony* 29, 12 (October 1974): 97–104. No recent examples of this activity were encountered on the selected sites, however. The retention problems observed were in connection with public condemnation and redevelopment efforts.

2 Inequalities in Rural Housing

The term "market outcomes" refers to the observable results of the operation of an area's housing market. Outcomes include residential location, tenure patterns, design and quality of housing occupied, and prices. This chapter presents a detailed examination of market outcomes for majority, minority and female-headed households.

The chapter is divided into five major sections. The first examines the extent of minority segregation. The second explores alternative explanations for the existence of segregation, including the hypothesis that segregation can be explained on the basis of income differentials. The third section is an analysis of the proposition that discrimination against minorities has resulted in their systematic confinement to a secondary or "dual" housing market, with evidence in the form of price differentials. The fourth describes the characteristics of occupants of substandard housing in rural areas. The final section explores the hypothesis that discrimination against minorities and households headed by women has severely restricted the ability of such households to own their homes in lieu of renting.

Residential Segregation in Rural Areas

Residential segregation in urban areas has been extensively studied and well documented. Using Census block statistics, Karl and Alma Taeuber calculated segregation indices for a large number of central cities in 1940, 1950, and 1960.[1] Their indices approximate the percentage of non-whites who would have to change their residence in order to achieve a uniform or unsegregated block distribution for the city. A value of 100 thus indicates complete segregation; a value of 0 a completely even distribution of non-whites. Of the 156 central cities studied in 1960, only 5 had indices below 70.

To date, residential segregation along racial lines in rural areas has not been satisfactorily documented in the literature. The only study which attempts to deal with the problem is an unpublished paper by Sumka and Stegman.[2] Utilizing Census enumeration district data, the authors determine that more than 60 percent of the population of North Carolina lives in districts in which blacks account for either less than 10 percent or more than 80 percent of the population. In attempting to deal with possible aggregation problems as well as to document changes in segregation patterns through time, Sumka and Stegman utilized information obtained from city directories from 1927-57; they have no similar data for the period since 1957.

The descriptions of segregation patterns presented below rely on three primary sources of data: (1) addresses of black and Spanish-surnamed families gathered on-site in North Carolina and New Mexico, (2) Census block statistics obtained for a number of individual towns in Tennessee, and (3) on-site interviews and observation by research teams in each study area.

The most significant and reliable source of evidence for segregation came from property record cards on file at the county assessor's office in the North Carolina study site (see figure 2-4 below). These cards were consulted for information on the structural characteristics of units recently sold, but it was found that the cards identified the race of both the owner and the current occupant of each piece of property in the county. (In addition, cards for black and white owners were filed separately.) Addresses were obtained and plotted for each property in the county seat listed as having a black occupant. The resulting pattern conformed exactly to neighborhood boundaries outlined *ex ante* from conversations with local real estate agents and others familiar with neighborhood composition.

The results appear in figure 2-1 and are consistent with the data for the Census enumeration districts which are superimposed on the map. Two important conclusions emerge. First, segregation is virtually complete; there is no apparent violation of established black-white neighborhood boundaries. The plotted addresses revealed not a single case of a black family living in a white area or of a white family living in a black area.

Second, even casual observation of the results presented in figure 2-1 reveals a serious bias problem associated with Census data available for rural areas. The enumeration district is the smallest unit for which the Census tabulates data in nearly all rural areas, and First Count Summary Tapes present tabulations of a large number of variables for individual enumeration districts. As a result, a good deal of the professional literature has come to rely heavily on such data. The problem is that existing enumeration district boundaries cut across clearly delineated neighborhoods and the resulting data fail to distinguish anything approaching true neighborhood characteristics.

This is most dramatically illustrated in figure 2-1 by ED 18, which contains the worst of the black neighborhoods separated by an industrial park from one of the most exclusive higher income white neighborhoods. The aggregate data for the ED paints a meaningless picture of a thoroughly mixed neighborhood.

Although enumeration district boundaries do not in general conform to true neighborhood boundaries, there are instances of rough correspondence. A particularly good example is the study site in Georgia. In figure 2-2 enumeration district boundaries are super-imposed on black-white neighborhood boundaries drawn *ex ante* from interview responses. The results reinforce the

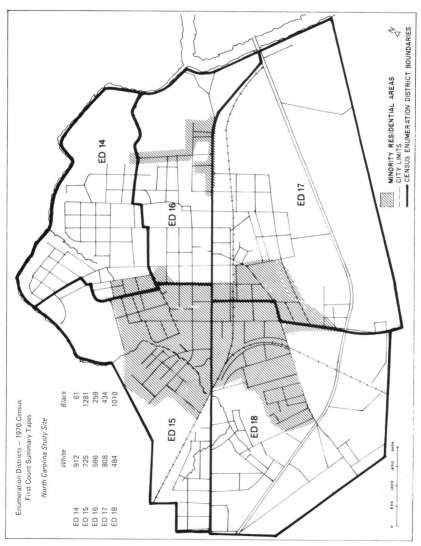

Enumeration Districts — 1970 Census
First Count Summary Tapes

North Carolina Study Site

	White	Black
ED 14	912	61
ED 15	725	1281
ED 16	596	259
ED 17	808	434
ED 18	484	1010

MINORITY RESIDENTIAL AREAS
CITY LIMITS
CENSUS ENUMERATION DISTRICT BOUNDARIES

ED 14

ED 16

ED 17

ED 15

ED 18

Figure 2-1. The North Carolina Study Site (Town NC)

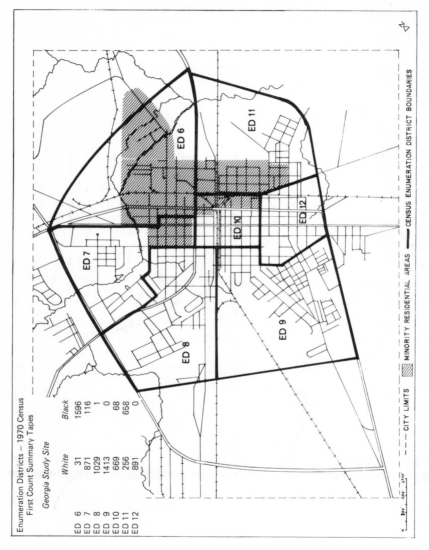

Figure 2-2. The Georgia Study Site (Town G)

conclusion that housing segregation along racial lines is virtually complete. The population of enumeration district number 6 is over 98 percent black, while numbers 8, 9, and 12 are 100 percent white.

Another source of information on segregation patterns is block statistics, i.e., Census data aggregated in geographic units much smaller than enumeration districts. Detailed block statistics are not generally available for nonmetropolitan and rural areas. However, when states and regions are willing to defray a portion of the cost, the Census tabulates and publishes such data for "selected areas." The 1970 Census contains such block statistics for a number of towns in Tennessee. Using a procedure similar to that employed by Taeuber and Taeuber, segregation indices were calculated for fifteen towns in Tennessee whose characteristics correspond closely to the "rural" site selection criteria used in this study. These indices can be roughly interpreted as the percentage of the minority population which would have to change residence in order to achieve a perfectly uniform geographical distribution of the black population.[a] Results are presented in table 2-1.

For towns ranging in 1970 population from 3,050 to 11,925 and from 1.5 percent to 34 percent black, there is a uniform pattern of fairly strict racial segregation. Indices range from a low of 0.77 to a high of 0.99, which corresponds roughly to the description of segregation in the urban South in 1960

---

[a]The indices presented in table 2-1 were calculated as follows:

$$\text{Let } \bar{P} = \text{\% black population in the town}$$
$$P_i = \text{\% black population in block } i$$
$$N_i = \text{Total population of block } i$$

$$N = \sum_i N_i = \text{Total population of the town}$$

$$\text{The Index } I = \frac{\sum_i (P_i - \bar{P})N_i}{(1 - \bar{P})\bar{P}N} \text{ for all } P_i > \bar{P}.$$

If one imagined a process of identifying each block with more than the town's average proportion of black residents and then moving individual black families one by one to blocks with less than the town's average proportion of blacks, in each case swapping residences with a white family, the numerator of the index could be thought of as the number of blacks (and thus whites) who would have to move to achieve a uniform distribution of black families. The denominator is the number of blacks who would have to move under such a process if segregation were initially complete. The index is thus bounded by 0 (complete integration) and 1.0 (complete segregation).

A detailed discussion of the methodological problems associated with summary measures of residential segregation is contained in Otis Dudley and Beverly Duncan, "Contributions to the Theory of Segregation Indexes," *Urban Analysis Report* (Chicago Community Inventory, University of Chicago, 1953). A more recent discussion can be found in a paper by Ann Schnare presented at the American Economic Association meeting, December, 1975.

Table 2-1
Segregation Indices for Selected Towns in Tennessee

Town	1970 Population	% Black	Segregation Index	% of Blocks with No Blacks
Athens	11,790	8	.87	76
Covington	5,801	34	.89	65
Dayton	4,361	9	.77	81
Fayetteville	7,030	25	.77	63
Hohenwald	3,385	2	.79	97
Humboldt	10,066	34	.99	63
Lawrenceburg	8,889	3.2	.89	89
Livingston	3,050	1.5	.87	94
McMinnville	10,662	6	.91	86
Paris	9,892	19	.84	79
Pulaski	6,989	25	.78	59
Trenton	4,226	30	.89	63
Union City	11,925	10	.89	76
Waverly	3,794	10	.87	87
Winchester	5,211	14	.83	79

Source: Department of Commerce, Bureau of the Census Series, 1970 Census of Population and Housing Series HC(3)-222, *Selected areas in Tennessee.*

given by Taeuber and Taeuber.[3] Even though Census blocks are considerably smaller than enumeration districts, block data, too, suffer from some aggregation bias. The index calculated for the Tennessee study site is in line with the figures given in table 2-1, but local respondents and personal observation verified that segregation is virtually complete.

Similar indices were calculated using *enumeration district* data for a number of county areas in North Carolina and Georgia (where block statistics are not available). The resulting indices ranged from 0.18 up to 0.90. It is apparent from the above discussion of the two study sites depicted in figures 2-1 and 2-2 that the validity of such indices depends critically upon how the ED boundaries happen to be drawn. The index computed from ED data for the North Carolina study site was 0.18 while that computed for the Georgia study site was 0.86; in both towns segregation was in fact virtually complete. It is fair to conclude, therefore, on the basis of black addresses in North Carolina, block statistics in Tennessee, and interviews and observation on all four sites, that residential segregation in the southern sites is strict and virtually complete.

In New Mexico, the focus of the study was on persons with Spanish sur-names. Unfortunately, Census data shed little light on the residential patterns of such families; no block statistics are available, and enumeration district data do not contain information on Spanish surname or heritage. However, research-ers obtained a list of the addresses of taxpayers with Spanish surnames from the county assessor's office in the New Mexico study site and plotted these on a town map. Results show a slightly denser concentration of such families in certain neighborhoods, but the overall pattern appears to be one of residential integration. The segregation index calculated for the site was only 0.37.

In South Dakota, the concern was with off-reservation American Indians.[b] Little information on the residential patterns of this minority is available from published data, although some was gathered through on-site inquiry. The residences of Indian families were concentrated in the lower-income area of the town, but were interspersed with white residences. There was no systematic segregation of Indians living off-reservation in private housing. Public housing was found to be somewhat more segregated, owing partly to income differences between whites and Indians, and partly to the existence of separate town and tribal housing authorities. Problems faced by American Indians in this area centered on access to ownership and on land retention, both of which are discussed in more detail later in this study; residential segregation was not an issue.

In summary, there is conclusive evidence from a variety of sources that residential segregation along racial lines in the southern sites is strict and virtually complete. There is little evidence of the residential segregation of either Spanish-surnamed families or of off-reservation American Indians in the areas studied.

Alternative Explanations: Income-Based Segregation and Self-Segregation

The presence of housing segregation does not in itself imply the existence of discrimination. Several "nondiscrimination" explanations have been offered for the segregation observed in urban areas. It might for example be argued that socioeconomic differences such as the low incomes of many blacks might explain differences in residential location patterns. This proposition has, however, received considerable empirical examination, and most studies for urban areas have concluded that differences in socioeconomic status account for only a small portion of observed racial segregation.[4] This section carefully examines the proposition that patterns of residential segregation observed in rural areas can be explained by differentials in the distribution of income accruing to blacks and other minorities. A second explanation contends that existing patterns of

---

[b]The reservation status of land in and around the South Dakota site was under litigation until March 1975 when the Supreme Court ruled that the original reservation had been terminated in 1892 and its boundaries are no longer valid (*De Coteau* v. *District County Court,* No. 73-1148, 1150 March 3, 1975). This decision had the effect of designating the study town and part of the county as "off-reservation" at the present time; their status had been unclear and had reversed several times since 1963.

segregation result from preferences among blacks, more specifically a desire to "live with one's own kind." This proposition is examined briefly here and in more detail in Chapter 3.

To test the first propostion, an index of the racial (or minority) segregation *which would result* if residential location patterns were determined by income alone was calculated for each of the rural towns in Tennessee for which Census block data were available.[c] The results, presented in figure 2-3 and table 2-2, range from a low of 0.15 to a high of 0.44. It is evident from a comparison of these with the indices of observed segregation that income differentials explain only a small fraction of existing racial segregation in the rural South. In New Mexico, however, the fact that certain areas contained a somewhat higher concentration of Spanish-surnamed population can be explained largely on the basis of income differentials.

The hypothesis that existing patterns of segregation result from similar preferences among blacks is a more difficult proposition conceptually. Professor Schelling has demonstrated with a simple checkerboard model that preferences for living in a neighborhood with some minimum proportion of residents of one's own color can result in segregated residential patterns even when that minimum is quite low (i.e., 35 percent).[5] It should be noted of course that preferences regarding segregation are not exogenous in any meaningful sense. That is, in the presence of discrimination and long-standing social barriers between blacks and whites, blacks may express no desire to live among whites, but this lack of expression may result more from the barriers than from inherent black preference. It is difficult if not impossible to establish what preferences would exist in the absence of social institutions which foster segregation. This point is discussed in more detail in Chapter 3.

In spite of these problems of endogeneity, there is some evidence that a majority of blacks would rather live in a neighborhood with some whites than live in an all-black neighborhood. In 1963, 50 percent of a random sample of southern nonurban blacks and 64 percent of a sample of all blacks in the United States indicated such a preference. By 1966, the corresponding figures had risen to 56 percent and 68 percent respectively.[6] Although this survey is by now somewhat dated, it is the most recent nationwide study of black attitudes. A more recent survey of New York City blacks revealed that 52 percent felt that residential integration was very important or somewhat important, while 51 percent felt that having white neighbors was very important or somewhat important.[7] In addition, the institutional analysis conducted in the course

---

[c]The indices presented were calculated using Census data on the distribution of money income accruing to blacks, whites, and households of Spanish heritage. The analysis assumes that households within a given income class reside together, i.e., all those with money incomes between $10,000 and $12,000 reside together. The index was calculated in the same way as the index of observed segregation discussed above.

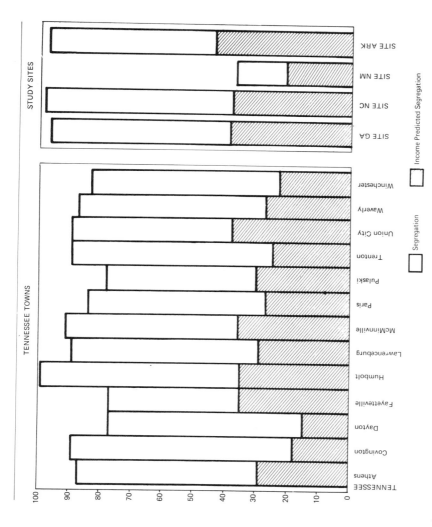

Figure 2-3. Income-Predicted Segregation vs. Actual Segregation

Table 2-2
Segregation and Income (1970)

	Income-Predicted Index	Actual Index
Tennessee		
Athens[1]	.29	.87
Covington	.18	.89
Dayton	.15	.77
Fayetteville	.35	.77
Humboldt[1]	.35	.99
Lawrenceburg	.29	.89
McMinnville[1]	.36	.91
Paris	.27	.84
Pulaski	.30	.78
Trenton	.25	.89
Union City[1]	.38	.89
Waverly	.27	.87
Winchester	.23	.83
Site, Georgia	.39	.96
Site, North Carolina	.38	.98
Site, New Mexico	.21	.37
Site, Arkansas	.44	.97

[1] Income distribution based on city data for towns over 10,000 population. All others based on County data.

Source: Data for Tennessee from Department of Commerce, Bureau of the Census Series HC(3)-222, and Series PC(1)-C, Tables 128, 124. Data gathered on site for Arkansas, Georgia, North Carolina, New Mexico.

of this study and presented in Chapter 3 found no significant preference among blacks for segregation. It is safe to say, in conclusion, that neither the self-segregation hypothesis nor the socioeconomic segregation hypothesis explains the extensive residential segregation patterns which exist in four of the sites under study.

A Dual Housing Market

This section examines the proposition that housing markets in rural areas are segmented along racial lines. It is an analysis of market prices which seeks to determine whether minorities are systematically confined to a "secondary" housing submarket. A segmented housing market, often referred to as a "dual" housing market, is one in which separate supply and demand forces operate in separate submarkets; such a situation will generally result in price differentials between submarkets. This section attempts to determine whether minorities are paying the same price as others for housing services.

Methodology and Results of Recent Urban Studies

These phenomena have been extensively studied in urban areas. Empirical studies of market segmentation in urban areas have followed one of two general methods of analysis: (1) studies of market prices in transitional neighborhoods over time,[8] and (2) cross-sectional analyses using hedonic price techniques to compare equilibrium prices of "identical" units in different submarkets.[9]

Of the former, Karlen's study of a Chicago South Side community stands out. Karlen observed the development of two virtually identical communities. One, a South Shore community, was initially all white but in the path of ghetto expansion in the 1960s. The second, a North Shore community, remained all white during the test period. Properties in the North Shore community were initially priced somewhat higher than those in the South Shore community. The period of observation lasted from 1956-66; the transition of the South Shore community from white to black took place around 1960-61. Karlen observed an initial decline in prices but a relative and absolute increase once the neighborhood was clearly marked for black occupancy. Karlen concludes, "Because Negro demand could not be diffused over the metropolitan area, it had to be concentrated on the few areas like South Shore where a breakthrough had been made, thus driving values up."[10]

The second general methodological approach which has been applied to these questions involves the estimation of hedonic price indices from detailed cross-sectional data. The method has been discussed in some detail by Griliches and more recently by Rosen, both of whom discuss the properties of the "implicit attribute prices" which result from the estimations.[11] Ideally, the procedure involves regressing the market value of individual housing units (or rents for rental housing) on their structural attributes and neighborhood characteristics (broadly defined to include such things as public service levels and accessibility). One of the neighborhood characteristics is, of course, racial composition. The estimated coefficients can be thought of as implicit short run equilibrium prices of the various housing attributes.

Using micro housing data from St. Louis, Kain and Quigley distinguish differences between black and white submarkets in two ways.[12] First, they estimate a single equation for the entire market area using a pooled sample of ghetto and non-ghetto housing, concluding that "similar units cost 4-6% more in an all-Black than in an all-White neighborhood."[13] Second, they estimate separate equations for the ghetto and non-ghetto samples and discover that the structure of attribute prices differs substantially between the two sub-markets. This, they claim, reflects in part the limited choice of housing attributes available in the ghetto housing.

Schnare's analysis makes use of the Census Bureau's one-in-a-hundred Public Use Sample for the Boston SMSA and Census tract data in a two-step procedure to estimate similar hedonic indices.[14] Her results using 1960 data indicate the presence of a substantial "ghetto" premium in Boston; she estimates that a unit of housing inside the ghetto costs approximately 12-14 percent more than an identical unit outside. The tests were repeated for 1970, but with the surprising result that the "ghetto premium" seems to have declined substantially or vanished altogether. Cursory examination of the data seems to indicate that the reason lies in an increase in the supply of housing available to blacks rather than a drastic decline in the rate of influx into Boston.

Based on a sample of individual housing observations from New Haven and using a reduced form equation incorporating arguments from both supply and demand sides, King and Miezkowski concluded that black families living inside the ghetto pay 19 percent more than white families living in all-white neighborhoods for identical housing. This figure is the highest estimate yet obtained for urban "ghetto premiums."[15]

Housing Market Segmentation in Rural Areas

To test for the existence of a segmented housing market in rural areas, a detailed cross-sectional analysis using the hedonic price technique to compare equilibrium prices of "identical" units in different submarkets was accomplished for five of the six study sites. The analysis employed data gathered on-site, including selling price and detailed structural and neighborhood characteristics for over 1,000 individual homes which were sold between 1971 and 1974.

A number of assumptions about the behavior of households and the nature of the housing supply function are implicit in the analysis. Traditional theories treat housing output as a single-valued, homogeneous good: "housing service." By assuming that all housing inputs except land are variable in the long run and that housing markets adjust instantaneously to long run equilibrium, it is possible to (1) ignore the effects of durable capital stocks and (2) measure the quantity of housing services consumed by the household's expenditure on housing. This approach clearly obfuscates a number of extremely important dimensions of housing market operation.

Use of hedonic price techniques on the other hand stresses the heterogeneous nature of existing housing stocks. Households obtain utility not from consuming some single-dimensional service; rather, utility is obtained from the consumption of a large number of identifiable attributes which when combined represent a multidimensional "housing bundle." In choosing a residence, households are choosing simultaneously a number of rooms, a segment of land, a structure type and a quality of construction, a set of neighbors, a local package of public services, a neighborhood environment, etc. In principle there is an implicit price associated with each specific attribute. These implicit prices are unobservable since attributes cannot be purchased individually; they must be imputed from differences in the cost of otherwise identical bundles.

In addition, the analysis to be employed does not rest on the assumption of long-run equilibrium. Housing stocks are durable and supply responses are sluggish; as a result, shifts in demand may result in positive or negative quasi-rents associated with specific geographic locations. The existence of such quasi-rents has been documented.[16]

Estimation of the attribute prices involves multiple regression analysis. Specifically, it attempts to "explain" the market value of housing bundles with a set of independent variables describing the dwelling unit itself and the characteristics of its neighborhood of location. Among the neighborhood characteristics is the racial or ethnic composition of the immediate neighborhood of each dwelling unit. The significance level of the estimated coefficient of this variable indicates whether or not housing market segmentation exists. The sign and absolute value of the coefficient indicates the precise effect of this segmentation on the market value of otherwise identical housing units inside and outside of the specifically separated market areas.

The Data

To estimate the hedonic indices above, it is necessary to obtain data on housing prices, structural attributes, and neighborhood characteristics. Ideally, the unit of observation should be the individual housing unit. Since there is no existing data source which contains everything required for such an analysis, it was necessary to gather information on individual housing transactions in each of the six study sites.

Housing prices were obtained from three basic sources. First, the registrar of deeds in most counties is required to accurately record the actual selling price on all deed transfers for taxation purposes. There was, however, obvious lack of enforcement in some areas (e.g., North Carolina and Arkansas). That is, there was evidence of tax avoidance through underreporting. In such areas, other sources were utilized.

Second, in most of the sites real estate agents were cooperative and permitted access to files on completed home sales. Finally, in three areas, home buyers were required to report the purchase price of newly acquired property to the county assessor's office. In all cases, care was taken to exclude observations on intrafamily transfers and parcels transferred through wills or estates.

The structural characteristics of each home in the sample were obtained from property record cards on file at county assessors' offices. A sample obtained from the study site in North Carolina is presented in figure 2-4. In all areas except Tennessee, the cards appeared to be well maintained and consistent. In most cases, the cards had been completed by outside appraisors within the last three years and updated by the county assessors.

In addition to objective measures such as square feet of interior and exterior space, each card contained a code indicating "quality of construction" and "condition" of the property. In each site, assessors had detailed procedures for estimation of the "quality" index which included explicit examination of foundation, exterior walls, roofing, floors, interior finish, attic, heating, plumbing, tiling, insulation and lighting. As such, the quality variable appears to be an excellent proxy for many omitted variables. In cases where the index was alphabetic (i.e., A, AA, B, etc.) it was converted to a numeric equivalent.

The data are primarily observations on single-family, owner-occupied units; however, they contain a few observations on single-family rental units. If it is assumed that the market value of such units is the capitalized value of future rents, the results may be generalized to include rental housing. Examination of the residuals for identifiable rental units indicates no observable bias. Since rental units, when sold, are offered to both potential owner-occupiers as well as potential lessors and since virtually no low income rental property in the study areas is of the multiple-family variety, there is little reason to suspect a great deal of difference between owner and renter markets.

It was initially decided to obtain neighborhood characteristics from Census enumeration district data. However, as discussed earlier in this chapter, severe aggregation bias would have resulted from such a procedure. Consequently it was decided to rely on information obtained on site. In each state the towns being studied were divided up into a fairly large number of homogeneous neighborhoods. The number ranged from sixteen in Georgia to thirty in Arkansas. Each neighborhood was given a condition rating based on direct inspection by researchers. This subjective condition variable was used in lieu of average market value because of the severe bias which the latter would introduce if included as an independent variable. In addition, each neighborhood was given an accessibility rating which corresponds roughly to the number of miles from the neighborhood center to the main business district in the nearest major town. Dummy variables were included for observations in separate towns. Information on paved and unpaved roads as well as accessibility to sewer trunk lines was obtained from assessment records.

The most important independent variable is the racial or ethnic composition of the immediate neighborhood. In the rural South, where segregation is virtually complete, it was quite easy to identify each neighborhood as either all black or all white. In North Carolina, the researchers found both the race of the owner and the race of the occupant recorded on the property record cards in the county assessor's office. A plot of the addresses of black residents coincided perfectly with the black/white neighborhood boundaries drawn *ex ante* from information supplied by real estate agents and others familiar with residential location patterns.

In New Mexico, the addresses of Spanish-surnamed taxpayers were similarly obtained and plotted on a county map. Since neighborhoods were not completely segregated, those where Spanish-surnamed families appear to make up a substantial majority were identified as "minority" neighborhoods.

An insufficient number of observations on off-reservation American Indians in the South Dakota site was obtained and the analysis was not accomplished.

Specification

The specification of the appropriate functional form of the regression equations is a difficult problem. The most reputable method of choosing functional form is to derive it from an underlying theoretical model. Unfortunately, there is nothing in the theoretical literature to provide anything but the most general guidance. Only one study to date has attempted to deal with the problem and it provides no help to housing market analysts.[17]

The problem is dealt with here by providing alternative estimates of the basic equations; both the linear and double log specifications were utilized. Coefficients of the linear specification can be thought of as individual attribute prices. Coefficients of continuous variables in the log-log specification can be thought of as elasticities; they show the percentage of change in market value which would result from a 1 percent change in the particular independent variable, *ceteris paribus*. Coefficients of dummy variables can be easily converted to fractions indicating the percentage of change in market value which will result from the "presence" of the attribute in question.

Standard pooling tests (Chow F-tests) seem to indicate the appropriateness of estimating separate equations for high and low value subsamples while pooling blacks and whites within each. This is a pleasing result since it is only through pooling blacks and whites that estimates of the *magnitude* of black/white price differentials can be obtained. For the remaining states the same stratification scheme was employed, except in Arkansas, where separate equations were estimated for each of the two towns in the sample area, and in Tennessee, where there were only four observations in the high value black subsample.

City _____

( ) inside   ( ) outside

TOWNSHIP _____

CARD NO _____ OF _____

RECORD OF OWNERSHIP

	W	C	OOK	PAGE	DATE	SALE PRICE OR STAMPS	MAP

DESCRIPTION

ADJOINING OWNERS

PROPERTY FACTORS AND INFORMATION

STREET OR ROAD

	IMPROVEMENTS		TOPOGRAPHY		TREND OF DIST
PAVED	WATER		LEVEL		IMPROVING
SEMI-IMP.	SEWER		HIGH		STATIC
DIRT	GAS		LOW		DECLINING
SIDEWALK	ELECTRICITY		ROLLING		INFO BY OWNER
	SEPTIC TANK		SWAMPY		TENNANT

BLOCK   LOT

ROAD LOCATED ON

RENTAL CAPITALIZATION

FLAT EXPENSE ITEMS		RENT
LAND COST	LAND	PRIOR TAX VAL.
BLDG. COST	VACANCY	LAND
	HEATING	BLDGS
SALE PRICE	WATER	TOTAL
	ELECTRICITY	
	JANITOR	LAND
	MANAGEMENT	BLDG
	TOTAL FLAT EXPENSE	TOTAL
	GROSS ANNUAL INCOME	LAND
	LESS FLAT EXPENSE	BLDG.
	BALANCE FOR CAP.	TOTAL
	CAP RATE	LAND
	REFLECTED CAP. VAL.	BLDG.
MEMORANDA		TOTAL
		LAND
		BLDG.
		TOTAL
		LAND
		BLDG
		TOTAL
		LAND
		BLDG.
		TOTAL
19	19	19

LAND VALUE COMPUTATIONS AND SUMMARY

FRONTAGE	DEPTH	UNIT PRICE	DEPTH FACTOR	FRONT FT. PRICE	NO. ACRES	RATE	TOTAL	DEPR.	TOTAL APPRAISAL
CLASSIFICATION									
BUILDING SITE									
LAND OPEN	GOOD								
	FAIR								
	POOR								
IMPROVED PASTURE									
UNIMPROVED PASTURE									
WOOD LAND									
TIMBER OR PULP									
CUT OVER WOODS									
WASTE LAND									
TOTAL ACREAGE									
TOTAL VALUE LAND									
TOTAL VALUE BUILDINGS									
TAX VALUE LAND AND BUILDINGS									
TAX VALUE									

Form AA–1GT.

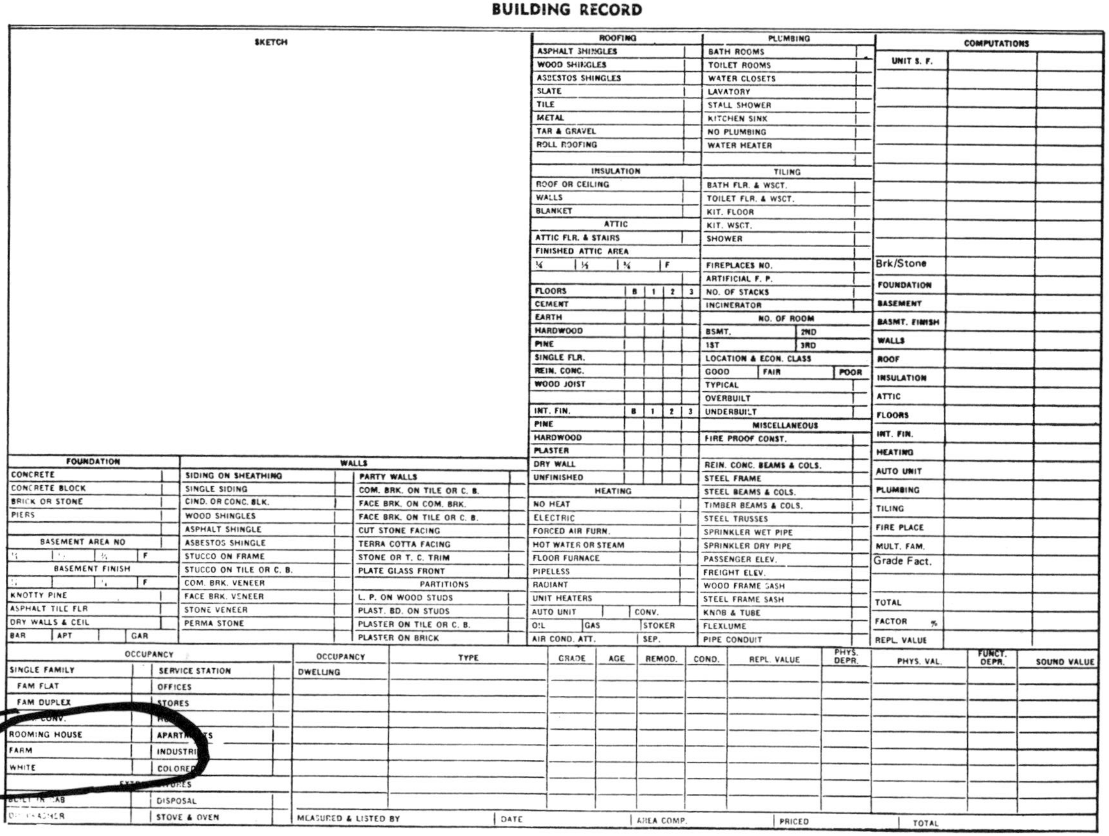

BUILDING RECORD

SKETCH

ROOFING — ASPHALT SHINGLES, WOOD SHINGLES, ASBESTOS SHINGLES, SLATE, TILE, METAL, TAR & GRAVEL, ROLL ROOFING

INSULATION — ROOF OR CEILING, WALLS, BLANKET, ATTIC

ATTIC FLR. & STAIRS, FINISHED ATTIC AREA — ¼ ½ ¾

FLOORS — CEMENT, EARTH, HARDWOOD, PINE, SINGLE FLR., REIN. CONC., WOOD JOIST

INT. FIN. — PINE, HARDWOOD, PLASTER, DRY WALL, UNFINISHED

HEATING — NO HEAT, ELECTRIC, FORCED AIR FURN., HOT WATER OR STEAM, FLOOR FURNACE, PIPELESS, RADIANT, UNIT HEATERS, AUTO UNIT — OIL, GAS, CONV., STOKER, AIR COND. ATT., SEP.

PLUMBING — BATH ROOMS, TOILET ROOMS, WATER CLOSETS, LAVATORY, STALL SHOWER, KITCHEN SINK, NO PLUMBING, WATER HEATER

TILING — BATH FLR. & WSCT., TOILET FLR. & WSCT., KIT. FLOOR, KIT. WSCT., SHOWER

FIREPLACES NO., ARTIFICIAL F.P., NO. OF STACKS, INCINERATOR

NO. OF ROOMS — BSMT., 1ST, 2ND, 3RD

LOCATION & ECON. CLASS — GOOD, FAIR, POOR, TYPICAL, OVERBUILT, UNDERBUILT

MISCELLANEOUS — FIRE PROOF CONST., REIN. CONC. BEAMS & COLS., STEEL FRAME, STEEL BEAMS & COLS., TIMBER BEAMS & COLS., STEEL TRUSSES, SPRINKLER WET PIPE, SPRINKLER DRY PIPE, PASSENGER ELEV., FREIGHT ELEV., WOOD FRAME SASH, STEEL FRAME SASH, KNOB & TUBE, FLEXLUME, PIPE CONDUIT

COMPUTATIONS — UNIT S.F., Brk/Stone, FOUNDATION, BASEMENT, BASMT. FINISH, WALLS, ROOF, INSULATION, ATTIC, FLOORS, INT. FIN., HEATING, AUTO UNIT, PLUMBING, TILING, FIRE PLACE, MULT. FAM., Grade Fact., TOTAL, FACTOR %, REPL. VALUE

PHYS. VAL. | FUNCT. DEPR. | SOUND VALUE

CRADE | AGE | REMOD. | COND. | REPL. VALUE | PHYS. DEPR.
PRICED | AREA COMP. | DATE | TOTAL

FOUNDATION — CONCRETE, CONCRETE BLOCK, BRICK OR STONE, PIERS

BASEMENT AREA NO., BASEMENT FINISH

DRY WALLS & CEIL., ASPHALT TILE FLR., KNOTTY PINE

BAR | APT | GAR

SIDING ON SHEATHING — SINGLE SIDING, CIND. OR CONC. BLK., WOOD SHINGLES, ASPHALT SHINGLE, ASBESTOS SHINGLE, STUCCO ON FRAME, STUCCO ON TILE OR C. B., COM. BRK. VENEER, FACE BRK. VENEER, STONE VENEER, PERMA STONE

WALLS — PARTY WALLS, COM. BRK. ON TILE OR C. B., FACE BRK. ON COM. BRK., FACE BRK. ON TILE OR C. B., CUT STONE FACING, TERRA COTTA FACING, STONE OR T. C. TRIM, PLATE GLASS FRONT

PARTITIONS — L. P. ON WOOD STUDS, PLAST. BD. ON STUDS, PLASTER ON TILE OR C. B., PLASTER ON BRICK

OCCUPANCY — DWELLING, SINGLE FAMILY, FAM FLAT, FAM DUPLEX, ROOMING HOUSE, FARM, WHITE

SERVICE STATION, OFFICES, STORES, APARTMENTS, INDUSTRIAL, COLORED

STOVE & OVEN, DISPOSAL

TYPE | OCCUPANCY

MEASURED & LISTED BY

Figure 2-4. Property Record Card

Results[d]

The results of the analysis are striking. In three of the six study sites (North Carolina, Georgia, and Arkansas) housing in the black submarket appears to be selling for significantly more than identical housing in the white submarket. What is most surprising and extremely important about these results is that in each of the study sites where a black submarket "premium" was observed, black population has been declining both relatively and absolutely. Statistically significant differentials are presented in table 2-3.

The most dramatic results were in Georgia where high-income black housing is selling for a 19 percent premium and low-income black housing for a 29 percent premium. The Georgia equations control for seventeen separate structural and neighborhood characteristics; the "premium" is significant at the 1 percent level in all equations. In the Georgia site, black population has declined only slightly relative to white.

In Arkansas, the results are similar but the premiums are smaller in absolute size. In Arkansas, low-income black housing is selling for about 11 percent more than identical white housing, while high-income black housing is commanding a 9 percent premium. The Arkansas equations contain twenty-two structural and neighborhood characteristics. The "race" variable is significant at a level of between 5 percent and 20 percent, depending upon the equation. (A premium was observed in two separate towns in the study county.) In Arkansas, the relative decline in black population was more dramatic than in Georgia. From 1960-1970 black population fell 15 percent, while white population increased by 14 percent.

In North Carolina, low-income housing in the black submarket seems to be commanding a small premium while high-income housing in the black submarket is selling at a discount. The 6 percent premium estimated in the low-income equation is mildly significant in the linear specification only. The 9 percent discount is statistically significant in both specifications at a level of 10-20 percent. From 1960-1970 in North Carolina black population fell 18 percent while white population remained constant.

The results in Tennessee were inconclusive because of weak data. Since there were only four observations on high-income black housing transactions, a separate set of equations for the high-income subsample was not estimated. Secondly, the property record cards on lower value properties were incomplete and data was often recorded in an inconsistent manner. This latter point is reflected in the weak power of the low-income equations ($R^2 = 0.64$), (see Appendix table D-5). In New Mexico, there appears to be no significant price differential between houses in neighborhoods with a high concentration of

---

[d]Detailed regression results are presented in Appendix D.

Table 2-3

Price Differentials Between Identical Housing Units in the Black Submarket and the White Submarket

(+ indicates higher price in Black submarket; - indicates lower; figures in parentheses are standard errors)

	% Price[1] Differential	$ Price[1] Differential
Georgia		
High Income:	+ .19 (.06)[2]	+ 2836 (1289)[3]
Low Income:	+ .29 (.12)[2]	+ 1127 (469)[2]
Arkansas		
High Income:	+ .09 (.06)[5]	+ 3726 (1774)[3]
Low Income:	+ .11 (.06)[4]	+ 443 (316)[5]
North Carolina		
High Income:	- .09 (.05)[4]	- 2446 (1630)[5]
Low Income:	+ .06 (.07)[6]	+ 772 (598)[5]
Tennessee		
Entire Sample:	- .09 (.11)[6]	+ 1754 (1252)[5]
Low Income:	- .11 (.12)[6]	+ 306 (1020)[6]
New Mexico		
Entire Sample	- .04 (4.0)[6]	+ 793 (1321)[6]

1. The percentage of price differential is a transformation of the race coefficient in the log/log specification; the $ price differential is the coefficient of the race variable in the simple linear specification.
2. Two-tailed *t* test significant at the 1% level.
3. Two-tailed *t* test significant at the 5% level.
4. Two-tailed *t* test significant at the 10% level.
5. Two-tailed *t* test significant at the 20% level.
6. Not significantly different from zero.

Spanish-surnamed families and those in other neighborhoods. No analysis was completed in South Dakota as the data failed to identify enough transactions for off-reservation Indians.

The results of the analysis allow us to draw two important conclusions. First, there is evidence that housing markets in rural portions of North Carolina, Georgia, and Arkansas are segmented along racial lines. In each area there seems to exist a "dual" housing market with characteristics similar to those which have been documented in urban areas.

Second is the surprising result that the price differentials indicating a segmented market are in most cases *premiums* for black housing. "Ghetto
premiums" documented in northern urban areas were explained on the basis
of black migration from the rural South to the urban North, creating "demand
pressure" in the constrained black submarket. However, in the four rural sites
studied, black population is *declining* both absolutely and relative to white.
With no evidence of large black/white differentials in either income growth or
elasticity of demand, the explanation would seem to lie in the responsiveness
of the housing supply available to blacks relative to whites.[e] Such a result is
highly suggestive and, if borne out in future research, will be of great importance to those concerned with evaluation of the "housing allowance" proposal,
since an allowance program relies on a responsive housing supply. The mechanisms through which the supply of housing to blacks is constrained are explored
in Chapters 3 and 4 of this study.

Occupancy of Substandard Housing

One of the most visible aspects of inequality in market outcomes is in the
quality of housing consumed by various groups. This section presents a brief
summary of the socioeconomic characteristics of households occupying "substandard" housing units. Data for the four southern states (Arkansas, Georgia,
North Carolina, and Tennessee) are combined here, while data for New Mexico
and South Dakota are presented separately. The results presented here summarize the findings; the detailed cross-tabulations are contained in Appendix F.

It should be emphasized that the figures presented here are intended
merely as a demographic profile of the population living in substandard housing.
No statistical analysis of these figures has been carried out, and no attempt has
been made to "control" for socioeconomic characteristics as variables explain-
ing the occupancy of low quality housing. The figures are simple cross-tabulations, and constitute a summary, not an analysis, of the data.

The data for these summaries consist of 3,100 records extracted from the
1970 Census one-in-one-thousand Public Use Sample based on the 5 percent
questionnaire. They cover the nonmetropolitan areas of the six states in question. Households were classified in accordance with seven socioeconomic
characteristics: (1) sex of head, (2) minority status of head, (3) family income,
(4) welfare status (whether the family had received any welfare income),
(5) employment status, (6) family size, and (7) age of head. Cross-tabulations

---

[e]Some argue that there are fewer and fewer black families living in extended family
situations. As time progresses, such a trend might conceivably result in an increased demand
for housing units even if population is declining. No evidence to either support or refute this
hypothesis was obtained in this study.

were based on five characteristics of the dwelling unit: (1) lack of toilet, (2) lack of bath or shower, (3) lack of a major piece of plumbing equipment, (4) lack of installed heat, and (5) more than 1.01 persons per room. A dwelling unit with one or more of these characteristics is considered "substandard." (It should be noted that (3) includes both (1) and (2).)

The South

The results for the South are dramatic if not terribly surprising. Female-headed households are more likely than male-headed households to live in substandard housing, as are households with a black head compared with those with a white head. Table 2-4 shows the aggregate percentages of households living in substandard housing by demographic group. It is readily apparent that race is on balance the stronger explanatory variable. Within each race, the difference between the sexes is small. However, since the proportion of female-headed households is higher in the black population than in the white population, the combined average for men appears lower than that for women. In fact, as table 2-4 makes clear, this difference is accounted for by the differing racial composition of the two sex subgroups. Females are more likely to live in substandard housing because they are more likely to be black, not necessarily because they are female.

Further, it appears that some of the difference between male- and female-headed households within a given race can be explained on the basis of income. For whites, and to a lesser degree for blacks, the percentage of female-headed households in each income class living in substandard housing appears to be *less* than the corresponding percentage for male-headed households. However, the income distribution for female-headed households is more skewed toward the lower income classes (where the probability of living in substandard housing is higher for both) than is the distribution for male-headed households, and thus the overall percentage of female-headed households living in substandard quarters is larger than that for the opposite sex.

Table 2-4
Percentage of Households Living in Substandard Housing in the Southern Four States

	Male Head	Female Head	Total
White	35.2	38.6	35.8
Black	75.5	74.4	75.2
Total	40.7	47.1	42.0

Inadequate heating is the most common attribute of substandard housing in the rural South: fully two-thirds of all substandard units lack installed heating.[f] Second in order of importance is the absence of some plumbing facilities, typically more than one. Overcrowding is a characteristic of about a third of the substandard units in the sample.

South Dakota

Because the sample of off-reservation American Indians responding to the 5 percent questionnaire in South Dakota is so small, there is little that can be said about their housing characteristics. Overall, female-headed households are more likely to live in substandard quarters (21.6 percent) than male-headed households (14.6 percent). It is intriguing that for both men and women the chances are better overall for living in standard housing than they are in the South, even if lack of installed heating is dropped from the list of criteria. Moreover, this relation holds within each income class as well as for the whole population.

New Mexico

Table 2-5 presents the percentage of households in substandard housing aggregated for New Mexico. As was the case for blacks and whites in the South, there appears to be more difference between nonminority male- and female-headed households than between Spanish-surnamed male- and female-headed households. Also as in the South, a good deal of the difference between male- and female-headed households aggregated over race lies in the differential racial composition of the two sex groups.

Table 2-5
Percentage of Households Living in Substandard Housing in New Mexico

	Male Head	Female Head	Total
Spanish surname	57.5	56.2	57.1
Other White	16.5	35.0	19.1
Total	26.7	44.4	29.9

[f]It has been argued that lack of installed heating equipment should not by itself define a unit as substandard. Others contend that climate, even in the southern states being studied, is in fact quite variable and, thus, such a criterion is indeed justified. In Appendix F each of five characteristics used to define substandard is cross-tabulated separately against household characteristics.

Race and Sex as Determinants of Home Ownership

Both direct and indirect forms of discrimination in rural areas may have very serious effects on the kinds of housing consumed by minority families and households headed by women. Specifically, discrimination may have a significant effect on a household's ability to own rather than rent housing, and thus to acquire the equity and participate in the tax savings which homeownership affords. Distortion in tenure may result from simple restrictions in the supply of owner-occupied housing available to minorities, and could be reinforced by discrimination in capital markets or in the administration of federal programs designed to subsidize homeownership.

In order to determine whether such forms of discrimination exist, the existing patterns of minority and female *homeownership* in rural areas, as well as current patterns of home *purchase*, were analyzed. Examination of patterns of tenure choice by families recently changing resident location (viz, purchase vs. renting) will reveal biases currently existing. Overall patterns of tenure (viz, ownership vs. renting) will uncover biases which have developed over time, such as the difficulties experienced by minorities in purchasing when racial covenants were legal, or in maintaining ownership during periods of cyclical downturn.

Methodologies and Results of Recent Urban Studies

A number of studies have investigated these phenomena in urban areas.[18] Most of the studies proceed by estimating the probability of homeownership or home purchase as a function of a complete set of socioeconomic characteristics including age, sex, race, and income. The probability of home purchase may be approximated as the conditional probability of homeownership given that the household has recently moved. Kain and Quigley attempt to isolate the effects of differential rates of mobility from differences in the probability of home purchase by concentrating on the subset of "movers."

Using a large sample of individual households from St. Louis, Kain and Quigley estimate that a black family with identical income, job stability, education, age, and life cycle as a white family will be nearly 9 percent less likely to own. Most surprising is their analysis of home purchase which indicates that only 8 percent of recent black movers purchase homes, while 20 percent would have if they had been white. These results indicate that current patterns of tenure are not simply a result of historical problems. In addition, Kain and Quigley estimate that households headed by females are less likely to own and to purchase than otherwise identical families headed by males.

The Kain-Quigley study proceeds by estimating a linear probability model. It is assumed that the true probability of homeownership (or home purchase) is a linear function of a number of independent variables describing the socio-economic characteristics of the household. Estimation is accomplished by regressing a binary dependent variable (1=own, 0=rent) on the set of independent variables. Such linear probability models present a number of severe problems. The present study has utilized the more efficient and correct LOGIT technique. The essential characteristic of the LOGIT analysis is that it is mathematically suited to the problem of predicting probabilities.

Analysis of Tenure in Rural Areas: Methodology and Data

Briefly, the approach used here was to use Bureau of the Census Public Use Sample data to estimate a LOGIT statistical model which could then be used to predict the probability that a household with any given set of characteristics would own its home. Within each of the six study states, and separately for movers and nonmovers, the analysis estimates the change in the probability of homeownership that would result from a change in the race, sex, age, education, employment, or veteran status of the head, or in the income or size of the family.

Movers (those who have moved within the three years preceding the collection of the data) and nonmovers are treated separately for two reasons. First, it is important to investigate whether the pattern of the recent past differs systematically from that of more distant history. Second, the "stability" of a given household in labor and capital markets is an important determinant of its ability to secure credit, and may be proxied by the "mover" variable.

The sections that follow discuss first the statistical model used in the analysis and then the data and specification used to estimate the parameters of that model. Finally, the results are presented. Some of the issues raised are fairly technical, and are dealt with in the body of this chapter at an intuitive level. The interested reader will find a more explicit and detailed discussion of the model, its interpretation, and its results in Appendix E.

The LOGIT Statistical Model

In estimating a "choice" model, in which one tries to ascertain the probability with which individuals with a particular set of characteristics are distributed between two classes (owning or renting), the standard least-squares (OLS) linear regression techniques are inappropriate. The problem with these techniques is that their estimates are not constrained to lie within the unit interval, and any estimates from a probability model that are either greater than one or less than zero are rather embarrassing. The fundamental error lies in the assumption that the true probabilities lie along a line; as figure 2-5 shows, this implies that for some values of the independent variable, z, the predicted probability will be outside of the unit interval. In the case depicted in figure 2-5, any value of z greater than $\bar{z}$ or less than $\underline{z}$ results in a predicted probability greater than one or less than zero. It should be noted that the implication is not simply that linear probability models are necessarily somewhat inaccurate. Rather, it is clear that the fundamental assumption upon which estimation is predicated in the use of the linear model—that the true probabilities do in fact lie along a line —*cannot possibly be correct*. This makes any estimates derived from such a model suspect.

The solution to the problem must involve a change in this fundamental assumption. The LOGIT technique, in particular, is based upon the assumption

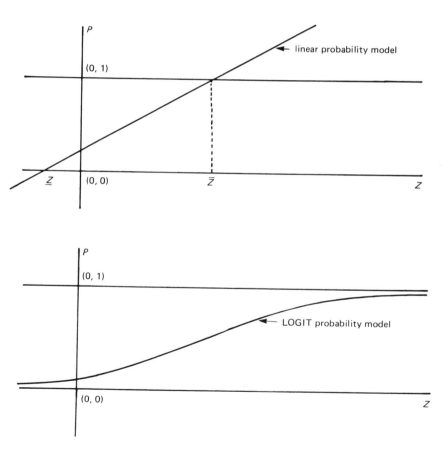

Figure 2-5. LOGIT vs. Linear Probability Model

that the true probabilities to be explored lie along a curve like the one depicted in figure 2-5. Clearly, there are many curves that look more or less like the one in figure 2-5, just as there are many possible lines in the case of a linear model. The LOGIT process restricts its consideration to a particular, though fairly large, subset of the possible curves, and then chooses from among the subset that which fits the data "best" in a precisely defined mathematical sense. Although computationally quite different, the method of choosing the best curve in the LOGIT estimation procedure is not unlike that for choosing the best line in the case of linear regression estimation.

In most data sets, the probabilities estimated by the two models are not substantially different when both are in the range of 0.25 to 0.75. It is toward the "edges," where the linear probability estimates approach and then cross the boundaries of the unit interval, while the LOGIT estimates do not, that the estimates typically differ importantly. Since the estimates of the two models typically agree fairly closely over the middle range of probabilities, and since one could always correct the OLS estimates by setting them to zero if they were less than zero and to one if they were greater than one, it might seem as if there were little to choose between the models. The important difference is in the way in which the models predict that the probability will *change* as a particular characteristic is changed. The OLS estimate of the *rate of change* of the probability with respect to a parameter is constant over the entire range of probabilities. By contrast, the LOGIT estimate of the rate of change of the probability with respect to the value of a parameter, the slope of the curve in figure 2-5, is small when the predicted probability is close either to 0 or to 1, and is larger when the predicted probability is in the middle range. To illustrate, the LOGIT model predicts that for persons of sufficiently high income, race and sex of the head are practically immaterial because the probability of ownership is already so high. The OLS model, on the other hand, makes the unlikely prediction that changing the sex of the head for a family with income of $5,000 has the same impact on the probability of ownership as for a family with $500,000 of income. Thus, the interpretation of the estimates of rate of change of the probability of ownership with respect to the values of the underlying parameters, while more complicated in the LOGIT model than in the OLS model, is also inherently more reasonable. This is a strong reason for preferring the LOGIT model to determine how the probability of ownership is affected by socio-economic status. This does not imply, however, that one need dispense with the strong empirical relation between the two models. In fact, as discussed in Appendix E, it provides the basis for the technique of estimating the parameters of the LOGIT model.

Data

This portion of the research relied upon data compiled by the Bureau of the Census and released as the one-in-one-thousand State Public Use Sample based upon the 15 percent sample questionnaire. All nonmetropolitan households with an identifiable head were examined for each of the states considered. The data extracted included the race, sex, educational attainment, income, age, and employment status of the head, family income from various sources, size of the family, whether the family had moved within the preceding three years, and other related socioeconomic characteristics. The characteristics of the Census "rural" sample were examined to see whether it might be better suited to the purpose of selecting the sample, but it contained numerous cases of families that were "rural" but "metropolitan." Since this might impart a significant bias to the results, the criterion of the Census "nonmetropolitan" characteristic was used. (According to the Census definitions, a "rural" household is one that lives outside a "place" of 2,500 or more while a "nonmetropolitan" household is one that does not live inside an SMSA.)

Specification

Selection of Variables. Two fundamental concerns governed the search for an appropriate set of variables within the context of the chosen LOGIT model. First, it is frequently acknowledged, but less frequently practiced, that selecting variables by observing directly how well they alone or in combination explain the data set involved in the analysis is not a theoretically defensible statistical procedure. In order for the tests of significance to have any statistically meaningful interpretation, they must be derived from a model and variables chosen *prior* to fitting the parameters and observing the results. This study has scrupulously avoided the temptation to make substitutions from the original set of variables chosen, with the exception of eliminating those that happened to have no variation whatsoever across a particular subgroup of data. (Inclusion of such a variable makes any estimation impossible because the resulting data moment matrix is singular.) Thus, the original formulation, which was both simple and straightforward, has remained the only specification. Second, in order to make comparisons across states, the model and the variables used had to be the same in each state. Otherwise, it would be impossible to separate the effect of adding or substituting variables from the true effect of changing states. Again, this argues for a simple and straightforward choice of variables. It is clear that one could have found sets of variables that resulted in higher "explanatory power," crudely measured by t and F statistics, but those statistics would then be interpretable only as the outcome of an ad hoc maximization process, and would have no true statistical significance.

A list of the variables selected, their position on the 15 percent Census PUS records, and the way in which each was measured follows:

H27	Tenure (Owner, Renter)
H71, H74	Race of head, measured at 1 if minority[g] and 0 otherwise,
P6	Sex of head, measured as 1 if female and 0 if male,
H85-87	Income of the family,[h] measured as a continuous variable, in hundreds of dollars,
P17-18	Education of the head, measured as his or her highest grade attended,
P62-63	Family size, measured as the total number of members,
P31	Employment status of the head, measured as 1 if unemployed and 0 otherwise,
P9-11	Age of the head, measured in years as a continuous variable,
P49-51	Presence of welfare income, measured as 1 if the family received any welfare income, and 0 otherwise, and
P80	Veteran status of head, measured as 1 if the head is a veteran, 0 otherwise.

The last two of these variables deserve further comment. Both are intended to capture the effects of credit markets in determining the ability of a family to buy a home. Casual observation suggests that credit agencies do not typically extend the large amounts of credit necessary for a mortgage to families on welfare; this variable is measured as a binary variable because of the obvious nonlinearity of the "bunching" of the continuous variable, welfare income received, at the value of 0. The veterans variable is an attempt to proxy the effect of the federal guaranteed loans program available to veterans.

In addition to stratification by state, the sample was also stratified into the group that had moved within the preceding three years and the group that had

---

[g]American Indian in South Dakota; Spanish-surnamed in New Mexico; black in the southern four states.

[h]The possibility that the income of the head is the more relevant variable was also investigated. However, there was no important difference between the results with family income held constant and the outcome with household head's income held constant.

not. This division was tested, as were the others, and was found to be highly significant. Classifying individuals as "movers" or "nonmovers" is in some ways an unusual criterion for dividing a sample in an investigation of the effect of socioeconomic characteristics. However, it is important for two reasons. First, it evidently proxies a number of otherwise practicably unobservable traits of the family, which, bundled together, might be referred to as "stability," both in labor and capital markets. Such a characteristic is clearly quite important in determining the likelihood of ownership. Second, and perhaps even more importantly for this study, the market outcomes for "movers" represent what is presently occurring in the housing markets. Thus, they present evidence of whether recent events are more or less similar to those more distant chronologically, or whether instead the effects of various socioeconomic characteristics are now different than they were previously. Unfortunately, of course, these two effects are confounded, and largely inseparable. The stratification of the cross-section sample into two chronologically separate groups is at best a poor approximation for time series data. Nonetheless, it appears potentially useful for both reasons, and has been maintained.

Analysis of Pooling. Extensive tests were carried out to determine the degree to which data samples should be divided into completely separate classes, or "pools." This amounts to testing whether the effect of a particular variable on the likelihood of ownership is adequately caught by simply including it as a single variable in the LOGIT model. For example, is the effect of having a female head of household simply that the constant term is different for that family than for one with a male head, or do the signs and the magnitudes of the other effects also differ for the two types of families? It is not unreasonable to assume that the effect of having the head of household be a veteran might well depend upon whether the head was male or female.

Standard Chow tests were employed to determine whether a constrained version of the model should be accepted or rejected in favor of an unconstrained version. Here, the unconstrained model permits the effects of income, education, and so on to vary with sex or race.[i]

---

[i]Formally, if Ω is the unconstrained and ω the constrained model, with df_Ω and df_ω degrees of freedom respectively, and with sums of squares of residuals SSE_Ω and SSE_ω then

$$\frac{SSE_\omega - SSE_\Omega}{\sigma^2}$$

is distributed approximately as chi-squared with $df_\omega - df_\Omega$ degrees of freedom, and is independent of SSE_Ω/σ^2 under the hypothesis that ω is true. But SSE_Ω/σ^2 is approximately chi-squared with df_Ω degrees of freedom, so that

$$\frac{SSE_\omega - SSE_\Omega}{df_\omega - df_\Omega} \Big/ SSE_\Omega/df_\Omega$$

is approximately F with $(df_\omega - df_\Omega, df_\Omega)$ degrees of freedom. This is the pooling test statistic.

Using the data for North Carolina, tests showed that one could pool male- and female-headed households at the 0.05 level. In addition, with the sample not yet pooled over sex, black and white households could be pooled at the 0.05 level. The results of tests for pooling over both race and sex were ambiguous. Technically, the test statistic rejected pooling at the 0.05 level. Interpretation of such test statistics, however, is not merely a matter of reading F tables. With a large sample, the tests can be expected to draw rather fine distinctions between coefficients of the two models being compared. Technically, the test reveals a statistical difference between the effects of the other socioeconomic characteristics on tenure choice for blacks and the effects for whites, already pooled over sex, and for men as against women already pooled over race. While statistically perceptible, however, this difference may be practically immaterial. Because of the large amount of data under observation, the test may be able to identify differences that are actually trivial in importance. This appears to be the case here. Moreover, the additional, and perhaps more important consideration of clarity in interpretation of the results, which would have been unduly complicated and yet in no way significantly different without pooling over both race and sex, argued strongly for the model in which the effects of race and sex are captured by allowing the constant term to shift. Thus, the model was fit with both race and sex as binary variables, rather than having separate equations for men and women or for whites and non-whites.

Analysis of Tenure in Rural Areas: Results

The estimation and interpretation of the parameters of the LOGIT statistical model are highly technical processes, and are dealt with in detail in Appendix F. This section concentrates on what appears to be the most useful parameterization of the results. After the coefficients of the model are estimated, it can be used to make predictions of the probability of homeownership for families with a given set of characteristics. In particular, one can identify an "average" family, i.e., one of average size and income, and having a head with average age, education, and so on, and then consider the effect of changing the race or sex of the head on the predicted probability of ownership. By so doing, the analysis presents in isolation the predicted effect of race or sex on the probability of ownership for the "average" family, holding all other socioeconomic characteristics fixed.

The results of this inquiry for rural portions of the four southern states under study are overwhelmingly conclusive. Race and sex have a substantial impact upon the probability of ownership even when other important socioeconomic factors are held constant. The results for race for off-reservation Indians in South Dakota and for Spanish-surnamed families in New Mexico are not conclusive, though the results for sex in these states are much the same as in the South. Because the statistical results are stronger in the South, the following discussion concentrates on them.

Figure 2-6 presents the results of the analysis for movers and nonmovers separately in each of the four southern states examined. The calculations are based on an "average family," that is, a family earning the mean income whose head has achieved the mean number of years of schooling, is of average age, etc.

Among *nonmovers*, the probability that a white family with average characteristics will own is above 0.90 in all states. The probability that an otherwise identical black family will own is 0.43 in Tennessee, 0.64 in Georgia, 0.68 in North Carolina, and 0.86 in Arkansas. Among *movers* the probability that a male-headed household with average characteristics will own is about 0.60 in each of the four states. The probability that an otherwise identical female-headed household will own is between 0.38 and 0.53. Among *nonmovers* the probability of ownership is above 0.90 in all states for male-headed households with average characteristics. In Georgia that probability is reduced to 0.71 for female heads, in North Carolina to 0.79. Sex has a very small effect among nonmovers in Tennessee and Arkansas.

Table 2-6 shows the predicted results of changing other important socio-economic characteristics on the probability of homeownership for the otherwise average family, in addition to the information already depicted in figure 2-6. These estimates are presented both for their intrinsic interest and because they illustrate the apparent sensibility of the predictions made by the LOGIT model. The fact that these estimated effects are reasonable is reassuring; though this is clearly a weak test of the procedure and results, one might be a good deal more suspicious of the estimates of the effects of race and sex if the estimates of the other effects had been wildly counterintuitive.

The analysis presented here, with its recurrent pattern of statistical significance and its overall sensibility, strongly suggests several broad conclusions.

1. First, and most important, there is convincing evidence that both minority and female-headed households are substantially less likely to own their homes in lieu of renting.
2. The effect of race appears to be somewhat larger than that of sex, although the difference between the two is small relative to the size of either.
3. The effect of sex does not appear to differ systematically between movers and nonmovers. In North Carolina, the effects of sex are the same, while in Georgia the effect is larger for nonmovers and in Arkansas and Tennessee it is larger for movers.
4. The effect of race appears to be smaller for movers than for nonmovers.

The third and fourth statements require further elucidation. It should be noted in particular that the evidence in their favor is suggestive rather than over-powering. Further research in a larger number of states would be required to

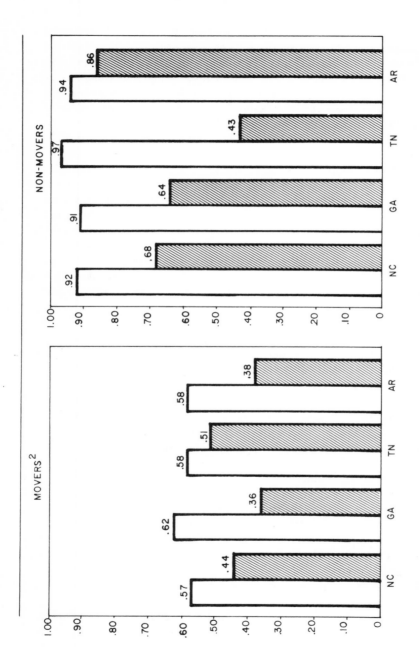

Figure 2-6. Probability of Homeownership for Otherwise Identical[1] Black and White Households

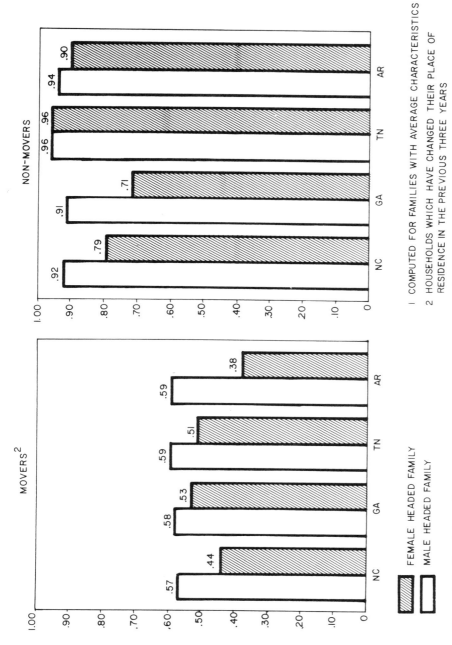

Figure 2-6. Proability of Homeownership for Otherwise Identical[1] Male- and Female-Headed Households

Table 2-6
Probability of Homeownership and Purchase

	NC		GA		TN		AR	
	Movers	Nonmovers	Movers	Nonmovers	Movers	Nonmovers	Movers	Nonmovers
Average	.54	.90	.57	.88	.57	.96	.56	.93
High Income	.76	.90	.68	.88	.81	.97	.52	.96
Low Income	.44	.89	.53	.88	.47	.95	.56	.92
Old	.67	.90	.67	.89	.67	.97	.66	.93
Young	.48	.86	.51	.81	.52	.91	.45	.95
Off Welfare	.55	.90	.58	.89	.58	.96	.56	.93
On Welfare	.26	.57	.53	.56	.41	.85	.51	.96
Male Head	.57	.92	.58	.91	.59	.96	.59	.94
Female Head	.44	.79	.53	.71	.51	.97	.38	.90
Minority	.44	.68	.36	.64	.51	.43	.38	.86
White or Other	.57	.92	.62	.91	.58	.97	.58	.94

Definitions:

Average: Mean for each variable
High Income: $20,000
Low Income: $2,000
Old: 60 years
Young: 30 years

Off Welfare: No welfare income
On Welfare: Receives some welfare income
Male Head: Head is male
Female Head: Head is female
Minority: Head is black, Hispanic, or American Indian

confirm them. However, if these results are not misleading they may be quite important, for they suggest that the effect of race may be less presently than it has been historically, while there is no evidence that the effect of sex is similarly declining. This would not be a terribly surprising conclusion, since the drive for equal racial opportunity appears to predate that for sex equality by a number of years, and since the latter was not specifically included in federal Fair Housing legislation until 1974.

To summarize, the evidence developed here is quite conclusive. It documents the existence of pervasive, systematic and important biases in the tenure patterns of blacks compared with whites, and male-headed compared with female-headed households, when other important socioeconomic characteristics are held constant, at least in the four southern states examined in this study. The evidence for sex inequality in New Mexico and South Dakota, presented in Appendix E, is entirely consistent with that from the South. There is, however, no evidence that tenure patterns are significantly different for the Spanish-surnamed population in New Mexico than for other whites. The data contained an insufficient number of observations on off-reservation American Indians in South Dakota to permit any generalization concerning this minority.

Notes

1. Karl E. and Alma F. Taeuber, *Negroes in Cities: Residential Segregation and Neighborhood Change* (Chicago: Aldine Publishing Co., 1965).
2. Howard J. Sumka and Michael A. Stegman, "Racial Segregation and Price Discrimination in Non-metropolitan Rental Housing Markets," North Carolina Housing Market Study, Working Paper #14, Oct., 1974.
3. Taeuber and Taeuber, *Negroes in Cities*.
4. See for example, Karl and Alma Taeuber, "The Negroes as an Immigrant Group," *American Journal of Sociology* 64, 4 (January 1964); A.H. Pascal, "The Economics of Housing Segregation," Memorandum RM-5510-RC (Santa Monica: the RAND Corporation, November 1967); Davis McEntire, *Residence and Race* (Berkeley: University of California Press, 1960).
5. Thomas C. Schelling, "Dynamic Models of Segregation," *Journal of Mathematical Sociology* 1 (1971).
6. William Brink and Louis Harris, *Black and White* (New York: Simon and Schuster, 1967).
7. Louis Harris, *Living in Harlem*, study completed for the Harlem Urban Development Corporation, November 1973.
8. Examples include:
   Luigi Laurenti, *Property Values and Race: Studies in Seven Cities* (Berkeley: University of California, 1960); "Effect of Integration on Property Values", *American Economic Review* 52, 4 (Sept. 1962); Davis H. Karlen, "Racial

Integration and Property Values in Chicago," Urban Economics Report #7, April 1968 (Chicago: University of Chicago Press); Joseph P. McKenna and Herbert D. Werner, "The Housing Market in Integrating Areas," *The Annals of Regional Science* 4, 2 (December 1970); Donald Phares, "Racial Change and Housing Values: Transition in an Inner Suburb," *Social Science Quarterly* (December 1971).

9. Studies using the hedonic price technique include Donald G. Ridker and John A. Henning, "The Determinants of Residential Property Values with Special Reference to Air Pollution", *The Review of Economics and Statistics* 44, 2 (May 1967); Thomas King and Peter Mieszkowski, "An Estimate of Racial Discrimination in Rental Housing," Cowles Foundation Discussion Paper 307, Yale University, February 1971; Mahlon Straszheim, *An Econometric Analysis of the Urban Housing Market*, National Bureau of Economic Research, 1974; Ann Schnare, *An Empirical Analysis of the Dimensions of Neighborhood Quality*, The Urban Institute, forthcoming; John F. Kain and John M. Quigley, *Discrimination and a Heterogeneous Housing Stock*, National Bureau of Economic Research, forthcoming.

10. Karlen, "Racial Integration," p. 16.

11. Zvi Griliches, "Hedonic Price Indexes Revisited: Some Notes on the State of the Art," *American Statistical Association, Proceedings of the Business Economics and Statistics Section*, 1967; Sherwin Rosen, "Hedonic Prices and Implicit Markets," *Journal of Political Economy* 82, 1 (January/February 1974).

12. Kain and Quigley, *Discrimination*, Chapter VIII.

13. Ibid.

14. Schnare, *An Empirical Analysis.*

15. King and Mieszkowski, "Estimate of Racial Discrimination."

16. See for example, John M. Quigley, "Residential Location: Multiple Work Places and a Heterogeneous Housing Stock," Ph.D. dissertation, Harvard University, 1972; Gregory K. Ingram, "A Simulation Model of a Metropolitan Housing Market," Ph.D dissertation, Harvard University, 1971; Straszheim, *An Econometric Analysis.*

17. Makoto Ohta, "Production Technologies of the U.S. Boiler and Turbogenerator Industries and Hedonic Price Indexes for These Products," *Journal of Political Economy*, (February 1975).

18. See, for example, Sherman J. Maisel, "Rates of Ownership, Mobility and Purchase," *Essays in Urban Land Economics* (Los Angeles: Real Estate Research Programs, University of California, 1966), pp. 76–108; Kain and Quigley, *Discrimination* Chapters 5 and 6; Tony Hum Lee, "Demand for Housing: A Cross-Section Analysis," *Review of Economics and Statistics* 45, 2 (May 1963): 190–96; Guy H. Orcutt et al., *Micro-analysis of Socioeconomic Systems* (New York: Harper & Bros., 1961); Martin David, *Family Composition and Consumption* (Amsterdam: North-Holland Publishing Company, 1962).

3 Housing Market Interactions

This chapter and those which follow analyze the operations of the six markets in an attempt to account for the inequalities documented above. They seek to identify the ways in which consumers, suppliers, and interveners interact in order to determine how and by whom inequality is brought about. (See figure 1-1). The activities of suppliers and interveners are covered in Chapters 4 and 5. This chapter examines specifically "market" interactions between consumers and suppliers—inquiries, purchases and rentals.

These interactions are patterned by (1) the means of *communication* or information exchange between potential consumers and the suppliers of housing, land and financing; and (2) *regulations* defining permissible interactions. Communications would include the ways in which consumers learn about supply, or are prevented from doing so. Regulations define whether a given attempt at purchase (etc.) would be permissible in the local market. Characteristically, these "regulations" are likely to be traditional, culturally-reinforced mores and "taboos" rather than formally propounded rules. However, the enactment of formal rules is the most frequent means by which the federal government attempts to intervene in market interactions.

The specific questions addressed in this chapter are the following. First, can the inequalities in market outcomes detailed in Chapter 2—racial segregation, the lower probability of homeownership for women and minorities and their higher probability in general of occupying substandard housing—be attributed to imperfections in the means by which such households receive information about housing and financing opportunities? Secondly, what is the role of informal regulations in relation to the observed inequalities in these market outcomes? Finally, special consideration is given here to the role of "self-segregation" in accounting for black locational patterns. The discussion is presented as a series of "assertions" whose validity was examined in this study.

Patterns of Information Exchange

In order to gain access to sales or rental housing, the potential consumer must become aware of available units and, in the case of housing to be built or purchased, of financing opportunities. Findings concerning the ways in which information is exchanged in rural markets are presented in this section.

Consumers most frequently learn of available housing through real estate agents.

False

ban areas, which are frequently large in land area and by definition densely populated, real estate agents typically play a significant role in disseminating information about available units. Discrimination on the part of agents in failing to inform minorities of certain units or in discouraging them from acquiring certain units has been suggested as a means by which unequal access is maintained in urban areas.[1] The information-exchange role of real estate brokers was found to be much less significant in rural markets, and to be highly selective in terms of the types of units listed and the types of customers served.

Brokers were found to be involved in a surprisingly small share of the market for existing housing, and hardly at all in the markets for new housing and rentals. New housing is normally sold directly by the builder, who prefers to locate customers on his own and avoid brokerage fees. Occasionally, a broker will refer a customer to a builder unable to dispose of a particular house built on speculation, but regularized interaction between builders and brokers was never encountered except in the rare cases where one office served both functions.

Rental housing is handled by brokers only in exceptional cases. No instances of brokers acting as agents for multifamily units were encountered, and only one of a broker acting as agent for an owner of a block of (mostly substandard) single-family units. Maintenance and collecting rents is a long-term, low-return activity which brokers avoid. Rental housing is typically listed and/or managed only in sporadic instances, such as a favor by the broker to a friend who wishes to rent out the family home while temporarily out of town.

Within the market for sales of existing homes, where brokers' activities are concentrated, their share of the market was found to be surprisingly small. Large proportions of existing-home sales—ranging from 25 percent to as high as 50 percent on one site—were found to be private sales in which brokers had no involvement at all. The average per site of private sales hovered around one-third, according to estimates by local brokers.

This discussion deals only with market transactions, excluding intrafamily transfers, wills, foreclosures, etc. Should these nonmarket transactions be included, the role of brokers would of course become even smaller.

In turning to look at the market from the demand side, the role of brokers becomes even more constricted. Demand for homes is generated by newly-arrived families, newly-formed families, and local families wishing to move. In-locating families—a small proportion of total consumers—almost invariably use brokers, and use their whole range of services: referral, negotiation, and closing.

Local families, either newly-formed or wishing to move, would often not use brokers—the private sales were mostly to them—and when they did, would be likely to use the broker for negotiation and closing but *not for referrals.* This is to say that very frequently the customer already knew which house he or she wanted, and consulted the broker because his name was given by the seller or posted on the property. In effect, the house "steered" the customer to the broker, rather than vice versa.

In sum, the role of brokers in alerting consumers to available units was found to be quite limited. They rarely dealt in rentals or new homes, and even within the existing home market, held collectively some 50-75 percent of the market, with the rest occurring as private sales. Most significantly, only a small proportion of their customers were new to the area. The bulk of the consumers who used brokers were familiar with the area, and had already located the desired unit through informal means: word-of-mouth or by simply driving around looking for "For Sale" signs.

This finding suggests two further questions: the role of brokers in relation to equal access within their market share, and the possibly unequal operation of the other, informal, means of access to information.

Assertion: *Real estate agents tend to preserve racially segregated neighbor-hood boundaries.*

Finding: *Qualified*

This hypothesis, also suggested by urban experience, must be strongly qualified in relation to rural markets. The ways in which brokers *might* maintain inequality are two: (1) refusing to serve minority customers, and (2) refusing to inform minorities of homes in white areas and/or discouraging minorities from attempting to acquire such homes. These will be discussed in turn.

Refusal of services is a blatantly illegal activity which is quite rare. Superficial observation shows that the majority of brokers' customers are white, but this does not necessarily indicate refusal of services (or reluctance to apply because of the expectation of discrimination). To some extent, it can be attributed to income distribution—brokers deal more often in higher-priced housing, and the higher-income families who can afford these homes tend to be white. In addition, blacks have a higher rate of renting in lieu of owning (possibly because of other inequalities in the market structure, particularly financing), and brokers almost never handle rental housing. Finally, the portion of brokers' business which comes from newly-arrived families includes almost no blacks. The small number of newly-arrived black families tend to be rural, low-income families moving into the towns from the counties; such families would not be in a position to purchase. The higher-income new families tend to be professionals transferred in by the area's industries, schools, and government offices, and these are, with very few exceptions, white.

There is also direct evidence that brokers do not as a rule refuse services to minorities. Practically all brokers interviewed had Equal Opportunity signs prominently displayed, claimed to serve black customers, and were supported in this claim by black respondents.[a] Perhaps more significantly, the black submarket is not served by a separate set of formal institutions: there were no black brokers (aside from one individual with a broker's license who was inactive in the market), and no white brokers who concentrated exclusively on the black submarket. Rational economic incentives to capture this market would operate against whatever personal disinclination a broker might have toward dealing with minorities. The economic incentive would be reinforced by the small size of the total market. In contrast to urban areas, where brokers often concentrate in particular neighborhoods or areas, rural brokers usually cover (or at least try to cover) the whole county.

The fact remains, however, that even though brokers typically serve both black and white submarkets, the submarkets remain separate. This suggests either that brokers are refusing to show blacks homes in white areas, or that this expectation has been internalized and blacks are not asking to see such homes.[b] There is some reason to believe that both are true. Black respondents frequently charged that brokers would refuse them service in white areas if they dared ask, although the study team lacked the investigatory authority to verify this independently. One such case led to a law suit recently in one of the study sites—a newly-arrived black family hired by the school system filed suit charging that a broker had shown them homes only in the black area. The case became moot, however, since the man was soon fired from his job and, unable to find other employment, had to leave the area. (The school system denied any connection.)

On the other hand, the most frequently-offered explanation by brokers for lack of residential integration was that blacks "want to live with their own kind," and thus show no interest in homes outside of the black areas. To the extent that this does reflect consumers' *stated* interests, it would indicate that market separation is being maintained as much or more by lack of black pressure as by overt white refusal.

There are two considerations, however, which tend to diminish the importance of possible inequality of services by brokers in accounting for residential

---

[a]There were exceptions, of course. One broker said in an unguarded moment that "We don't deal in Niggertown," though his main explanation for the lack of black customers was that blacks could not afford the high-income housing his office listed. Given the income distribution of the area, this claim is probably true, and his willingness to serve black customers was therefore left untested. ("Niggertown" in this area refers to the entire black section of the town, not just the rundown neighborhood which is known as "the Hole.")

[b]The situation could also result from self-segregation among blacks, but self-segregation is difficult to distinguish from internalized discrimination. This problem is discussed further in the section "The Self-Segregation Hypothesis."

segregation. The first is the relatively low share of the market handled by brokers, as discussed above. The second is that in the very few cases in the study sites where blacks had moved into white areas—*they were referred to these homes by brokers.* No cases of blacks moving on their own into white areas were found, but four cases of blacks moving into white areas with the assistance of brokers were found.

This finding tends to take some of the burden of rural discrimination off the real estate industry, especially in light of the fact that the reprisals taken by irate neighbors were more against the broker than against the black family. This serves to underline, of course, the fact that no element of the housing market acts in a vacuum, and that brokers who do discriminate are following not only whatever personal feelings they might have, but also reacting to the market "rules" of the area, which can be quite vigorously enforced.

Assertion: *Separation in the informal communication networks deprives minorities of information about available housing.*

Finding: *Qualified*

The above discussions have suggested that most communication about available housing units is informal; separations in the informal networks could deprive minorities of information available to whites, and thus serve to effect and maintain segregation. Findings suggest, however, that this assertion need be somewhat qualified in relation to rural markets.

The social context of which the housing market is a part is one of racial and income-class separation. This is to say that there is little personal friendship or social interaction among whites and blacks and American Indians, and little such interaction between high- and low-income groups within racial categories. (Personal friendship and social interaction among Spanish-surnamed population and other whites were much more frequent on the New Mexico site.) Interactions between members of different racial and income groups, while not uncommon, tend to be in formal nonpersonal relationships such as employer/employee, customer/vendor, etc. Since minorities are disproportionately lower income (this is true in all six sites), they are thus cut off by both racial and income barriers from informal sources of information.

To the extent that information about available housing is available *only* by word-of-mouth, this social separation would indeed deprive minorities of equal access to white-occupied housing (and, of course, whites to minority housing). However, this assertion needs to be qualified because *most respondents interviewed knew about most houses for sale, regardless of racial barriers.* Like the hypothesized importance of real estate brokers, the hypothesized importance of word-of-mouth communication derives from the urban experience, where the geographical expanse and comparatively dense population makes for greater problems in information transfer. In rural areas these factors do not apply. The towns are small in land area and can easily be covered by car and even on foot. Respondents of both races were generally aware of what new housing was being built and of what homes were for sale or rent simply from personal observation. Families were deprived of information through social separation only if a home purchase or rental was arranged between people known to each other and thus never came on the open market. The shortage of housing in relation to need *and* effective demand is becoming so severe in all the areas studied that this type of transfer is becoming more and more common, although its numerical relationship to formally and informally advertised housing could not be determined.

Assertion: *Separation in the informal networks of communication deprives minorities of information concerning financing opportunities and programs.*

Finding: *True*

Unlike housing, available financing is not visible to the naked eye and is rarely advertised. As a result, informal word-of-mouth communication is the most important means by which such information is disseminated. However, such information rarely reaches out beyond those who are professionally concerned with it: consumers normally knew which lenders made home mortgages, but did not know as a matter of general information what terms were available, what federal subsidy or guarantee programs they might be eligible for, etc.

Naturally, people with personal friends in the financial and real estate circles could more easily find this information when they needed to know. In this context, it is important to note that minorities were never found in responsible positions in lending institutions or in real estate, and only one black builder was encountered. (This discussion does not apply to the New Mexico site where Spanish-surnamed were frequently found in the supply industries, and where social barriers in any case appear to be based more on income than on ethnic background.) However, lack of consumer information, particularly in relation to the federal programs in operation at the time covered by this study, is a general problem which is only slightly more serious for minorities.

Assertion: *Public agencies and private community organizations serve as sources of housing-related information for consumers.*

Finding: *False*

This finding is important in light of the general unawareness of consumers of financing opportunities, and also because of the general lack of organization among consumers, which leaves each household responsible for dealing with the housing market as best it can.

An exception to this finding, which points up its importance in the other areas, is the operation of the Indian tribal organization on the South Dakota site. Tribal officials keep up to date on benefits and services which may be available from the federal programs, and *coordinate the acquisition of services and/or information* for Indian consumers. Thus, the tribe can inform a consumer of programs aimed at individual households—such as the FmHA 502 homeownership program—as well as administer a federally-funded Housing Improvement Program for rehabilitation and sponsor a Tribal Housing Authority for constructing and managing HUD Public Housing.

No comparable function is performed in the other areas by either public or private organizations, leaving the individual household more-or-less cut off from any source of general information. Again, the effect on minority households is slightly greater than on white households because of the lesser probability that minorities will be in industries or on boards where the information would be available; the problem is, however, a general one. Only one of the areas is within the target area of a specifically housing-related community organization, and this organization had not yet become active in the study site. In another area, a community action agency did attempt to disseminate information in the black community about program eligibility, but interviews revealed a startling ignorance and misinformation about program benefits and eligibility requirements on the part of out-reach workers. More generally, no organization performed this communication function.

The result is not only to deprive households of information needed to make optimal choices among housing alternatives, but in some cases to prevent access to improved housing altogether. For instance, in one area a number of HUD 235 homes were standing vacant, although they were available to black consumers. Interviews revealed that there was considerable misinformation in the community about the terms of 235 ownership—that you don't really own the house and can't leave it to your children, that you own the house but not the land, etc. With no source of information to correct these misimpressions, black families were discouraged from purchase.

Another commonly-encountered problem was that, even after purchase, households were still unaware of many of their rights and obligations. Many failed to consider utility and sewerage costs, for instance, or did not understand that 235 payments increase with income. Nor did families generally know their legal rights in relation to tax and mortgage foreclosure. Again, this lack of access to information is a general problem which is only slightly greater for minorities.

Assertion: *Housing-program and financing information is provided almost exclusively by local supply institutions: builders, lenders, and real estate agents.*

Finding: *True*

The information gap is dealt with only by these supply institutions and only in the course of their normal business. Bankers may recommend and arrange FHA-insured financing, builders may suggest taking advantage of HUD 235 or FmHA 502 homeownership programs, real estate agents may arrange out-of-town financing on better terms than are available locally, etc.

The limitation of the communication function to these organizations makes for two inadequacies in information exchange. The first is that each organization generally has one or two specialties among the plethora of alternatives available, and would naturally make a point of informing consumers only of the services which the organization can arrange.[c] Consumers do not therefore receive the overview of benefits which would permit an optimal choice of financing mechanisms or sources.

Secondly, the reach of these organizations into the community is somewhat restricted along racial lines as noted above. For reasons which may be but are not necessarily deliberately discriminatory, the households served by builders, lenders, and real estate brokers are disproportionately white. The effect, therefore, is that minority households are somewhat less likely than white households to become aware of financing information, and thus to acquire housing on the best terms for which they are eligible. This is a paradigm case of indirect or by-product discrimination: unequal access which results from the institutional structure of the housing market, rather than from direct discrimination on the part of housing market actors.

Conclusion

This discussion has indicated that unequal access to housing on the part of minority households is only partially attributable to imperfections in the information exchange function of the market. The availability of housing itself is generally disseminated across racial lines, and lack of information about financing alternatives is only partially racially-selective. However, racial segregation and tenure differences persist. This suggests that to the extent that market interactions contribute to inequality of access, the answer is more apt to lie in the informal regulations which define a permissible interaction than in the communication function.

---

[c]Aside from their particular specialties, many suppliers were no more familiar than consumers with programs and terms. Even a bank president on one site was unaware of FmHA as distinct from HUD.

Housing Market Regulations

"The law" is that which designates permissible and prohibited interactions among persons; "the Law," as the term is commonly used, refers to that which is written and duly enacted. This is to say that "the law" is by definition an institution—a regularized pattern of interactions among persons—while "the Law" may or may not be institutionalized, depending on the extent to which it has more than paper reality. In the selected sites, with the exception of New Mexico, the unwritten regulations which in reality govern the housing market prescribe unequal access to housing.

Until recently, the informal or unwritten regulations applicable to housing market interactions could be translated directly into formal regulations: restrictive covenants, Jim Crow laws, etc., and the legal machinery of the public sector was available for enforcing them. Since the passage of Civil Rights and Fair Housing legislation on the federal level, and with the declared unconstitutionality of state and local race-related regulations, the formal and informal rules are in conflict and the enforcement mechanisms of both are in some disarray. This section considers the role of informal, traditional "regulations"; formal Fair Housing regulations are discussed under market interventions in Chapter 5.

Assertion: *Racial discrimination is deeply ingrained in traditional patterns of social interaction.*

Finding: *True*

This obvious point is worth stressing here because the regulations applying to the housing market in an area are a subset of its more general traditions of race relationships. In five of the six areas visited (the exception is New Mexico), racial discrimination is palpably obvious and supported by long tradition. Blacks and Indians were frequently spoken of in the most disparaging terms by whites— "dumb-ass Niggers" and "drunken Indians" were among the sobriquets used even by local officials in conversations with strangers (the research team). Social aversion was translated into denial of equal opportunity: minorities consistently held more menial jobs (if any jobs at all in the case of Indians), lived in worse housing (and in segregated housing in the case of blacks), and were granted only token representation (if that) in decision-making institutions—major employment providers, public and private boards, appointive public offices, etc.

It should be noted, of course, that this situation is by no means limited to rural areas, or to the South, or to areas abutting Indian Reservations. Racial discrimination in the urban North, for instance, has become increasingly visible in recent years, and many Indians who had left the South Dakota site's reservation have been returning from metropolitan areas in disappointment (according to tribal officials). It should also be pointed out that discrimination is by no means universal on the sites visited—more than a few whites maintained relationships of mutual respect with minorities, and worked for minority rights at some cost to themselves. The fact remains, however, that in these sites as in many or most other places, race is a factor in the access to social benefits.

The role of sex in prescribing access to social benefits and to housing in particular was almost impossible to define, although its invisibility is itself indicative. Neither men nor women interviewed were conscious of women as a distinctive social group differentially treated in the housing market, although the statistical analysis in Chapter 2 demonstrates that this is so. However, the role and status of women is so entangled with factors other than sex—race, income, status of husband or previous husband, status within the role of wife, etc.—that the particular effects of sex could not be isolated. There were no women's political groups on the sites, and individual women interviewed expressed the general view that women should not be discriminated against, but on the other hand, should not compete with men for jobs, housing, or other benefits. Housing market suppliers and interveners were typically unconscious of women *qua* heads of household. When asked if many applications from women were received, lenders typically responded "Yes, many women come in during the day when their husbands are at work," even though seven to eighteen percent of the towns' households are headed by women. It is clear that the general unwritten regulation applicable to women demands that they be subordinate, invisible, and (preferably) married; this was so ingrained and widely adhered to that the protests and reactions by which unwritten rules become visible were absent on the sites studied.

Assertion: *Residential segregation is dictated by the informal rules governing housing market interactions.*

Finding: *True*

In the four sites where segregation was observed, black-white neighborhood boundaries have never changed within the memory of local respondents, and racial segregation is virtually complete. (See Chapter 2 for a more detailed discussion of the extent of residential segregation.) While segregation was most often explained by white respondents as the result of black preference, other comments as well as the general traditions of interaction noted above suggest that such preference, if it exists, is by no means endogenous. "No white would ever sell to a black," "Integration?! Why that goes against all tradition" are among the statements of white respondents which suggest a market rule; black respondents were in general quite convinced that their entry into white neighborhoods would be actively discouraged. In one site, the rule was explicit: a sign prominently displayed in front of a new subdivision read: "RESTRICTED – FOR YOUR PROTECTION."

Like all operative regulations, the segregation rule is accompanied by enforcement procedures, although Fair Housing legislation and the Supreme Court's banning of racial covenants and Jim Crow laws tends to prevent the use of public authority for this purpose. In two cases where blacks had moved into white neighborhoods—both were the first examples of integration on the respective sites and both were within the last year—the family *and* the broker who had referred them were intimidated and harassed. Reprisals were taken against the brokers in the form of canceled insurance policies (both brokers were also insurance agents) and abusive phone calls, and physical reprisals were threatened against the families and the homes.

It is significant that the threats and reprisals, while damaging, appeared to be anomic. No organization could be detected behind the protests—the Ku Klux Klan, for instance, was inactive on all sites—and such collusion as there may have been among the "enforcers of traditional law" was discontinuous and ineffectual. The reactions had the appearance of discrete personal acts, not supported or melded into a greater whole by organization. Most significantly, the public powers once used in support of tradition were now arrayed against it: the fact that physical reprisals were *not* taken against the black family was attributed by respondents on one site to the long period of protection which their home received from local police and the FBI. (The lack of organization apparent among the protesters was also seen among the public servants. At one point, police arrested a suspicious character lurking on the premises; he turned out to be an FBI agent.)

In a symbolic move perhaps as much indicative of frustration as hostility, a cross was burned on one realtor's lawn. This type of action, once a sinister warning of events to come, was in this case simply another anomic protest, without follow-up and therefore without effectiveness beyond such fear as it may have instilled. However, the fear itself, whether or not produced by effective actions, is a powerful deterrent: a single person, with or without organized backing, can kill another; and economic reprisals, while in the aggregate smaller than they would be if coordinated, are still not insignificant to an individual person.

No general lessening of racial restrictions has therefore occurred on these two sites, even in the face of the apparent lack of coordinated support for the tradition. However, the structure of the institution is being minutely chipped away: within a few months, each of the black families was followed by another black family—referred by the same brokers—and another, but more muted, round of threats and protests began. The pace of change is extremely slow since it depends on individuals who are willing to risk certain threats and possible reprisals; such persons are at this point bearing the full cost of social "deviance"

on these two sites. On the other two southern sites, the costs are apparently
perceived as greater, or the opposition as more effective: the segregation rule
there has never been broken.

While organized preservation of discriminatory traditions was not observed in
the southern sites, the beginnings of such organization *were* observed in South Dakota. The South Dakota site is not segregated, but there is considerable hostility
generated by Indian attempts to regain reservation land that has been lost or sold
over the years and by other efforts to promote Indian rights. A rather large underground organization of local whites, perhaps best described as a "vigilante group,"
has been formed; meanwhile the American Indian Movement has been gaining
some support and organizing protest activities by Indians. While local respondents
described the area as not discriminatory, "not like the South," the South Dakota
site is the only one where, within the last year, gunshots have been exchanged on
racial grounds.

This discussion has concentrated on the more spectacular instances of discrimination and reprisals, since it is through these that the informal rules governing market interactions become visible. Local actors are, however, well aware of
the unwritten rules, and the comparative infrequency of such instances as described above indicates their understanding and compliance. This is to say what
is perhaps obvious: where race is a factor in access to housing and land, it is
enforced not merely by discriminatory acts on the part of individuals, but also
by community pressure which subjects individual actors—suppliers as well as
consumers—to costs and reprisals should they transgress the unwritten rules.

The Self-Segregation Hypothesis

The proposition that racial segregation results from black preferences de-
serves particular consideration since it could, logically, account for some of the
inequalities in market outputs;[d] and more importantly, because it was the explanation most commonly offered by housing market actors. In addition, the extreme rarity of integration-related incidents on the sites surveyed, coupled with
the failure of black interview respondents to mention residential integration
among their concerns, lends some superficial credence to this point of view.

The previous section concluded that segregation is an unwritten but effective rule of the market, and that any such preference blacks may in fact feel is
less endogenous than imposed. Black respondents among the poor and the
elderly were the most likely to have internalized the rule to the point where

---

[d]Self-segregation would of course result directly in segregation and housing market
segmentation, and, in the presence of inflexible housing stocks, in price differentials
between submarkets as well. In addition, self-segregation would result indirectly in
differences in the quality of housing occupied and in the likelihood of ownership to the
extent that supply and demand relationships differ among submarkets.

segregation was accepted as the natural order of things. Younger and middle-class respondents were less fatalistic, but still, with very few exceptions, acquiesced. The four instances mentioned above were the *only* examples of integration in private housing in two of the sites;[e] the other two had none at all. This section explores the reasons for this seeming acquiescence.

Assertion: *Racial minorities are in a position of dependence which serves to paralyze protest.*

Finding: *True*

The social pattern most commonly encountered was a complete absence of black-controlled or Indian-controlled institutions which could provide employment, social services, and organized support to individuals; in addition, nowhere did blacks or Indians have more than token representation in the formal institutions on which they depend. An exception was the Indian tribal government itself. Outside of the tribe, the study site contained no organizations owned or controlled by Indians. In some cases, a minority person had been elected to the town council or appointed to a public or private board; more often than not, however, such representatives do not articulate specifically minority interests and have little influence on eventual decisions. Black-owned businesses tend to be very small retail and service establishments serving the black areas and do not, in the aggregate, account for much employment. Indian-controlled employers, apart from the tribe, were nonexistent.

This situation of dependency leaves individuals especially vulnerable to reprisals should they become known as "troublemakers." When asked what would happen should a black attempt to move into a white neighborhood, most black respondents cited loss of job. (On one site with no integration, an unusually outspoken black respondent assured the study team that any such "troublemaker" would be killed.) Even on sites with no integration-related activity, other examples of retaliatory denial of social benefits had been observed—welfare recipients had been threatened with loss of benefits, school children suspended in large numbers, etc. The fear of job loss was therefore supported by the general experience of blacks, although it was rarely directly tested. Significantly, the first black to break the neighborhood barriers in one town was self-employed outside of the area; the one who filed a discrimination suit in another area lost his job and was unable to find another.

Over time, this position of actual dependence and enforced social subordination can lead—through a not-too-obscure process—to a state of psychological dependency and fatalistic acceptance of one's role and its rules. This was evident particularly among the elderly, who in addition found social support from

---

[e]Segregation in public housing is discussed in Chapter 5.

proximity of long-time neighbors and friends. In one site where a black organization attempted to recruit low-income tenants to integrate a new public housing project, they had considerable difficulty in convincing the elderly to move.

Younger, middle-class blacks, especially the educated, are much less fatalistic. It is this group, in fact, which is most likely to leave the area. Those who remain are perforce in a position of dependence on white-controlled institutions, and thus vulnerable to economic reprisals. Such persons were found to be extremely unlikely to undertake protest on their own behalf, and even less likely to provide leadership to the poor and elderly. In fact, some middle-class blacks attempted to preserve their own hard-won security by disassociating themselves as far as possible from the interests of the low-income blacks. (An NAACP chapter president explained the town's black slum with: "You know those people—they don't care how they live.")

In contrast, two of the sites showed evidence of active attempts on the part of middle-class blacks to promote black interests in general (including those of the poor). On one site, the leadership was employed at an out-of-town federal installation, and thus not vulnerable to local reprisals; on the other, the effort was conducted by a minister serving the black community and the leadership of a large, outside-funded community action agency. The social process at work thus becomes clear. In general, there is a lack of social protest. This can be attributed to economic dependency, which may be translated to some extent into psychological dependency or into refusal to admit commonality with other, poorer, blacks. However, where economic dependence is minimized or removed, leadership and protest have begun to emerge.

The situation of the American Indians is particularly instructive in relation to the role of dependency. Of all the minority groups surveyed, it was the Indians who were closest to economic desperation. Official unemployment rates hover around 50 percent but are estimated unofficially at closer to 65 percent or 70 percent. This reflects the depressed economic condition of the area in general, and, in addition, discrimination in employment. Outside of the tribe and the BIA office, only a handful of Indians are employed at jobs other than seasonal farm labor. In addition, Indians are routinely denied equal services and public accommodations, and are openly insulted in dealings with merchants, landlords, etc. In contrast with the situation of blacks, where protest is dampened by expectation of loss, many Indians are very close to the point of having nothing left to lose. Thus the social protest on the South Dakota site, which, however sporadic and as yet ineffective, goes far beyond anything observed on the southern sites.

This discussion has indicated that the general lack of social protest on the part of blacks against segregation and other forms of residential discrimination can be attributed to the perceived costs of such protest. The exceptions merely serve to underline the rule, since in the areas where the beginnings of protest have been observed, the leadership is provided by those who are shielded from direct economic reprisals.

There are two other factors which also contribute to the observed low levels of protest against residential segregation. These can be summed as a lack of pressure *toward* integration, in contrast with white community pressure *against* integration detailed above. They are discussed in the following sections.

Assertion: *Expansion of black residential areas occurs through transitional, "gray," neighborhoods.*

Finding: *False*

This assertion derives directly from the urban experience, where black neighborhoods are typically the old central cities, surrounded by concentric circles of new development. As whites move out from the center, their place is taken by in-coming blacks. If, however, black inmigration exceeds white outmigration, there is, in the absence of housing supply responses, population pressure tending to increase the absolute size of the black area.[f] Since the black area is typically surrounded by occupied white areas, the success of such expansion would take the form of neighborhood transition from all-white through some degree of (usually restless) integration toward, in most cases, all-black residency. In addition to general population pressure, the demand of individual black households for significantly improved housing is often expressed in the form of attempts to move out of the central city and into the surrounding white areas.

This pattern does not obtain in any of the rural sites visited. As noted repeatedly, there has been almost no crossing of neighborhood boundaries by blacks, and therefore no such phenomenon as a "transitional" or "gray" neighborhood has materialized. This can be attributed to some extent to the much lesser population pressure than is found in the major urban areas. The figures in Chapter 1 indicate substantial absolute decline of black population in the decade 1960-70—the continuation of a long process of massive outmigration from these areas.

The pattern in the towns appears to be somewhat less dramatic than that shown in these county-level figures. Black town population figures for 1960 and 1970 cannot be directly compared since most of the towns have annexed territory in that period. However, interview responses indicate that black outmigration from the towns is slightly less than from the farms and open country, and that some of the movement off the farms takes the form of intracounty movement to the towns. (The reverse movement from the towns into the counties is almost exclusively a white, high-income phenomenon.) Whatever the exact migration patterns may be, however, the observable pattern in housing is that black residential areas in the towns have in fact expanded over the last century and are continuing to do so.[g]

---

[f]There would also be a price response, usually called the "ghetto premium," as the urban literature has demonstrated (see Chapter 2).

[g]Some of the black neighborhood expansion reflects the increase in median income

However, in contrast to the typical urban area, *the black areas in the towns surveyed are not encircled*—all of the towns have black areas which abut on undeveloped land. The maps in figures 3-1 through 3-4 illustrate this point clearly. Two of the towns, those in Arkansas and Georgia, each have a single black neighborhood in a corner of town which has expanded onto the adjoining undeveloped land over the history of the town. The North Carolina and Tennessee towns each have more than one black neighborhood, but in both cases, the major black area abuts open and developable land. In fact, in the local traditions which define "black areas" and "white areas," such *expansion is provided for* by extending the designations to the land abutting existing neighborhoods. Whites will not move onto land designated as "black territory," and blacks are not permitted to move onto land abutting white areas.

The fact that black neighborhoods are not encircled, and that black expansion is permitted by tradition onto specifically-designated "black" undeveloped areas, means that pressure for expansion can reasonably be channeled in directions other than into existing white neighborhoods. Given the perceived costs of crossing racial boundaries, the existence of an alternative has a defusing effect on black efforts to achieve integration. As one respondent summed it up when asked what would happen if a black attempted to move into a white neighborhood: "Why should they? There's nice houses for Colored out Fourth Street."

Assertion: *Residential segregation deprives blacks of equal access to jobs and public facilities.*

Finding: *False*

This assertion, also clearly derived from the urban experience, is often used as an extension of a normative argument against racial segregation. In urban areas, industries, jobs, tax bases, schools, and other amenities are increasingly following the white population farther and farther from the central city where blacks are confined. The secondary effects of housing discrimination in denying blacks access to these amenities have received considerable attention in fair housing discussions.[h]

In rural areas, lacking the "noose effect" and the "expanding circles" phenomenon, these secondary impacts do not occur. The towns are small in land area and, unlike a metropolitan area, comprise a single jurisdiction. The

---

accruing to blacks over the last decade. The black median has increased by 48 percent, 55 percent, 58 percent, and 42 percent in the four southern counties (reflecting as much the outmigration of the poor as increased affluence). In addition, overcrowding has decreased somewhat, again reflecting both outmigration and movement to additional housing units.

[h]The Civil Rights Commission Report, *Understanding Fair Housing*, p. 1, gives these problems greater weight than specifically housing-related problems in discussing the impact of segregation.

Figure 3-1. The Arkansas Study Town (Town A)

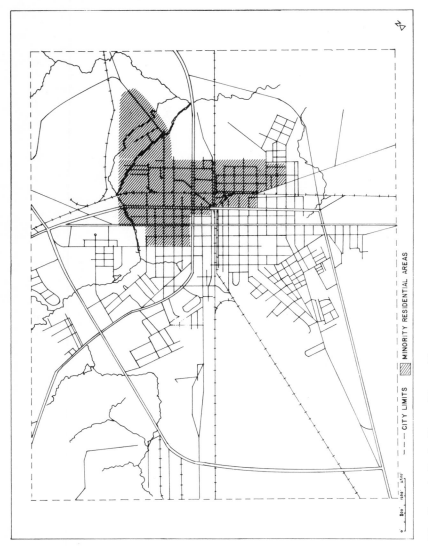

---- CITY LIMITS   ▨ MINORITY RESIDENTIAL AREAS

Figure 3-2. The Georgia Study Town (Town G)

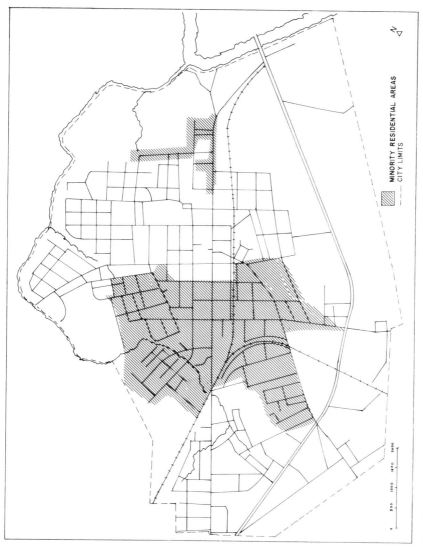

Figure 3-3. The North Carolina Study Town (Town NC)

MINORITY RESIDENTIAL AREAS

CITY LIMITS

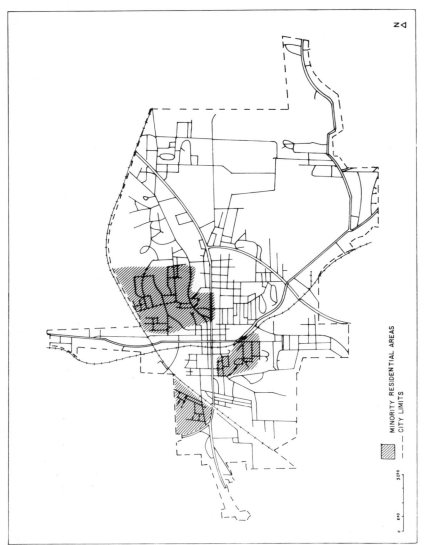

Figure 3-4. The Tennessee Study Town (Town T)

expansion that is occurring tends to be residential developments adjoining the existing neighborhoods, followed at least in the white areas by shopping centers and other commercial developments. However, the distances are not large, and the new developments are accessible to blacks for both shopping and jobs. Industrial jobs, the major source of employment in the four southern sites, are if anything more accessible from the black areas than from the white.

Movement of tax bases and therefore public services has not become a problem as yet, since the towns are a single jurisdiction and annexation has largely kept up with expansion. It is true that the town's school tends to be in the white area,[i] and that the public facilities there are often superior to the comparable facilities in black areas, but the dimensions of the problem suggested by the urban experience are of a wholly different order of magnitude than was encountered in rural areas.

Since jobs and facilities are accessible from the currently delineated black neighborhoods, the pressure for integration which occurs in urban areas as blacks attempt to follow these necessary amenities (thereby crossing into designated white areas) is absent. Again, it is unfair to conclude from the lack of black pressure for integration that the self-segregation hypothesis obtains. Rather, given the costs of attempting to cross neighborhood boundaries in relation to the marginal change in access to benefits, black residents have chosen the rational course.

Assertion: *Self-segregation accounts for observed residential segregation.*

Finding: *False*

This finding can be stated with considerable certainty because of a recent development in rural housing markets: the emergence of mobile home parks. The difficulty in discussing self-segregation *vs.* internalized discrimination in relation to existing neighborhood boundaries stems from the problem of distinguishing inherent preferences from the effect on actions of long-standing social barriers and the perceived (and verified) penalties for crossing them. However, since 1970, mobile home parks—a comparatively new phenomenon in the towns visited—have been springing up in large numbers. Given the recency of this development, the applicability of segregation rules had not yet been tested and ingrained. Significantly, when the parks began to open, even in designated "white areas," *blacks attempted to move in.* Two results were

---

[i]When school integration was achieved into the 1960s, it was invariably the white school which was designated "the school" and the black school discontinued. Thus, the town high school is found in the white area—but serves both white and black students. When multiple elementary schools exist, they still tend to be in separate parts of town. The extent to which racial patterns in elementary schools reflect the racial composition of the immediate neighborhood was not investigated in the course of this study.

observed. In one case, all the whites moved out, leaving an all-black park. More commonly, the black applicant would find that the half-empty park was "full." (Rebuffs of black applicants were reported by both black and white respondents, with varying degrees of approval.) The result is that mobile home parks are totally segregated, despite active black attempts to gain equal access.

Notes

1. United States Commission on Civil Rights, *Understanding Fair Housing,* Clearinghouse Publication 42, February 1973, p. 3.

4 Housing Supply and Demand

It is housing supply actors—builders, lenders, landowners, and municipal governments—who, along with real estate brokers, deal directly with consumers and through whom (if not by whom) unequal opportunity is therefore most directly effected and maintained. It does not follow, however, that inequality necessarily originates here, since the market interaction patterns discussed above in relation to brokers apply also to suppliers. This is to say that suppliers in general acquiesce to community pressure which demands segregated neighborhoods—pressure which is in many cases reflected in the apparent "self-segregation" of their customers. This section explores whether any additional factors exist on the supply side (in relation to demand) which result in housing inequality.

Assertion: *Suppliers tend to divide markets in terms of geography and race.*

Finding: *False*

Lenders and builders, like real estate brokers, were found to cover, or attempt to cover, the whole county in their market activities. The urban phenomenon of market division, with some actors avoiding black neighborhoods and others concentrating on them, was not encountered. However, for the reasons given in relation to brokers, the customers of the suppliers were disproportionately white. This can be attributed in large part to the economics of the housing supply industries in relation to local income distributions. For instance, since the cessation of HUD-subsidized home construction in 1973, all builders—with the few exceptions of those who specialize in FmHA 502 housing—have moved toward construction of higher-priced housing. The lowest price currently quoted for a new unsubsidized single-family house on any of the sites was $30,000 and on several sites the lowest price was upwards of $35,000. *Black customers who can afford these prices are served*; needless to say, not many customers of either race are served, and those who are, are disproportionately white.

The same pattern was observed among lending institutions. Unlike urban areas, where lenders appear to avoid black neighborhoods and especially transitional neighborhoods, lenders in rural towns have some confidence that neighborhood boundaries are unlikely to change. No lender was encountered who did not have some mortgage loans outstanding in the town's black area; although, again, the proportion was consistently lower than the black proportion of the population.

Assertion: *Suppliers provide unequal services to black customers.*

Finding: *Qualified*

No evidence was found that builders provide unequal services. Practically all builders are now operating (if they are operating at all) in the high-priced bracket, but no respondents asserted that blacks are charged more for equivalent *new* housing, and no other indications were found suggesting that this was the case.

Private sellers often charge more for existing black housing than do their counterparts selling white housing, as Chapter 2 amply demonstrates. This is not so much direct discrimination, however, as a price response to differences in supply and demand relationships in clearly separate submarkets. In practically all cases, the owner selling a single-family home to a purchaser would be of the same race; racial price differences are more the result of indirect or by-product discrimination than of direct seller discrimination. Price differentials do not, in fact, become clear until after extensive analysis; no one on the sites suspected their existence.

Supplier patterns in rentals tend somewhat closer to the typical urban pattern of some landlords specializing in one area (and therefore race) and others in the other. And in fact, some of the owners of black rental housing are white and do charge rents which tenants claim are excessive considering the often substandard condition of the units. Discrimination is not provable by comparison since almost no cases of whites living in severely dilapidated rental housing were encountered in the towns. A charge of "exploitation" may be more appropriate than discrimination; however, this is again difficult to assert with confidence since landlords typically claim that the low rent levels do not permit rehabilitation.[a] The only clear evidence on this issue came from a town where welfare benefits include full payment of rent, whatever it may be. In that town, rents for substandard housing often exceed $100 per month, and improvements have not been forthcoming.

Close comparison with the "urban slumlord" phenomenon is not justified, however (assuming that even the urban phenomenon exists in reality as clearly as it does in pervasive belief). *It was rare to find substantial white ownership of*

---

[a]Landlords' reaction to a rare instance of code enforcement is noted in the next section—the building inspector was forced to resign. In another town, a building inspector left the job after a few months, unable to endure the hostility and abuse his activities generated among white landlords.

black rental housing, and even rarer to find a single landlord renting out more than a handful of units. Multifamily tenements do not exist. Practically all rental housing consists of single-family units (see Appendix A), most landlords own no more than two to five units, and most landlords in the black neighborhoods are black. While instances of white abuse were noted (along with one case of a black "slumlord"), the most common situation encountered was that of a black family which owned (often by inheritance) another house or two near the one the family itself occupied. These would be rented out at the going market rates, which were high or low, depending on what the market in general would bear.

The most persistent reports of supplier discrimination were in relation to lending institutions. While all banks and savings and loans in the towns surveyed did have minority customers, minorities were in many cases convinced that race was an independent factor in risk assessment, and the blacks therefore had a more difficult time securing a loan than would a comparable white applicant.[b] Bankers just as frequently denied this. All that can be said with certainty by the study team is that there is no evidence of "redlining" or systematic avoidance of minority *areas*, and that *some* minority applicants receive mortgage financing. The frequent assertion that risk assessment was racially discriminatory is somewhat persuasive, given the general traditions of discrimination visible on the sites, but could not be independently verified.

Lending institutions were also charged with responsibility for the almost total absence of black builders on the sites surveyed. Two sites had no black builders; one had a builder who had been, by his own report, driven out of the market; and the fourth had a black builder who reported considerable difficulty obtaining construction financing but who was still managing to keep in business. According to the builders and to several other respondents, black businesses were not encouraged by local lenders, and black builders had trouble not only with construction financing but also with mortgage financing for their customers. Not surprisingly, this was also denied by lenders.

Circumstantial evidence of some discrimination in financing exists, and considering the frequency and the detail with which charges were made, this evidence is fairly convincing as a general description of market operations. However, it should be noted that black respondents, given the discriminatory traditions of the area, sometimes assumed discrimination when their needs were not met without determining that discrimination was the actual explanation. For instance, a black businessman reported discrimination because his request for a commercial loan had been turned down by a savings and loan. (It is worth noting, of course, that the S&L president did not refer the applicant to

---

[b]The South Dakota banks had no loans outstanding to Indians. However, it should in fairness be noted that housing purchase and construction have been almost completely suspended for several years while the reservation status of the town was under litigation.

the commercial bank.) One of the black builders charged discrimination on
the grounds that his customers had trouble with loans unless he agreed to purchase materials at a specified place, apparently not realizing that this practice is
not uncommon in the building industry and certainly not limited to blacks.

The supply of municipal services was also noticeably unequal in several
sites; this must be attributed to direct discrimination since all towns visited
comprised a single jurisdiction and therefore a single tax-and-expenditures unit.
Unpaved streets, irregular garbage removal, open storm drainage ditches, etc.,
were all more frequently encountered in minority areas. However, in only one
case was evidence found that inequality in municipal services directly affected
the supply of housing. In this instance, the town had not installed sewerage in
the area to which the black neighborhood was expanding, thus forcing black
homebuilders to bear the cost of septic tanks. (The area in question was within
the town limits, and sewerage was provided in the areas on which white expansion was occurring.) In other areas, inequalities in municipal services resulted
more in a lower level of amenity in black areas than in direct restrictions on
supply of housing.

Some evidence exists, therefore, that supply institutions are providing
services unequally and are therefore responsible for some of the inequality
detailed in Chapter 2. The supply side also enters the issue in another and
totally different way. This is through the fact that occupancy patterns are
traditionally and currently unequal in terms of location, quality, and price of
housing occupied. To the extent that supply restrictions exist, they would tend
to freeze these current patterns by presenting difficulties to any household
(including, of course, minority households) which might wish to move to
upgrade its housing conditions. Findings concerning general supply restrictions
occupy the remainder of this chapter.

Assertion: *Outmigration and population decline tend to free up
                     existing housing and thus result in a housing surplus.*

Finding: *False*

All areas surveyed showed evidence of persistent housing *shortages*, with
impacts on the housing situation of all but the very affluent. Evidence of
shortages was pervasive, and took various forms: practically all respondents—
suppliers, consumers, town officials, and "overview" respondents—pointed it
out, and consumers and their spokespersons regaled the study team with
numerous examples of households at practically all income levels seeking but
unable to find housing they could afford. Direct evidence came in the form
of major real estate agencies carrying only two or three listings, builders
unemployed for months, very low levels of mortgage lending for both new
and existing housing in comparison with past years, and a vacancy rate so low

that available housing (even abandoned substandard housing) remained available for no more than a few days.

Despite the population trends noted above in Chapter 1, very little housing is being freed up. Outmigration in the areas studied was primarily composed of two groups: young people generally, especially the educated; and poor people generally, especially minorities. The young are leaving from their parents' homes and consequently not freeing up housing. Many of the poor are leaving sub-standard units (which are in any case immediately claimed by squatters unless condemned and demolished); others are leaving units which are currently over-crowded, again not freeing up housing stock.

The county population trends may not obtain as clearly in the towns; some towns in fact appear to be experiencing inmigration.[1] Such migration patterns reflect partially a small movement of minorities from the open country into the towns (although most appear to leave the area when leaving the tenant farms and other open-country residences); and several towns appear to be experiencing net inmigration of white professional personnel in connection with local indus-tries. The latter phenomenon combines with local upgrading to put severe pressure on the moderate- and middle-income housing supply.

The unavailability of housing is having the effect of freezing current occu-pancy patterns. Its impact on future housing conditions might be even more deleterious. Traditionally, new housing has always been purchased only by the relatively high income consumer. As stock ages, it tends to change hands and eventually to provide services for those of lower income levels. Obviously this process of "filtering" or succession in ownership will provide acceptable housing to those of moderate and low income only if changes in ownership take place before substantial depreciation, and only if a suitable number of units enters the system to begin with. Recently, the market for new construction has tightened so severely that many of the very affluent refuse to build. This has led to a tightening at every level of housing stock succession, and may thus be expected to have a serious impact on the level of housing services consumed by middle and lower income households within the near future.

Assertion: *Housing shortages can be attributed to problems with land titles, lack of building capacity, and/or capital shortages in rural areas.*

Finding: *False*

None of the traditional explanations accounts for the low level of new construction or the low turnover of existing housing on the sites surveyed. Land titles were generally clear in all areas, except in South Dakota where multiple heirships tended to cloud titles of Indian-owned land. However, in this site, as in all others, a considerable amount of clear-title land was available —more than was being used for new construction.

Building capacity is also not responsible for low construction levels. While rural builders are generally not able to undertake very large projects—all Public Housing projects, for instance, were contracted to outside builders—the present capacity of the local industry has yet to be reached. The population of builders shifts somewhat in response to demand pressures. Many of the sites had in addition to the regular builders and site developers a large number of independent contractors, building one or two houses at a time on contract, who enter and leave the market as needed. At present, almost no independent contractors are operating, and the regular builders report very low levels of business compared with previous years. Some of these have in fact left the market along with the independent contractors.

The third frequent explanation—capital shortages—is also not valid. Five of the six areas showed a capital surplus and net outflow. The sixth area was served by lenders from nearby towns and from metropolitan areas in the state; funds were reportedly available, especially from private mortgage credit companies. Local lenders reported that exportation of capital reflects constricted demand locally, rather that preference for outside investments. This claim is fairly persuasive for two reasons. First, exportation of rural capital cannot be attributed necessarily to a preference for other investments over home mortgages, since such *exportation was as common among S&L's as among commercial banks.* (In fact, two of the commercial banks which make long-term home mortgages (both home offices) said they did so because of insufficient demand for *commercial* loans locally.) Secondly, most of the S&L's encountered on the sites were branches. For such a lender to "export" does not mean that the local manager makes outside investments but rather that the local surplus is pooled with the assets of the home office, and the local manager loses control of its disposition. There is, therefore, strong incentive for the local manager to make local investment to the maximum extent possible. For these reasons the above explanation offered by local lenders—that capital exportation results from a local surplus in relation to constricted demand—is therefore plausible.

This discussion does not imply, of course, that local resources in terms of land, building capacity and capital are sufficient to meet the entire "need," however defined, of the area. It does demonstrate, however, that the factors often considered responsible for housing shortages are not the actual bottlenecks.

According to local builders and lenders, the problem is due to building costs and credit costs, both of which are invariably reported to have skyrocketed in the last few years. Costs of financing are in line with mortgage prices and terms in urban markets, as table 4-1 illustrates. Building costs have also increased substantially to the point where it is extremely unusual to find an unsubsidized

Table 4-1
Mortgage Terms in Local Lending Institutions

Site	*AR*				*GA*			*NC*			*NM*			*SD*		*TN*		
Lenders	*CB**	*CB*	*Branch S&L*	*Branch S&L*	*CB*	*Branch CB***	*Branch S&L*	*Branch CB*	*Branch CB*	*S&L*	*CB*	*Branch CB*	*S&L*	*CB*	*Branch S&L*	*CB*	*CB*	*S&L*
Interest (%)	8¾	-	9	9¼	9	-	8¾	-	-	8¼	9	-	9	9	8¾	8½	8½	9
Term (years)	15	-	30	30	8	-	30	-	-	25	15	-	25	25	25	15	15	30
Down Payment (%)	20	-	10	5	20	-	5	-	-	25	25	-	10	20	20	25	25	25

"-" indicates none.
*Commercial Bank
**Mortgages available through referral to home office.

new house for under $35,000.[c] It is these factors which are preventing practically all households from either building or purchasing, thus serving to perpetuate unequal housing conditions for minorities and relegating even many white middle-income households to housing they consider unsuitable.

Notes

1.   Recent Census calculations indicate that between 1970 and 1973, two of the study counties (Georgia and Tennessee) showed net inmigration of 2.8 percent and 4.9 percent respectively. The other four continued to show negative net migration. See *Current Population Reports.* Federal-State Cooperative Program for Population Estimates, Series P-26, U.S. Bureau of the Census. For a more general discussion of post-1970 rural population trends, see "Rural Areas' Population Gains Now Outpacing Urban Regions," *New York Times* , May 18, 1975, pp. 1 and 44.

---

[c]Builders report as the reasons for price increases both a substantial increase in building costs and a preferable profit margin for high income housing since the cessation of the HUD 235 program. Only three builders in all six sites specialize in FmHA 502 housing. Two of these are also building suppliers and report that without their savings on materials, they would not be able to produce this moderate-priced ($18-20,000) housing profitably. While inquiry into the components of building cost increases and systematic comparisons with urban areas were beyond the scope of this study, it might be noted that the national *median* price for a new single-family home was $41,300 in 1974, an increase of 16 percent over the 1970 median. (*Source:* Congressional Joint Economic Committee.)

5 Housing Market Interventions

The term "market interventions" refers to activities by market elements other than suppliers and consumers which are intended to shift in some way the distribution of housing benefits. Interventions are found most commonly on the supply side of the market (e.g., federally-subsidized construction) or in relation to market interactions (e.g., organized attempts to disseminate information or to alter the rules governing interactions). The activities of three types of interveners—community organizations, local governments, and the federal government—are considered here.

Community Organizations

One might expect on the basis of the urban experience that community organizations would play a significant role in the operations of the housing market. However, findings indicate that the activities of organizations representing the interests of consumers (especially minority consumers) are very limited. Organizations of suppliers are similarly rare on the sites studied. The reasons for this, and the consequences for equal opportunity in housing, are explored in this section.

Assertion: *Housing-related community organizations intervene in the market on consumers' behalf.*

Finding: *False*

As a basic human need, shelter might be expected to be the focus of organized concern. Urban areas, for instance, often exhibit numerous organizations concentrating on housing issues; in addition, the major priorities of more general groups in urban areas often include housing.[1] In addition, some regional groups concerned with housing and land problems in rural areas do exist. (Examples include A.C.O.R.N. in Arkansas and the Emergency Land Fund in Georgia.) However, in the small and comparatively remote sites visited for this study, only two housing-related organizations were found.

One of these was a nonprofit housing assistance and development corporation, covering an eight-county area on subcontract from a community action agency. The functions of this group include site development and housing acquisition-renovation-resale, both with federal funding assistance (FmHA 502, 504, and 524, and HUD 235), as well as more general outreach and information exchange on housing programs and issues. This group is recently formed and has, not surprisingly, concentrated on the portion of its target area nearest the home office. However, the group's failure to become active in the study site can be attributed largely to the total lack of community organization in the town in question. The group could find no one in the study town, not even a minister, willing to serve as spokesperson for the black and low-income communities, or able to provide the information necessary for an assessment of housing problems and opportunities. While multicounty organization may in general be appropriate to sparsely-populated rural areas, in this instance it was frustrated by the lack of local organizations through which to work.

The only other example of a specifically housing-related private group was found in a site whose black area is undergoing large-scale "urban" renewal. The redevelopment program had begun with minimal input from the population affected, but its continuation was successfully challenged by an ad hoc neighborhood group led by a black minister and backed by a powerful community action agency. The group demanded and received recognition from the HUD area office as the official voice of redevelopment-area residents, and redevelopment plans must now secure its approval. This group was not originally intended as an ongoing organization, but rather as a response to a specific situation. (Any group which changes its name three times in two years is clearly suffering identity problems.) It is unclear at this point whether the organization will continue to articulate minority interests after the completion of the redevelopment project.

Other than these two examples—one inactive in the study site and the other issue-specific and possibly temporary—there were no examples of housing-related community organization on the sites visited. The possible reasons for this were alluded to in Chapter 3 in relation to the self-segregation hypothesis, and will be expanded later in this section.

Assertion: *General-focus community organizations tend to include housing issues among their priorities.*

Finding: *False*

There was a slightly greater population of more general community organizations than of specifically housing-related groups, although the number was still quite small and many of the groups existed on paper only. The community organizations concerned with minority interests on the six sites are easily counted; each of the southern towns had a chapter of the NAACP, all sites had (or were within the target area of) community action agencies, and two contained community-oriented churches. The total of *active* groups includes two community action agencies (one allied with a church), a second church on another site, and, on a third site, a small-but-growing NAACP. In addition, it is appropriate to include the Indian tribal organization on the South Dakota site, even though tribes are legally local governments, since this group performs some of the political functions of a community organization (see table 5-1.)

It was noted in Chapter 3 that in the four southern sites, the economic (and in some cases, physical) vulnerability of blacks to reprisals has tended to discourage individual protest. The same factor also, not surprisingly, discourages the formation of community organizations. Those who are not resigned to political and economic powerlessness tend to migrate from the area, leaving a population which is disproportionately elderly, poor, poorly educated, and passive. This is not the most important factor, however: even those who remain and might wish to lead organized protest are frustrated by the vulnerability of themselves and of their potential constituents. What one sympathetic observer termed the "rampant apathy" of a study town's black population can thus be explained by frustration, translated in some cases into resignation.

Community organizations have formed, however, under two sets of circumstances. The first is the establishment of economic independence from local institutions. The NAACP group mentioned above and in Chapter 3 is an example of an organization forming when protection from reprisals is obtained. The leaders of this group are either self-employed or employed outside of the area; they are, however, having difficulty recruiting membership because of the vulnerability of most other blacks. The clearest example of this process is the community action agency on one site, which was originally formed by a local

Table 5-1
Active Community Organizations

	AR	GA	NC	NM	SD	TN
Housing (permanent)		X*				
Housing (ad hoc)	X**		X			
CAA			X	X		
NAACP						X
Church			X	X		
Tribe					X	

*Not active on study site.
**Now dissolved.

white activist to provide community services to the black population. Within
a short time, threatened reprisals from other whites had led the director to
resign, and the organization came under black control. Its funding and activities
were somewhat reduced with the phasing out of OEO; however, the organization is continuing with funding from the Community Services Administration
and a variety of programs funded by other federal agencies.[a]

The other circumstance under which community organizations might form
is the sudden emergence of an issue judged serious enough to demand organization, whatever its possible costs. Individuals will then coalesce into an ad hoc
group, sometimes formed around the core of an existing paper organization.
This type of activity was seen on a site with no permanent community organizations, passive churches, a vestigal CAA, etc. The town and the housing
authority were using scattered-site public housing as a form of neighborhood
redevelopment, purchasing and demolishing substandard units and replacing
them with public housing units. Several elderly black residents, not wishing to
give up their houses, met with the titular leader of the inactive NAACP and
were referred to a law firm in a metropolitan area of the state. They successfully filed a discrimination suit—the charge was discrimination in that no public
housing units were in white areas although the actual impetus was a desire to
halt condemnation and acquisition of black owner-occupied units. Once an
agreement was reached, public housing expansion was stopped and the group
dissolved.

The tendency for community organizations *not* to become involved
in housing-related activities can be discussed in terms of each of these
types of groups. The ad hoc group will naturally concentrate on the issue that
gives rise to it, and generally not continue after the issue has been resolved.
In any case, such groups are comparatively rare, and those that exist are more
often concerned with employment and education issues than with housing. The
two groups formed in response to redevelopment efforts were the only examples
of this type of group focused on housing. Of these, one has already dissolved,
although the other, given the continuing nature of the town's redevelopment
effort, could possibly gain organizational permanence.

The response of general-purpose organizations to housing—the CAA and
the NAACP were the only ongoing groups in the four southern sites—has been
minimal. The NAACP has not been active on housing issues, except for an

---

[a]The community action agencies on the other sites do not conform to this pattern:
all were severely curtailed with the phasing out of OEO, only one is black-controlled, and
none serves the political function of articulating black interests. The CAA on the New
Mexico site does serve as a representative of Spanish-surnamed interests; it has not, however, become active on housing issues. The South Dakota CAA does not represent Indian
interests (neither the tribe nor the Bureau of Indian Affairs was familiar with the organization).

effort to recruit black tenants for a new public housing project. The CAA does do outreach work in an attempt to inform people about program benefits, including housing, but aside from backing the ad hoc group has not itself become actively involved in housing market intervention. In both cases, the explanation was the same: housing inequality is regarded as an important issue, but given the wide range of equally or more important issues in relation to scarce political resources, both groups have relegated housing issues to a lower priority. Both are more concerned at present with employment (and credit) discrimination— resolution of these issues is judged to have greater and more direct impact on the living conditions of blacks, including (indirectly) their housing situation. As the leader of one group noted: "We ain't got nuthin' till we gets the bread."

In addition to being to some extent a derivative of the financial situation of consumers, housing issues are also more complicated politically than the issue of direct employment discrimination. Employment discrimination can be, and is, countered by direct pressure on major employers, backed by law suits if necessary, to institute equal opportunity and affirmative action. Responsibility for inequality in housing is apt to be diffused throughout the system, and is in addition seriously complicated by supply restrictions on the market in general. Integration per se is judged by black leaders to be only the beginning of true equality in housing; all were opposed to segregation (especially enforced segregation), but all saw the full accomplishment of housing equality as a demanding project which, given lack of resources, must defer at present to the issue of employment discrimination.

Unlike blacks, Indians have the legal machinery for separate (tribal) organization and earmarked funding for the tribe and Indian needs. The tribal organization, dormant for a hundred years, has recently become reactivated through the efforts of a group of educated "returnees" (tribal members returning from sojourns in other areas). Indians are served through the tribe or the Bureau of Indian Affairs (BIA) by federal funding. The BIA, for instance, administers a General Assistance program for those in need of welfare but not eligible for the county-administered AFDC program, and the tribe sponsors various housing programs as well as providing some 200 jobs for Indians. The tribe has been increasingly successful in gaining control of programs formerly administered by the BIA.

The tribal organization, with its nonlocal sources of funding, is to some extent comparable with the community action agency mentioned above: its leaders are beyond local reprisals, and it attempts to provide services and support to tribal members. The particular forms which their protests in relation to the white community take are also comparable: they tend toward political protest and pressure and the building of a separate economic base, but retain the goal of eventual reconciliation of interests. Some of the more frustrated or more nearly dispossessed of the Indians regard the tribe as too slow or too conciliatory in its activities. It is this group which has garnered the support of the American Indian

Movement, and somewhat to the annoyance of tribal officials, begun open confrontations with whites. This political schism among the Indians is an example
of the classic split among lower-caste groups, and is partially reflected in the
split between middle-class and poorer blacks mentioned in Chapter 3. The
difference appears to be that the poor blacks are somewhat more likely to be
employed than Indians, and have in any case a longer and more thoroughly
internalized tradition of accepting subordinate status. Indians, who were historically more likely to be removed than enslaved, have a greater tradition of
protest on which to draw.

Assertion: *Organizations of suppliers intervene on their members'*
                   behalf in the market.

Finding: *Qualified*

Housing supply organizations—builders, lenders, land owners, real estate
agents—were comparatively rare on the sites visited. Individuals would
occasionally (not consistently) be members of national trade organizations like
the National Association of Real Estate Brokers and various associations of
builders and lenders, but these groups were rarely if ever called upon for local
needs. In addition, local organizations of suppliers were also not in evidence.
Several factors account for this.

The first is the general paucity of consumer-oriented organizations, either
white or minority. In the absence of consumer-oriented organizations, controversy to which suppliers would need to respond is less likely to be generated
and there is, therefore, less need for suppliers to organize to promote their
interests. Most of the organizational needs of suppliers are handled by existing
general purpose business organizations such as the Chamber of Commerce,
civic groups, social clubs, etc.

This is not to say that supplier interests are not represented in the political
process of the towns visited. Evidence of supplier influence was in fact pervasive. Such influence could often be inferred from the particular types of
codes and ordinances adopted (and often not enforced) by the towns. Very
occasionally, the influence became evident. In one case, the study team's
every mention of the word "HUD" to town officials was met with an almost-
automatic "We don't need any more public housing." Town officials later
admitted in confidence that pressure from owners of rental housing had forced
the town and its housing authority to cease providing this type of competition.
In another instance, a town administrator doubling as building inspector
attempted to enforce housing codes against the owners of several blocks of substandard housing; according to all local respondents he was, as a direct result,
forced to resign from office.

The expression of supplier interests also requires little organization because of the small number of individuals involved and the lesser complexity of political institutions as compared with metropolitan areas. Pressure on local, state, and federal government offices tends to be informal, taking the form of representations by individuals or ad hoc groups.[2] It is not necessary to postulate any untoward activities on the part of suppliers to account for the frequently supplier-oriented outcomes of public policy, although such incidents are not unheard of. (One builder, for instance, attempted to use state-level pressure against a Farmers Home county supervisor when the supervisor refused to approve the builder's departures from specifications; the effort was, however, unsuccessful.) More generally, the outcomes can be attributed to the lack of organizations effectively representing consumer interests opposed to supplier interests in the political process. This factor also contributes to the generally low visibility of supplier representations—should controversy ever arise it is quite possible that suppliers would organize in response or at least that their role in decision-making would become more visible.

Assertion: *Efforts to form community organizations expressing the interests of minorities are actively discouraged.*

Finding: *True*

Minority organization is indirectly discouraged in a number of ways already touched upon, particularly the fear of exciting economic reprisals and discouragement about the possibilities of accomplishment in the context of generalized discrimination and minority powerlessness. In addition, minority organization is also discouraged in some direct ways.

Most blatantly, reprisals have been threatened even for the act of organizing. A white CAA director was forced to resign, as mentioned above, although the result in this case was the emergence of a black-controlled organization. More commonly, no such organization is able to get established. In two sites, for instance, schoolteachers whose contracts are up for renewal are asked specifically if they are members of the NAACP. Not surprisingly, the NAACP is inactive on these sites.

Ministers are active on only two of the six sites. On the others, the ministers are either nonlocal commuters, or share the general discouragement noted among minorities. In one case, the minister of the town's largest (white) church hired an assistant pastor specifically to organize outreach and community service activities among the minority population. The minister was stunned by the hostility of his congregation's reaction and has been unable to pursue the activity. The only other active church is in New Mexico, where the situation of Spanish-surnamed appears to be due at least as much to income barriers as to ethnic background. (The connection between these factors is not as immediately obvious on this site as it is on the others.)

Contributing to the problem of effective organization is the frequent refusal by white organizations or governments to recognize spokespersons. The black minister mentioned above protested to the mayor about town redevelopment activities in the poor black area, but was met with "Why Reverend, how can you speak for those people—you don't even live down there." His response was "Why Mr. Mayor, neither do you." With the backing of his own large church and the community action agency, the minister was able to demand recognition. The Indian tribal officials are similarly successful in gaining recognition, largely because of their legal status as a government; other Indian organizations, including those associated with the American Indian Movement, have great difficulty in achieving recognition.

Nonrecognition is a common situation among blacks. Frequently, the titular head of the NAACP will attend council meetings and other such activities and claim to represent minority interests; recognition of the person's status as spokesperson is, however, often denied. Recognition tends to be given, if at all, to conciliatory representatives. One site has what appears to be a perfectly stable social arrangement where a black professional is recognized by both blacks and whites as the spokesperson for black interests, but, as one black pointed out, "To be in a position like that, you have to be kind of safe." No active encouragement of minority interests has been forthcoming, and potentially more active leaders have been discouraged from entering the political arena.

In other areas, minority representation is allotted to persons best described as token; that is, they are recognized as leaders by whites but not by minorities. In most cases, these persons held elective or appointive office but were careful to disassociate themselves from minority interests when speaking with the study team, and by all reports do not actively represent minority interests in decision-making. Tokenism has a defusing effect on minority organization, since recognition, once given to an ineffectual leader, is difficult for a potentially more active leader to obtain. Only in the case of the CAA and the NAACP mentioned above is effective leadership developing and forcing recognition.

Local Governments

The potential intervention functions of local governments derive from their powers to set and enforce housing-related regulations, and their power to disburse public funds. Local governments on the sites visited possessed and used these powers, but their role in effecting unequal access to housing was found to be much smaller than one would expect based on the urban experience.

Assertion: *Local governments act to maintain segregated neighborhoods.*

Finding: *False*

Urban local governments have been found to play some part in both the "neighborhood succession process," progressive deterioration of a neighborhood usually accompanying its changeover from white to black occupancy, and in the confinement of blacks to the central cities. Neighborhood succession is often postulated to result from the actions of a restless *ménage à trois* comprising governments, lenders, and insurance companies.[3] Should any one of these withdraw services from a neighborhood, it serves as incentive for the others to do likewise; as a result, neighborhood decline becomes almost inevitable and—the direction of causation is unclear—black occupancy tends to increase. In the sites visited, several cases of unequal public services were encountered—less frequent garbage removal in the black neighborhood, for instance, and fewer paved streets. The effects of these inequalities were, however, far less than the urban experience might suggest. Because of other factors noted above, there are no racially transitional neighborhoods in the study sites; the possible role of local government in contributing to neighborhood succession is therefore meaningless in this context.

In addition, the powers of local government, particularly the zoning and building-code powers, may be used in metropolitan areas to contribute to the containment of black neighborhoods. Again, the point is not relevant to rural areas, where containment is effectively accomplished by unwritten rules without requiring active support from local governments. ("Channeling" is perhaps a better term in these sites since black expansion is possible and provided for.) The powers of local governments may, however, be called upon when tradition is threatened. In one area, for instance, white residents strongly resisted a proposed zoning change to permit construction of a 236 project, on the assumption that "government housing" would necessarily be "for blacks." However, the developer involved was successful in convincing the council to grant the change, and local blacks, having gotten the message, made no attempt to move in. In most cases, public powers are not needed to maintain segregation; and in one case, as noted above, were used in protection of the first black family to break neighborhood barriers. In general, local governments play no active role on either side of the segregation/integration question, since the "issue" is settled by tradition without in most cases becoming politically alive.

Assertion: *Local government regulations served to inhibit housing development.*

Finding: *False*

Aside from the question of segregation, equal access to housing requires that sufficient housing be developed and available to both (or either) whites and minorities. Unequal provision of public *services* has, in one instance,

inhibited such development in the black neighborhood, as noted above in
Chapter 4. Local *regulations* do not, however, have this effect.

All of the towns visited have housing and building codes, subdivision regulations, and zoning regulations. (In addition, new housing must meet state-
enforced public health standards.) Typically, town powers extend a mile or
more beyond the town limits and cover the entire developed and developing
areas. Suppliers often object to regulations which increase their costs, e.g.,
subdivision regulations requiring expensive site improvements, zoning regulations requiring three lots as platted to comprise a building lot, etc.–but,
significantly, none stopped building on that account. Builders might attempt
to reduce costs by acquiring land already subdivided (and thus not subject to
the regulations), but would in any case pass the increased cost along to the
consumer. This proved to be a successful business practice until building costs
and mortgage rates brought the new home market in most cases to a halt.

In addition, zoning regulations in particular tend to be only intermittently
enforced, and building codes, while enforced, are not unusually stringent. Only
in New Mexico are regulations credited with dampening development. In that
state, a state subdivision law has been enacted, reportedly in an attempt to curb
abuses of nationally-advertised retirement property. The law requires the
developer to put in escrow 125 percent of the full cost of site developments
before proceeding. This regulation has not yet had full impact locally, however,
since builders are still covering land already subdivided and improved. The New
Mexico site, in fact, showed more building activity than any other town visited.

Assertion: *Code enforcement has racially-selective impact.*

Finding: *True*

In most sites visited, housing codes are not enforced on existing housing,
even if obviously dilapidated. Building inspectors report that many substandard
houses are beyond repair, or require such large investment that the low-income
owner-occupants could not be expected to defray the costs. Typically, building
inspectors allow substandard property to remain as is, but immediately con-
demn a house if its occupants abandon it. In all sites visited, inspectors and
others reported that an abandoned house, even if thoroughly dilapidated, would
have a new "squatter" occupant within a few hours if not condemned (and
sometimes even despite condemnation).

Codes are also rarely enforced against owners of rental property. The one
attempt to do so resulted in the resignation of the town manager/building
inspector, as noted above. Lack of enforcement was generally claimed, however,
to reflect the inability of owners to afford rehabilitation, given the very low
rents of substandard housing. Rents for substandard housing tended to range
from $25-50/month on most sites. In one area, however, rents for substandard

housing were found to be extremely high—over $100/month plus heat and utilities, for example. On this site, the welfare schedule allows for full payment of the family's rent, whatever it is. The price response has been strong, but no new housing or improvement of existing housing has resulted.

In most cases, therefore, codes are not enforced on existing housing because of the professed or actual inability of owners to afford rehabilitation, and the unwillingness of officials to force low-income families out. All areas except two lack public funds to provide alternative housing. The two with redevelopment programs in operation do use code enforcement in connection with these programs, and the effects are racially selective in that the blighted areas slated for condemnation and renewal are minority areas.

In both cases, minority resentment is strong. In one, the ad hoc neighborhood group mentioned above has been formed and has demanded the right to participate in program development. In addition, the group provides assistance to individuals who feel confused or threatened in their dealings with the redevelopment authority, especially when the condemnation powers of the town are being used in acquisition. In the other case, as mentioned, the group successfully stopped the use of condemnation and acquisition in the redevelopment process.

It is significant that in both cases, minorities resisted even though families displaced by redevelopment were relocated in new housing in the same neighborhood. The aggrieved parties include many homeowners, especially the elderly, who prefer ownership to rental, even if the public housing is promised to be an improvement in housing quality. In addition, resistance is bred by the fact that both redevelopment efforts are planned and administered by whites, with only token black representation. Based on long experience, blacks have less than total faith in white goodwill, and in any case resent having plans simply presented as *faits accomplis*. It is possible to construe public housing regulations, for instance, as "The Man" telling black families how many bedrooms they should have and otherwise interfering in traditionally private decisions.

Assertion: *Local governments are active in the housing market and on housing-related issues.*

Finding: *False*

The two instances discussed above were the only active local interventions on the supply side of the market (other than the sponsorship of local housing authorities). One of these was a duly-funded "urban renewal" effort; the other, the planned use of scattered site public housing in combination with town condemnation powers to achieve a de facto "urban" renewal. Other instances of local intervention were not encountered. In one site, the council had resisted urban renewal, despite pressure from the housing authority and others to "clean up" the blighted areas; reportedly, the local government was unable or unwilling to provide the necessary matching funds. On the other sites, applications for urban renewal and for code enforcement monies have been made, but have been turned down, reportedly for lack of funds, by HUD offices.

As a result, only one of the areas surveyed is eligible for CDBG monies under the "hold harmless" provision of Title I of the Housing and Community Development Act of 1974. Given the competition for nonmetropolitan discretionary funds under the program, the other sites do not expect to benefit. Considerable resentment was expressed over this situation, particularly because some of the towns have become more concerned with housing and community development issues than they were before. (Revenue-sharing provisions tend in any case to be more popular with governments than categorical programs, especially when the latter require matching funds.) The local governments do feel, however, that their needs do not receive equitable consideration in the 1974 Act.

Localities are particularly distressed by the cessation of conventional public housing and its replacement by leased housing under Section 8 of Title II of the 1974 Act. Only one town expressed a wish for no more public housing (as noted above). All others need and want more units: several had recently applied but had been turned down on the grounds that limited funds were being allotted to other towns in greater need. Currently, only the Indian tribal housing authority is able to arrange additional units. Spokespersons considered the cessation of public housing to be, in effect, a form of punishing rural areas for the sins of urban areas, since every site contained fully-occupied, well-maintained, and solvent public projects. The provisions of Section 8 were as yet poorly understood, but local Authorities realized that they would no longer be able to build and manage projects as they had in the past. Their hopes that private supply mechanisms would respond by providing new units or by making existing units available for subsidized occupancy were slim.

The Federal Government

Federal intervention in local housing markets has taken two forms: intervention on the supply side through housing subsidy and loan guarantee programs, and intervention in interactions through the passage of Fair Housing legislation. These will be discussed in turn.

Assertion: *Federal housing programs meet some of the needs of women and minorities.*

Finding: *True*

The federal programs most commonly encountered on the local sites were HUD 235 and FmHA 502 (both homeownership programs) and HUD Public Housing. Less important were FmHA 504, a rehabilitation program used only occasionally; FmHA 515 and HUD 236, multifamily rental programs of which three projects were encountered; and FmHA 524, a site development program currently under negotiation by the eight-county housing development corporation but not located in the study county.

In no case were minorities and women excluded from federal programs, and in some cases, such households were served in greater numbers than their proportion of the population.[b] The role of these programs in local housing markets is affected by the fact that they are implemented by local actors, and rarely did local actors systematically refuse service to minorities. Builders, the main conduits of 235 and 502 housing, tend to serve any consumer who can afford a house; while local housing authorities, the providers of public housing, often saw their programs as primarily oriented toward minorities even though the administrators themselves were invariably white.

Some inequalities were observed, however, in spite of these generalizations. HUD 235 and FmHA 502 housing was most typically initiated by builders, who would then find a customer, rather than by a customer who would then find a builder (although the latter pattern did sometimes occur). In one site, no builders were active in the black area and there was, therefore, no subsidized housing available for blacks. In South Dakota, there are two housing authorities, the town's and the tribe's, which by agreement concentrate on elderly housing and family housing respectively. The proportion of Indians in the elderly housing is slightly lower than the Indian proportion of the population (and probably much smaller than the proportion of Indians among the elderly poor), although both town and tribal officials commented on the difficulties of uprooting and moving the elderly, especially those who are not bilingual. The tribal projects are 13 percent non-Indian (one of the seven projects was entirely white-occupied), which was explained by the (white) official who is executive director of both authorities to be the result of compliance with Fair Housing legislation. Tribal public housing which is built on reservation land is exempted from Fair Housing requirements; the exemption status of projects built on non-reservation land, which most of these projects are, is unresolved and currently under litigation in Oklahoma.

The efforts of the FmHA county supervisor in South Dakota show an unusual degree of flexibility and responsiveness to minority needs. The supervisor,

---

[b]It was not possible to calculate the proportion in relation to the programs' *target* population, which in view of demographic income distributions are disproportionately minority and female. Exact program figures were generally not available, and the nature of eligibility requirements makes it impossible to calculate target populations from Census sources.

whose caseload is disproportionately though not entirely Indian, has made special efforts to provide counseling and technical assistance to Indian clients and has arranged to use lease-hold income as security in lieu of a mortgage. In addition, this supervisor is assisting the tribe in reacquiring Indian land by means of community development funding. Of the supervisors in the other five sites, two had the reputation of also making special efforts to meet minority needs (and both complained of the low level of FmHA funding for staff and programs). Two others were reputed to be "by-the-book" officials, not discriminatory but also not especially helpful to minority clients. The remaining supervisor was repeatedly charged with discriminatory decisions on loan applications, although the study team lacked the authority to verify this independently.

Despite the fact that most federal programs have served minorities and women at least equally, it should be noted that the total number of units produced under these programs is relatively small. Table 5-2 provides estimates of the units built as of 1975. (All public and 235 units were newly built, as were practically all 502 units.) Of these figures, the public housing figures are most nearly exact, since they were provided by the housing authorities who manage the units; 502 estimates are slightly rougher but were still provided by a single source (the county supervisor); 235 estimates are extremely rough since there was no single source of estimates—on three sites no estimates at all could be obtained, although the total is almost certainly under 100. As a very rough standard of comparison for these figures, table 5-2 contains the figures for overcrowded units and those lacking complete plumbing from the 1970 Census. Even given the roughness of Census figures as a proxy for "need," it is immediately obvious that the impact of federal programs has been small. (See Apprendix A for an indication of the relative incidence of substandard condition of minority-occupied housing.)

Assertion: *Public programs have not affected black-white neighborhood boundaries where segregation exists.*

Finding: *True*

Since the immedicate delivery mechanisms of subsidized or guaranteed housing—builders, housing authorities and Farmers Home supervisors—are local, one might expect that the unwritten laws prescribing segregation in private housing would apply also to these programs. This is in fact true. It is easiest to understand in relation to 235 and 502 housing since these are handled by the market in much the same fashion and by much the same institutions as private housing. Builders in general take the initiative in securing 502 or 235 commitments to build on land they already own; selection of sites is dictated almost entirely by economic factors, after which selection of potential consumers is dictated by the same market regulations which maintain segregation in private

Table 5-2
Federal Programs: Estimated Caseload as of 1975

	AR	GA	NM	NC	SD	TN
HUD Public:	124	110	156	92	305*	196
HUD 235:	?	100	?	?	0	40
FmHA 502:	510	15	160	550	168	275
1970 Substandard Units						
Lack Plumbing:	1,063	1,125	647	2,595	1,035	1,747
Overcrowded:	937	211	591	3,134	436	734

*240 — Tribe
  65 — Town

housing. Where customers take the initiative and acquire a lot before arranging for a builder, blacks have invariably selected lots in the black areas and whites in the white areas. It would be surprising if this were otherwise, given the institutions detailed above in Chapters 3 and 4.

Segregation in public housing is equally widespread, even though the institution by which it is provided differs from those of the private market. However, the administrators and board members of local housing authorities are all local persons, steeped in the traditions which govern the market generally. It was a housing authority director who responded to a question about integration with, "but that goes against all tradition."

The exact placement of projects and therefore their racial distribution differs among the sites visited. One site has two projects, one on the white side of town and the other on the black side. The units are identical in construction and maintenance, and the numbers provided for blacks and whites are equal. Two other towns have all-black public housing. These are the towns which have used public housing in connection with redevelopment efforts; all units are therefore located in traditionally black neighborhoods. Both directors report that whites had applied for the projects initially, but as soon as it become obvious that the projects would be located in black areas, white applications ceased. It is interesting to note that it is in these two towns that public housing was most strongly condemned as a "government giveaway," suggesting that the "giveaway" form of resentment stems as much from hostility toward the recipients as toward the source.

The fourth southern site was the only area where some attempt has been made at integration. This town has had two separate black and white projects for many years. When application was made recently for a third, the HUD area office insisted that the Authority choose a site which did not lie within a currently segregated neighborhood, and that it produce an integrated list of potential tenants. Choosing such a site posed some difficulty since, as noted repeatedly, there are no "gray areas" in the towns, and even the undeveloped areas adjoining the towns are tacitly designated "for blacks" and "for whites." The Authority finally settled on a site located at some distance from the developed part of town—a selection which displeased everybody about equally. Black representatives felt that the elderly in particular could be better served if not forced to move far away from long-time neighbors; but, rather than see the project become de facto segregated, blacks did exert considerable effort to recruit prospective tenants. The project is now in operation with about half-and-half black and white occupancy, and while turnover is considerably higher than in the other two projects, no racial incidents have occurred.

Assertion: *Federal Fair Housing regulations have not greatly affected local market interactions.*

Finding: *True*

Given the direct contradiction between federal law and the traditional or unwritten law of five of the six sites studied, as well as the lack of effective enforcement procedures for Fair Housing legislation, the impact of federal intervention in market interactions has so far been minimal. Fair Housing enforcement relies on complaints, which are not generated in the context of general and internalized discrimination.

Further, the housing market actors to which affirmative marketing regulations apply—builders, real estate agents, and lenders—*do*, almost without exception, serve both black and white customers. The fact that blacks are expected to confine their housing aspirations to the traditionally black neighborhoods is generally understood on both sides of the local interactions. Suppliers can therefore contend that they are serving the expressed wishes of their customers —and in fact they are to the extent that blacks adhere to the traditions. Because of the prevalence of informal communication of housing availability, black customeers often approach a broker or a lender with a house already in mind—invariably a house in the black area. Internalized discrimination therefore precedes and obviates supplier discrimination. Should a black consumer request and be refused access to "white housing," he or she is unlikely to file a complaint in the context of general discrimination. Only one case of supplier discrimination has resulted in a law suit, and, as noted above, the case was quickly dropped when the plaintiff lost his job.

Indian customers were rarely served by the homeownership market. This was attributed by suppliers to lack of applications, which in turn reflects the extremely low income levels of most Indians. It reflects as well a long tradition and deeply internalized discrimination. When asked how he goes about evaluating an Indian's credit history, for instance, one lender responded, "Indians have no credit history."

It is difficult to imagine how federal regulations, as currently written and enforced, could have much greater impact than they presently do. There is little obvious, prima facie evidence of discrimination on the part of suppliers, and black pressure for services outside of the black areas is limited, reflecting the degree to which discrimination is internalized. Fair Housing is recent legislation opposing centuries-old tradition. It is, at this stage in the social process, an attempt to restructure institutional relationships by directives from above, with a minimum of local support and with a considerable burden placed on the first few individuals who become "test cases." In addition, it attempts to restructure relationships among a large and shifting population of actors, with no central organization on which legal and executive pressure can be applied. In this, the housing market contrasts with the areas' public school systems, where desegregation was accomplished, without enthusiasm but without incident, in the 1960s.

On the other hand, the effectiveness of "on-paper" intervention into a situation this long-standing, amorphous, and deeply entrenched should not be immediately dismissed, since it at least provides backing to local actors who wish to promote equal access to housing. The broker who had referred a black family to a white neighborhood and had as a result suffered economic reprisals and personal abuse, said with a smile and an exaggerated shrug, "What else could I do—it's the law."

Notes

1. Melvin Mogulof, "Coalition to Adversary: Citizen Participation in Three Federal Programs," *AIP Journal*, July 1969. Charles Levine, "Community Organization in Chicago," Ph.D. dissertation in progress, Stanford University. *The Politics of Housing*, Special Issue of *Transaction: Social Science and Modern Society* 9 (July/August, 1972).
2. A lucid discussion of the political process represented here is contained in Charles Lindblom, "Bargaining: The Hidden Hand in Government," Research Memorandum, RM-1434-RC. (The Rand Corporation, Santa Monica, 1955); and Lindblom, *The Intelligence of Democracy: Decision-Making Through Mutual Adjustment* (New York, Free Press, 1965). The possible shortcomings of government through interest group accommodation, from both an administrative and social welfare point of view, are explored in Theodore J. Lowi, *The End of Liberalism: Ideology, Policy, and the Crisis of Public Authority* (New York: W.W. Norton & Company, Inc., 1969).
3. Levine, "Community Organization in Chicago."

6

Case Study of a Rural Housing Market in South Dakota

The South Dakota site is the most extreme of the six in terms of racial tension and political instability. It contrasts both with the New Mexico site, where ethnic discrimination was not encountered, and with the four southern sites, where racial tensions have so far been contained within a stable socio-political structure. The southern blacks studied have a rung in the sociopolitical hierarchy which, however disadvantaged, does at least guarantee minimal recognition from the dominant institutions toward those who keep their place. The South Dakota Indians, in contrast, have had no defined place in the local white-dominated structures, and until recently have been largely invisible: passive, heavily unemployed, and interacting mostly with tribal and federal agencies. When this group recently became visible and active, considerable strain was placed on local institutions, as these had no provision for recognizing or interacting with the Indians.

The local housing market, like other institutions, has little history of accommodating Indians, except for some rental transactions. Few Indians purchase homes on the private market, and most white interveners (the town, the town housing authority, etc.) are paralleled by Indian organizations. At the same time, the chronically depressed economy of the area has left even the white housing market in a state of stagnation. Private housing transactions have been even further dampened by the political tension between whites and Indians, with the result that practically the only housing-related activities now being conducted arise from public interveners: the tribe, the town, the public housing authorities, and the Farmers Home Administration.

The Setting

Site SD was described by one resident as "the Appalachia of South Dakota." It has a severely depressed economy, long-term decline in population, fiscally starved towns, and no immediate prospects for improvement. In some ways, its problems go beyond even those of Appalachia, however, for it also has a racial minority—a Sioux Indian tribe whose original reservation covered most of County SD and smaller parts of six other counties nearby.

The Economy

This area of South Dakota has been, from its original settlement in the mid-nineteenth century, a farming area. It was first settled by the Sioux tribe (actually, two closely related bands), who moved at that time from their former home in Minnesota.[1] During the Minnesota Sioux uprising of 1862, this tribe had not joined the insurgents, and some members had, in fact, served the government as scouts. After the U.S. victory, such distinctions were ignored, and all Minnesota tribes found their lands confiscated. In a belated act of reparation fives years later, in 1867, the government officially recognized "friendly Indians" and designated a 918,000-acre tract across the border in South Dakota as a reservation for this tribe.

By culture, the Indians were not farmers but hunters, and therefore better adapted to the wooded hills of Minnesota than to the prairie of South Dakota. At the same time, the westward migration of white settlers, in search of good farmland, began to reach the reservation. Hence, competition for the Indians' land began almost as soon as they themselves received it. Some whites bought or leased land from the Indians for farming; others took it by less legitimate methods.

Throughout the latter part of the nineteenth century, white population grew, and the Indians—unused to farming, suffering disease and bad harvests, and often finding that promised federal aid never arrived—became more and more desperate. Finally, in 1891, the tribe signed an agreement with the United States, under which the reservation was declared "open" to white settlement; and about 600,000 acres were sold to the government for resale to white homesteaders. An allotment of 160 acres was reserved as the property of each Indian person; much of this was leased to white settlers. After this, farming became the mainstay of what had been, until then, a fitful economy. In spite of the harsh climate, the land is fertile and water abundant. Tiny towns sprang up to serve as farm trade centers, including Town SD, first platted in 1908.

After this comparatively vigorous beginning in the early twentieth century, a long, slow decline set in, which has not yet reversed. Family farms became less and less viable; the Depression took its toll; and white outmigration began. For Indian farmers, the beginning of the end (if indeed, there had ever been a beginning) was World War II, when many young men were called up. This depleted the already struggling farm families of necessary labor, and large numbers of Indians left the open land and moved into the towns or out of the area. With the farms untended, according to one Indian official, there was actual famine after the War; and desperate families moved to the town for welfare assistance, or out of the area hoping for jobs.

The economy has never recovered. Employment is still primarily in agriculture (37 percent of the employed labor force in 1970), but the land is still mostly in small farms, which are barely profitable. The area has no industry—the

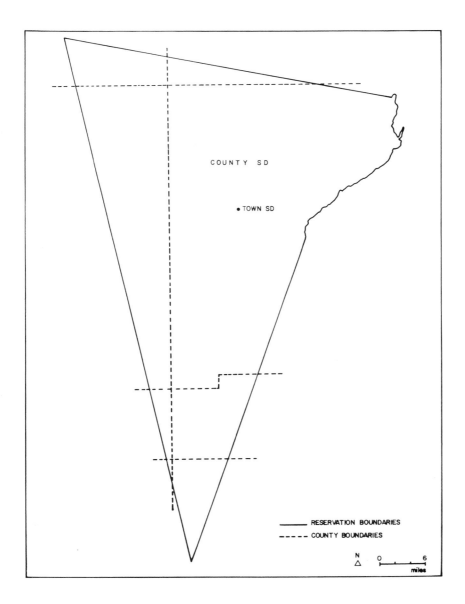

Figure 6-1. Original Reservation Boundaries: South Dakota Study Area

largest manufacturer is a creamery employing about thirty, and total employment in this sector is 3 percent—and no other economic base. According to the
1970 Census, overall unemployment in the county was only 4 percent, but
48 percent of the population over sixteen years of age were not in the labor
force. For Indians, the situation is much worse. Official 1974 figures from the
Bureau of Indian Affairs show that, for the whole tribe (over the seven-county
area covered by the reservation), only 27 percent are in the labor force; and,
of these, 56 percent are unemployed.[2] Unofficial estimates by the local BIA
office put the figure closer to 65 or 70 percent, and many of the rest are under-
employed. The tribe employs about 200 Indians and the BIA office about 20
more. Other than these, only a handful of Indians have jobs other than seasonal
farm labor. Walking around Town SD, the study team saw many Indians but
could find none working in stores, offices, etc. Indian respondents explained
that this is because there are none to be seen—discrimination in employment
is rampant.

Population Trends

In spite of this 100-year history of unrelieved distress, Indians are migrating
into site SD, while whites continue to migrate out. White population has shown
absolute decrease in every decade since 1920; Indians have also migrated out but,
in times of national economic downturn, tend to remain; and some who have
left tend to return.[3] As one Indian put it, "If you're going to be unemployed,
it may as well be among your friends and relatives." Thus, Indian population
increased through inmigration in the 1930s and, after decline in the period 1940
to 1970, has once again begun to increase in the last three to four years.[4]
The total county population in 1970 was 11,678; of these, 13 percent or
1,567 were Indians. In Town SD, the corresponding figures were 3,094 and
742 (24 percent).[5] The latest population estimate of Indians on or near the
reservation (the seven-county area) is 3,482 in 1974,[6] estimated by the local
BIA to be an increase of about 1,200 over the 1970 level.
White population trends are clear and clearly explained by local officials:
"The old folks stay on the farms till they die, but the kids get out. There's
nothing to do here—no future." White population in fact declined 14 percent
between 1960 and 1970, and, despite Indian inmigration, total population
declined another 0.4 percent between 1970 and 1973.[7] Indian trends are more
complex. General outmigration, except in times of national recession, has
already been noted. At one point in the 1950s, the BIA instituted migration
assistance and job training programs in metropolitan areas. Many members of
this tribe moved to Minneapolis and Cleveland and some as far away as Los
Angeles. Many of these came back because, according to one Indian official,
"It just didn't work. They were real plebians in the cities—couldn't get jobs,

cut off from their roots and families, all alone—it just didn't work." Since about 1972, even more have returned as employment conditions worsened in many cities. According to the BIA welfare director, who administers General Assistance over the seven-county area, the Indian caseload has increased from 78 families in 1970 to 334 in 1975—practically all of the new cases are returnees. Another 150+ Indian families in County SD alone receive county-administered AFDC. Even without considering the number receiving AFDC in the other counties, these 484+ cases are more than half of the total of Indian families, estimated by the tribe as 875 in September 1974.[a] As one caseworker noted, "These poor people are just jumping from the fire back into the frying pan."

Another event has occurred since 1970 which is both a result of Indian return and a cause of further return. This is the revitalization of tribal government by a group of active, educated returnees. As late as 1971, the tribal council existed only on paper, and practically all Indian affairs and programs were handled by the BIA. By now, an active administration has formed. They have gained control of many programs formerly handled by the BIA, actively pursued federal assistance for which Indians are eligible, and administered many areas of tribal governance. The effect of this on population trends has been to attract even more returnees. The tribe provides employment for some 200 Indians, and future prospects for jobs and well-being, while not entirely good, are at least not as totally dismal as they appeared to be only five years ago.

The Social-Political Structure

The most visible result of the emergence of the tribal government has been its effect on the social-political structure, both of the area in general and within the Indian community. A formerly stable arrangement of white dominance and Indian passivity has been replaced by political activity and schism—within the white group, within the tribe, and between whites and Indians.

White Dominance and Indian Resurgence

White Dominance. Until a very few years ago, practically all decision-making power in the site was in the hands of a relatively large group of white men, mostly

---

[a]A count of "families" is somewhat ambiguous given different cultural definitions. The traditional structure in this tribe is matrifocal—a grandmother, her daughters, and their children constitute a family. The position of males is ambiguous. Many, but not all, Indians are now accepting the white American structure. The above count of 875 families includes 650 "families" in the white sense, both male and female headed; 155 single adults living with a family; and 70 single adults with children living with a family.

businessmen. The town and county government offices are almost entirely held by these men, as is much of the town's rental property, and practically all businesses, banks, and other economic institutions. Although farming is the base of the economy, most farms are small family farms (average acreage in 1969 was 466) rather than agribusinesses, and neither farmers nor farm organizations are prominent in decision-making institutions.

There is no "power structure" in the sense of a closed elite. Power is shared with many federal officials, particularly those of the BIA, most of whom are non-local in origin. In addition, a nonlocal town manager was hired in 1972; he also serves as the town planner, the zoning administrator, and the building and housing inspector. Finally, several white ministers and priests are active in community affairs. Indians play no part in this structure, but are merely the recipients of whatever services or disservices these institutions choose to provide.[b]

There are splits among the white decisionmakers on the question of relationships with Indians—splits which have been exacerbated by the emergence of a separate Indian power base and independent activity. As far as the study team could determine, the situation until about 1972 was that the businessmen were generally oblivious or hostile to Indians, as was the town (under a previous town manager with businessmen as councilmen). The BIA saw itself as overseer of Indian affairs and caretaker of Indian interests, as perceived and defined by the BIA. Only the white ministers appeared to show genuine empathy for Indian problems, but their efforts to serve Indian needs were often blocked by other whites—in one case by resistance from a minister's own congregation.

The Indians were politically powerless, and many were economically destitute. In addition, their culture had received continuous assaults since their displacement onto farmland in the 1860s. Adjustment to agriculture was difficult, and many Indians leased or sold their land rather than farm it. Traditional family structure was undermined, and, according to staff of a local Indian museum, important tribal rituals and religious observances were forbidden, even on the reservation.

One of the most emotionally-charged issues is in relation to child welfare practices of the State Department of Public Welfare. Indian children are separated from their natural families—often the culturally sanctioned matrifocal families—and put up for adoption at a rate several times higher than are white children, according to various sources. Welfare workers in County SD confirmed that all of their Child Protective Services activities are with Indian children. It is partially out of concern for this situation that the tribe has recently begun encouraging monogamous unions and "white" family structure.

---

[b]An Indian woman heads the Public Health hospital and sits on many of the town boards. She was described (not without sympathy) as a "sell-out" by other Indians. One businessman introduced her to the study team and put her through a caricature of an interview where he supplied her answers as well as the questions, occasionally giving her a chance to nod. Her involvement in decision-making is clearly token.

Indian Resurgence. It was just as the tribal government was forming in 1972 that a child welfare issue exploded into litigation which questioned the legal existence of the reservation, and was not finally resolved until the U.S. Supreme Court decision in March of 1975 (one week before the study team's arrival). An Indian woman whose children had been separated from her by the Welfare Department petitioned in court for their return, claiming that the state had no jurisdiction over Indians on reservation land.[8] The tribe assisted her, and passed a formal resolution in her support. Her attorney testified at the later Senate hearings that the tribe was concerned because of the frequency of this child welfare practice.

It had been generally taken for granted until about 1963 that the reservation established in 1867 was still intact despite the 1891 agreement to open unallotted land for homesteading. However, tribal government had no real existence, and the state had regularly exercised jurisdiction over Indians on the unallotted—i.e., non-Indian-owned—land within its boundaries. Allotted land, which is held in trust for the Indian owners by the government and administered by the BIA, consists of small plots scattered in a random, crazy-quilt pattern over the seven counties. It covers in the aggregate about 100,000 acres of the original 900,000; about 300,000 acres were allotted to Indians in 1891, but two-thirds of this has been sold over time. Only a few blocks of Town SD are trust—i.e., Indian-owned—land. Legally, only federal and tribal law applies to Indians on reservation land. The question thus became: are the boundaries of the reservation those originally drawn in 1867, or does the reservation now consist only of the scattered plots of trust land?

In 1963, a Federal District Court had ruled in two cases of criminal jurisdiction that the state *did* have jurisdiction over Indians on nontrust land within the 1867 boundaries, but was reversed by a Federal Court of Appeals. The jurisdiction covering Indians in the seven-county area—most of whom do not live on trust land—was thus opened to question, and appeals and new cases added to the controversy. The March 1975 Supreme Court decision finally held that the original reservation boundaries had been terminated in 1891, and the reservation (and thus tribal law) covers only Indians living on trust land, while state law covers Indians on nontrust land.

The 1973 DeCoteau decision in State Court was that the original reservation was intact, and thus the state had no jurisdiction. (It was the state that appealed to the U.S. Supreme Court.) The reception of this decision among Indians was mixed. The tribe was pleased over the apparent victory in the child welfare case, but not entirely enthusiastic about setting up the legal machinery—police and courts—necessary to cover the seven-county area. Some Indians felt that the decision was just deliverance from the second-class citizenship they had long endured; others felt that it was a Pyrrhic victory in that financial and other resources would have to be diverted away from necessary services to Indians. (Now that the Supreme Court has overruled the state court, the same

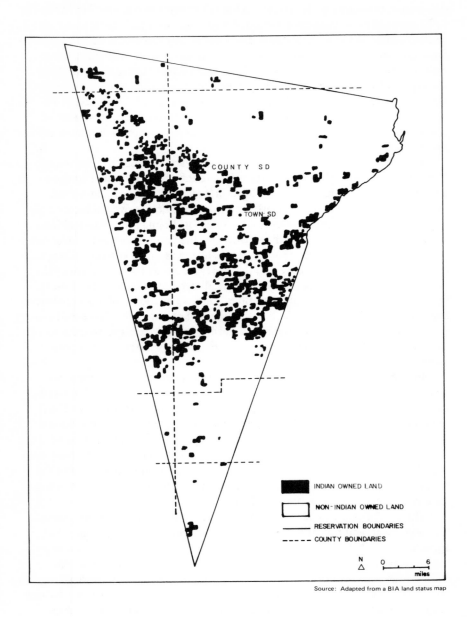

Source: Adapted from a BIA land status map

Figure 6-2. Original and Current Reservation Boundaries: South Dakota
Study Area.

disagreement remains. Some Indians are now outraged, while others are pleased, for exactly the reasons noted above.)

The most immediate and visible effect of the 1973 decision was not, however, this disagreement among Indians. Its major impact was to exacerbate beyond all previous experience the hostility between Indians and whites. The reaction of many, and perhaps most, whites to the news that they were living on 'a reservation was stunned anger. Indians, who had hardly been visible to many except as destitute and despairing "drunken bums," were now in some vague way "in charge," at least of themselves and perhaps of the future viability of the area.

Indian Schism and Confrontation

The Tribal Government. Whether Indians could exert much real power, even had they wanted to, is of course another question. The emergence of the tribal government coincided in time with the jurisdictional dispute and may have added to the *appearance* of Indian power and thus to white resentment. In fact, however, the government is still very new and on less-than-solid footing, even within the tribe. Most or all of the administrators were born on the reservation, but practically all are very recent returnees. The "old-timer" of the group has been back several years; most arrived no more than a year or two ago.

Efforts have been made to establish grassroots support, though some Indians say that the effort is more to establish just the appearance. In any case, the 900,000-acre area is divided into seven districts, each of which elects a councilperson to the legislative body. The tribal chairman is elected at large and oversees the administration. This is not a stable or well-accepted arrangement, as evidenced by the fact that the districts have recently elected a parallel set of district "chairmen," who also caucus regularly and whose official relationship to the council is far from clear. However, some Indians say that neither group has much impact on the decisions of the tribal chairman and the administrative staff. This may be due to closed elitism, as implied, or may perhaps be an inevitable outcome of the rapid establishment from above of governing institutions. The merits of the various arguments are not to be resolved here, but what is abundantly clear is that there is considerable political dissension within the tribe. The most vocal opponents of the recently established administration are members or sympathizers of the American Indian Movement.

The stated goal of the tribal administration is "employment for every Indian," and their strategy for accomplishing this is to establish a separate economic base and to maximize independence from local white-controlled institutions. Taking advantage of the federal commitment to Indian self-determination, the tribe has taken over some programs from the BIA and is independently pursuing federal funding for other activities. This year's total

revenues of just over $3 million[c] finance such activities as education, public
works, law enforcement, health and welfare, and economic development.
Relationships with the BIA and the town are outwardly cordial, although conflict of interest is acknowledged. However, the tribe tends to remain aloof from
either cooperation or conflict with local whites as much as possible while
pursuing its own objectives.

First among these goals is the establishment of a separate economic base—
plus as many other social benefits as federal monies can be acquired for—in
order to remove Indians from what had been until recently their total dependence on local white-controlled institutions. Feeling that the county's economic
development efforts are misdirected, and even if successful are unlikely to
benefit Indians, the tribe is pursuing its own economic development activities
with an EDA grant. More importantly, the tribe is concentrating effort at
present on plans to buy back and consolidate as much as possible of the land
that has been sold or whose title has been clouded by multiple heirships.
(This effort is being assisted by the Farmers Home Administration, and is discussed in more detail below.) Given these objectives, it is not surprising that
tribal administrators expressed no great objection to the Supreme Court's 1975
decision. It was a defeat on the child welfare issue, but it relieved them of the
need to divert substantial resources into law enforcement.

The Opposition. The position of the AIM group is that, despite the
potential appeal of these long-range plans, many Indians are suffering severe
and immediate problems which the tribe is not addressing. (They also suspect
the personal motives of the administrators, a sentiment which is thoroughly
reciprocated.) As noted above, unemployment and welfare dependency are
extremely high, much of the housing can only be described as wretched, and
Indians are routinely subjected to blatant discrimination and insults in their
daily activities. The study team overheard much casual banter about Indians'
inherent inadequacy as humans—"They're like babies; they really need a strong
hand over them or they just can't do anything"—and observed polite, well-
dressed Indians being refused service by merchants. One (white) respondent
warned against drawing conclusions from the sight of Indians drunk on the
streets: "Lots of White people get drunk too, but they have somewhere to go."
The situation is summed up with some delicacy by the county's "701" Comprehensive Plan, prepared by the regional development district. It notes: "The
short time that has passed since the two divergent cultures came into contact
has not allowed for a reciprocal adjustment and comprehension of social and
economic norms," and, "Additional problems may arise because of the two
cultures conflicting."

---

[c]About one-fourth of this was a one-time lump sum payment of $800,000 from the
United States, in compensation for the original lands confiscated in Minnesota in 1862.
"They got a bargain," remarked one Indian.

Such problems have already arisen. The AIM group directs most of its protest activities against the tribal government, but anger toward whites is strong. Corresponding white hostility is generated by the very existence of the tribal government, fanned by Indian involvement with AIM, and raised to a pitch by the jurisdictional dispute. As a result, a number of racial incidents have occurred. In one case, an unplanned incident escalated into a major confrontation. According to various reports, a white merchant refused an Indian's check and told him it was "because you're an Indian." The Indian returned later with some friends; the white man responded by brandishing a gun; more friends and more guns appeared (on both sides); and it was a tense stand-off most of the night until the county sheriff broke it up by arresting the white man. (The tribe immediately claimed jurisdiction over the prisoner under the 1973 decision, but found that he had been secretly transferred to a jail in another county.) Another incident started as a symbolic gesture to dramatize Indian ownership of leased land. A group organized by AIM briefly took possession of a field. It was reported by whites that the Indians were armed and had shot at whites driving by; and, by at least one Indian, that whites riding past in pick-up trucks had fired on the Indians.

Such incidents have fanned white hostility even further, and led to splits between whites who are sympathetic to Indians and those who are violently anti-Indian. (Included among the latter are many farmers, who had not in the past generally been involved in political activities.) The more extreme of the anti-Indian faction have formed into an underground organization best described as a vigilante group. Its activities and membership are secret, although it was learned that several public officials are members. They did surface recently to give the local congressman, a liberal Republican, some uncomfortable moments during his visit to town.

Noting this response, the tribal government feels that open confrontation solves nothing and only exacerbates problems while deflecting energy away from the effort to achieve self-sufficiency. The overall situation bears some resemblance to the politics of black civil rights activity in the 1960s. The Indians are split between the "moderates" and the "radicals"; the split appears to follow the line between the "ins" and the "outs" in the Indian society, although all Indians are "outs" in relation to the whites. An important difference between this and the black experience is that neither group is seeking integration into white society, and the moderates are even more separatist than the radicals.

The Housing Market

In this tense political atmosphere and chronically depressed economy, there are very few activities which could be called a housing "market" in the usual sense. Supply activities and transactions among private persons and institutions are very limited. The major actors in relation to housing are the public interveners; the major determinants of "who lives where and in what" are factors in the economic and political context analyzed above.

Land and Housing Stock

Land. Land ownership in site SD is extremely complicated and a source of much political tension. At the time of the opening of the reservation in 1891, 160-acre plots were allotted to Indian individuals, with title held in trust by the U.S. government. As noted above, these allotments comprised about one-third of the reservation land, and were scattered in no apparent pattern over the 900,000-acre area. Unallotted or "fee" land became the property of white homesteaders, and is subject to local taxes. Allotted or "trust" land was the property of individual Indians (although individuals did not actually hold title) and not taxable. The tribe owned no land as a corporate entity.

Allotted land was of no greater direct use to Indians after 1891 than it had been before. Many lived on their land and a few tried farming, but most leased their allotment to white farmers. In their continuing poverty, many of the Indian owners sold their land. (Whether or not this was encouraged by the government, which held the title, and whether terms were equitable could not be determined, but this particular point is not a live issue today.) During and after World War II, many Indians moved off the land and into the towns or out of the area. The resulting situation is that only about 100,000 acres remain in trust, and most members of the tribe do not actually live on trust land.

Ownership of trust land was divided equally among the heirs of the original owner, resulting by this time in a serious problem of "fractionated heirships." It is rare to find a plot owned outright by a single Indian. Most plots are the joint property of six to ten co-heirs, none of whom can use or dispose of the property without the consent of all others. The record is one plot jointly owned by over 300 individuals.

The local BIA office, administering the trust on behalf of the U.S. government, keeps track of the ownership of each property, administers leases, and distributes the leasehold income among the heirs. Current rates are $4-5 per acre per year for pastureland and $14-15 per acre per year for cropland. Gross income from land leases is about $300,000 per year, although this does not amount to much income for any individual. According to the BIA land agent, no more than ten Indians make as much as $1,000/year from this source. In addition, Indians who wish to live on or use the land must usually buy or lease it from their co-heirs.

A major effort is currently being made by the tribal government to consolidate land ownership. A special act of Congress in 1974 allowed land owned corporately by the tribe to be placed in trust, and thus off the local tax roles. Among the long-term goals of the tribe are such income- and employment-producing uses as a large tribal farm; plans are also developed for an industrial park. The major problem at present is getting title. With assistance and $1,250,000 from the FmHA, the tribe began last year to attempt to buy land.

Legal complications of purchase are immense, and white resentment is strong, particularly among farmers. Some feel the strong but nonspecific resentment expressed by one white, "Why are they trying to take our land away?" The issue of ownership is apparently a very emotional one on both sides, as evidenced by the AIM-supported "sit-in" to dramatize Indian ownership of white-leased land, and the events following. More practically, some whites are worried about the tax question. Tax revenues are already very low; about one-half of the land in Town SD is already nontaxable (because it is either public or Indian-owned), as are substantial chunks of the county land. Partly as a result, public services are very limited. The town cannot afford badly needed housing code enforcement and the public schools, which are predominantly white, are supported by Johnson-O'Malley monies—federal subsidies for Indian education. (This subsidy is unlikely to survive the 1975 Supreme Court decision. Since the proportion of whites in the schools is too high, a special waiver was needed to permit Johnson-O'Malley subsidies. The waiver was granted only because the schools were on a reservation; they no longer are.)

Because of such emotions and problems, white resistance to Indian land purchase is strong and is a major contributor to the political tensions discussed above. Legalities of purchase, from Indian co-owners as well as from whites, are also complex. So far, the tribe has not yet actually purchased any land from whites or from co-heirs, although some scattered plots had been purchased from Indian sole owners. Indian owners wishing to sell are encouraged by the tribe and the BIA to sell to the tribe rather than to whites, as the latter course would remove the land from trust status.

Housing. Town SD is still the neatly platted town first laid out in 1908. One new (1960s) subdivision is the only change from the original town limits, although a majority of the lots in it have not been sold. Beyond the town limits, there is no residential or commercial sprawl, but rather open farm country dotted with widely separated houses. Within the town, the better quality homes are generally on the east side, and the poorer ones on the west. However, good and poor quality homes often adjoin, sometimes facing a vacant and vandalized shack across the street and perhaps a mobile home nearby. (There are few mobile homes in the area because of the harsh winters; it is apparently impossible to keep the pipes from freezing.)

Housing is closely but indirectly related to land. Housing problems in the area result most directly from poverty. The predominant land use in the county is farming (92 percent of the acreage in 1969),[9] but farms are generally small. Income is low, and for most Indian owners limited to leaseholds. It is possible

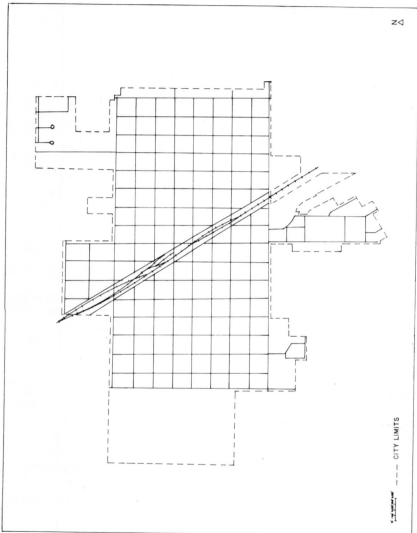

N△

- - - - CITY LIMITS

Figure 6-3. The South Dakota Study Town (Town SD)

that usage other than leasing individual small plots might result in more efficient land use and greater income—this is certainly the hope of the tribe—although scattered and multiple ownership at present prevents consolidated land use.

Among whites, the situation is better only by comparison. Many whites are the actual farmers and have higher income from the land than the Indian owners. However, most white farmers own their land outright, and even for these, incomes are not high. According to the 1970 Census, 20 percent of county SD's total population were poor. According to the Welfare figures given above, the incidence of poverty among Indians was then and is still much higher. In 1970, median income for all families was $5,628; for white families it was $5,879.

Poor housing for both whites and Indians is clearly visible both in the town and out in the county. (There is no racial segregation, although Indians are poorer and more frequently found in the poorer parts of town.) "This is a rural slum," stated one official bluntly. Most of the housing stock is old and much of it is deteriorating. According to U.S. Census of Housing figures, 83 percent of the county's 1970 stock was built prior to 1950. According to local respondents, most was built between 1910 and 1940. Only 8 percent of the 3,868 units dated from 1960 or later.

A town survey in 1970 revealed that 256 of the 943 units are deteriorating or dilapidated. The private stock available to the poor—including most Indians—can only be described as shacks. Many lack insulation and some or all plumbing. The study team noted many dilapidated shacks, occupied by families who were clearly paying high utility bills since in below-0° weather, the snow was melted off the roofs. According to a recent tribal survey, practically every Indian in the area, except those in federally-subsidized units, lives in housing which fails to meet state health and fire codes. Much low- and moderate-income private housing in town, including that occupied by most Indians, fails to meet town housing codes.

Housing, even poor housing, is in very tight supply. Despite decades-long outmigration, the 1970 town survey revealed only seven homes for sale, six of which were below codes. The current housing stock is clearly in need of rehabilitation or replacement, and many new units are needed. The tribe estimated a minimum need in 1971 for major rehabilitation or replacement of about 200 existing Indian-occupied units, plus about 100 new units for families living doubled up. This was before the inmigration which increased by almost 50 percent the number of Indians on site SD. The town estimated a need in 1970 for major repair or replacement housing for 175 families in the town, about 100 of whom were Indians.

Participants and Interactions

Very little of the apparent need is being met. The private market is quite

literally not functioning, except for some rental turnover. Public intervention is
somewhat more successful but only by comparison.

The Private Market. Officials and bankers estimate that there have been
perhaps five houses built in the private market in the last three or four years,
and about fifteen existing houses sold. The first respondent interviewed
remarked "Everybody will probably tell you it's because of the jurisdictional dispute"—as in fact most later respondents did—"but that's just the excuse." Prob-
ing of later respondents revealed that the current level of activity is not much
decreased from that previously, and that the market has been stagnant for decades.

The private housing market is currently not functioning at all. Builders are
concentrating on farm and commercial structures, the commercial bank and the
savings and loan report "ample" funds for long-term mortgages but no applications,[d] and the two largest real estate agents in town have three listings between
them. The jurisdictional dispute is probably responsible for the almost complete
cessation of activity. People were reportedly afraid to make large financial
commitments for fear that reservation status would discourage business and
further depress the area's economic prospects. In addition, any contractual
dealings with Indians, either in the housing market or in other areas, were
avoided because they would not be enforceable under state law. (Whites are not
willing to trust their financial fate to the tribal court, but prefer to bring Indians
to the county court.)

However, it is clear that the effect of the jurisdictional dispute on the housing market has only been to reduce activity from very little to even less. The
most important reason for stagnation is the chronically depressed economy,
high unemployment and low wage levels in relation to the cost of building (estimated to have doubled in the last five years) and of financing. This is not to
imply that costs are high in any absolute sense, although interest rates are comparable to current national levels. No dollar estimate of building costs could be
obtained (no one is building), although one banker guessed that the total cost
of building a 2-3 bedroom house would at present be $24-25,000.

On the question of costs, the fate of the new subdivision is instructive.
Officers of the commercial bank, hoping to increase mortgage activity, developed
an eighty-acre site in 1964. All site improvements were included, along with
seven acres for a park. Lots of 72x140 feet were offered at just above cost—
$1,200. The developers had expected twelve to fifteen new houses a year, but
only twelve lots were sold in ten years. It is clear from this experience that the
problem is not necessarily absolute cost, but cost in relation to the low incomes
in the area. It also implies, given the shortage of even middle- and high-income
housing, that persons of this income level are "making do" until they leave the

---

[d]Both offer twenty-year mortgages with 20 percent downpayment. Bank interest is
9 percent, while the S&L charges 8.75 percent.

area. Many such people are public employees temporarily assigned. As an example, the head of the BIA was unable to find and unwilling to build a suitable home when he was assigned. He therefore left his family in their home at the place of his previous assignment and, while in the site SD, rents a mobile home.

The rental market is similarly tight: no new privately-financed units have been built, and turnover is low. Rental housing, most of which is single-family, is in general far inferior to owner-occupied housing; and its occupants are mostly, though not entirely, the poor. (The manager of the S&L could not find a suitable house for sale when he and his family arrived, and so lived for six months in a poor quality rental building.) Most of the dilapidated housing is rental, and many, but not all, of its occupants are Indians. Rents, however, tend to be extremely high. Many of the low-income renters are Welfare recipients, either from the BIA or the county. (All BIA recipients are Indians, as are about 80 percent of the county AFDC cases.) Both Welfare offices have the policy of determining a family's housing allotment by the actual rent, whatever it is, although the BIA imposes a $103 ceiling. As a direct result, rents are unusually high.

It is not unusual to find a family living in a deteriorating house with poor insulation, but paying over $100/month (plus utilities). Some two and three room houses without plumbing rent for over $80. These homes are owned by many different individuals (all white), but a few names stand out. (One is on the town planning board.) When asked why improvements in the housing are not made, the manager of one block of rentals did *not* say the reason was cost in relation to rents. He said, rather, that it was no use because the tenants would just get drunk and tear the place up again.

Indians are clearly at the bottom of the housing filtration chain, not only because of greater poverty but also because of expectations such as this. "No one with a decent house would ever rent it to an Indian," said one knowledgeable respondent with no sign of defensiveness. "Once you rent to Indians you don't even know how many of them will be in there and you can never get them out. Sooner or later, they'll tear the house apart." There is thus a tacit designation of individual houses as either "for whites" or "for Indians," although there is no neighborhood segregation. Poor whites live among poor Indians, though usually in slightly better houses; while on the east side of town, a few middle-income Indians live among middle-income whites. A very few Indians own rather than rent: according to the 1970 Census, 13 of the 146 Indian households in the town owned, as did 67 of the 267 in the county.

Public Intervention. With the private ownership market stagnant for decades and rental turnover very low, it is clear that current decisions affecting "who lives where and in what" are not private market decisions but public interventions. It is for this reason that public policies and the local social-political structure have much closer and more direct impact on housing than was observed elsewhere in this study. These factors *are*, in effect, the housing "market." The actors consist of the town, the tribe, the housing authorities that each sponsor and the Farmers Home Administration.

Except for public housing, there has been no HUD involvement with the local housing needs. This has left the town's efforts ineffective. About three years ago, the town applied for Neighborhood Redevelopment and Concentrated Code Enforcement monies. The necessary codes were duly passed, a survey of housing conditions and needs taken and plans developed for renewal of the most blighted area in the western part of town. There was no visible opposition. Most of the property to be condemned or rehabilitated was rental, and at least some owners sat on the board who oversaw the plans. Owner-occupants of the area in question tended to be in the good quality housing mixed in with shacks, and felt that redevelopment could only help their properties. Applications were submitted in 1972 but were rejected for reasons not clear.

A more recent effort by the town to apply for community development (CDBG) funds to deal with substandard housing was thwarted by the opinion of a nonresident city engineer, ostensibly encouraged by the HUD area office, that HUD would not be receptive to an application for dealing with substandard housing. Housing is not a priority for HUD, he had said; they would be more likely to fund an application centering around water and sewer needs. A pre-application for discretionary CDBG funds for water treatment was submitted, but turned down by HUD. Hence, the town is stymied in its efforts to deal directly with its housing problems, including those of the Indian population living in the poor areas of town.

Visibly more successful is the HUD-funded public housing program. There are two local housing authorities, the town's and the tribe's, although they share the same (white) executive director. The town's Authority dates from 1968, and the tribe's from 1971; by agreement, they concentrate on elderly and family housing respectively. They are currently 305 units (240 under the tribe and 65 under the town), with 50 more tribal units under construction. Indians sit on the boards of both Authorities, though form a majority of neither. The chairman of the Tribal Authority board is an Indian; the chairman of the town's board is a white minister.

Several respondents report that the director makes most of the decisions (including those on who is admitted to public housing), with little input from the boards. However, he was only rarely criticized. Whites had no objection to his policies, though some felt he was too "pro-Indian." Tribal officials said that they wished he were "a little more cooperative"—the man is an ex-army sergeant of strong personality—but had no specific criticism of his decisions, and no desire to have him replaced. An Indian councilperson, who considered the director "anti-Indian," objected to the fact of white occupancy of tribal units and to some specific choices of comparatively high-income families for admission.

The family (tribal) units are 87 percent Indian-occupied, while the elderly (town) units are 12 percent Indian-occupied. The waiting list is over 400 for family units, and about 62 for elderly. Most of those on the waiting list are Indians. The Authority operates in the black, and to offset the 20 percent "low low-income," admits some of more moderate income. Rent is a flat 25 percent of income for all.

The family units are built in seven scattered clusters, while the elderly project is a single high rise. The tribe said that Indians prefer detached units, and their extended family structure would be better served by larger units. However, HUD policy for the area dictates cluster developments to reduce costs, and the tribe recognizes that the same money will produce more units if clustered. Therefore, though they are not entirely satisfied with the public housing, they have not objected. "The housing situation is so desperate," said one administrator, "that we will take anything we can get."

These 305 public housing units are practically the only new housing built since the town and tribal surveys (quoted above) pointed out severe housing needs. Those estimates were self-described as minimal emergency needs, and the Indian population has increased sharply since then. Public housing, while clearly inadequate to the total need, has been the single most effective response among housing institutions.

The only rehabilitation work on existing housing has been under the tribe and the FmHA. Under the HIP program, the tribe provides small grants (e.g., $1,500) for insulation and other minor repairs, while recognizing that much of the housing so affected is severely deteriorating. It is another case of taking "a drop in the bucket" as at least better than nothing. FmHA has granted only ten Section 504 rehabilitation loans because the amount needed to make the homes of most eligible applicants "safe and habitable," as required by FmHA regulations, is far above the 504 loan ceiling.

The FmHA has been far more active with the 502 homeownership program and in efforts to assist with tribal land consolidation. The county supervisor is a local white man who appears to know and get along with practically everybody in the area. He appears unusually sympathetic to Indian needs—and has made active efforts to provide assistance—while at the same time is well thought of by the whites. He was even permitted to attend a meeting of the white underground organization—not as a sympathizer but as an interested observer. The only criticism heard of FmHA was that there is not enough of it, and that perhaps the supervisor should explore the possibilities from other FmHA programs in addition to the ones he administers.

In total, the FmHA has made 168 Section 502 loans, 30-40 of these with interest credit, and 18 percent of the total to Indians. There are also three "four-plexes", multifamily rental units funded by FmHA. Of the 502's, most were for purchase of existing housing, although some new construction was financed. The supervisor claims that he has never turned down an Indian applicant, "because they have nowhere else to go." Instead, he attempts to reduce the cost of the home or repair, accepts promissory notes and assignment of lease-hold income in lieu of a mortgage, and makes other special efforts to adapt the program to Indian needs. He reports no problems with delinquency or foreclosure.

However, the programs do not serve—nor were they designed to serve—the low income. Maximum adjusted income for an FmHA 502 loan is $11,300; for interest credit the maximum is $8,500. The lowest acceptable income is about $5,000, which is not much below the median income of the area. Below that, the supervisor reports the family would be paying more than 20 percent of their income for the best costs he can arrange, and that would have to lead to problems either with the family's mortgage payment or their ability to meet their other needs. Other than income, the main criterion for judging white applications is credit history. No Indians have been rejected on this criterion, however, because "Indians have no credit history."

Access to Housing

The question of whether there is unequal treatment of Indians in the site SD housing *market* is somewhat beside the point, since there really is no market in the usual sense of the word. Most current decisions as to whether housing is made available are in the hands of public officials, and are influenced by the officials' positions in the somewhat sundered political structure, as well as by the constraints and opportunities presented by the programs they administer.

Clearly, Indians suffer racial discrimination in many visible ways; equally clearly, their housing conditions and probability of ownership are much lower than whites.[e] However, Indians are also for the most part desperately poor. The extra contribution to housing problems presented by housing discrimination is not, therefore, immediately obvious.

Nonspecific allegations of discrimination in private mortgage credit decisions were made by a few respondents. However, so few Indians are in a financial position to buy that these allegations, even if verified, would not go far to explain Indian housing conditions. Another suggestion was made to explain why the rental housing occupied by poor whites was slightly superior to that occupied by Indians. According to this respondent, it is because poor whites can at least get a small repair loan and fix the house themselves if the landlord refuses. Again, this is not entirely plausible, since any poor person, and especially any poor

---

[e]Numerous whites claimed that Indians do not want to own—that individual ownership is in conflict with their traditional culture. This was denied by every Indian interviewed, including the token Indian woman in the presence of the businessman who suggested this opinion to her.

person on Welfare, is likely to have trouble with credit even if white. In addition, all respondents agreed that the rental housing occupied by the poor of both races is either beyond repair or in such deteriorating condition that a small personal loan is not likely to have much effect on its condition.

However, the reported difference in the quality of rental housing available to whites as opposed to Indians, however small, does appear to be a case of direct housing market discrimination. Indians were frequently described as poor housekeepers and destructive of property and, because of this belief, are placed behind whites in order of preference as tenants. In this connection, it is interesting to note that the newest and in many respects the best quality housing available to anyone are the public housing units, and the director reports no serious problems with poor housekeeping among Indian tenants.

Also, poor Indians often pay exhorbitant rents, but this is pass-through money from the Welfare agencies and such rents are also paid by whites on Welfare. There is, however, a direct financial burden on the tenants of very poor quality housing, since there is a ceiling on heat and utility payments in Welfare allotments. The refusal to make repairs despite high rents indicates gross exploitation of the powerless—particularly when the refusal is attributed to the inherent faults of the tenants themselves.

More generally, the housing conditions of many Indians, for better and for worse, can be largely attributed to public policy and the success or failure of the various public interveners in their respective efforts. The town, for instance, was unsuccessful in applications for funds to improve blighted housing (much of it Indian-occupied). Both the town and the tribe have succeeded in providing public housing. Although the design is not ideal and some Indians feel that admissions are not equitable, the fact remains that tribal public housing is the major source of improvement in housing conditions in site SD and that it is almost entirely occupied by Indians.

The FmHA, occupying a delicate middle position among all the hostile factions, has served Indians in greater numbers than their proportion of the population. However, the nature of FmHA programs is such that the very low income—i.e., most Indians— cannot be served. It is possible that the only real hope for more general improvement in Indian housing would be the success (which is still in doubt) of the long-range economic development and land consolidation plans of the tribe. As stated by one tribal official: "Of course we need housing—desperately—and we'll take anything we can get. But until we get the jobs and the money to pay for it, we'll never get enough."

Notes

1. Historical information in this section is drawn from the Supreme Court decision, *DeCoteau* v. *District County Court*, No. 73-1148, 1150, March 3, 1975; and from on-site interviews.

2. BIA Area Office, Aberdeen, South Dakota, "Aberdeen Area Statistical Data," July 1974.
3. County SD, *Comprehensive Plan*, prepared with the assistance of a HUD "701" Planning Grant, November 1974.
4. Source: Tribal and BIA officials.
5. U.S. Census of Population, 1970.
6. BIA Aberdeen Area office, "Statistical Data." Total tribal membership is about 6,000. Most of those not in site SD are in Minneapolis, although some are scattered as far away as Los Angeles.
7. U.S. Census.
8. The legal history of the case is summarized in *DeCoteau* v. *District County Court*. Ms. DeCoteau has testified at a Senate hearing that one child was taken away when she left him with a baby-sitter. She was not informed of a formal hearing (held seven months later) on the need for emergency custody, and did not see the child for several years because Welfare officials refused to tell her where he was. Again according to her testimony, she was required to sign some papers by a Welfare worker, and was then told that they were papers giving up her second child for adoption. Source: *Indian Child Welfare Program*, Hearings before the Subcommittee on Indian Affairs of the Committee on Interior and Insular Affairs, United States Senate, April 8, 1974.
9. *U.S. Census.*

7

Case Study of a Rural Housing Market in Georgia

The Georgia site presents a sharp contrast to the political confrontation and market breakdown shown in South Dakota. While racial inequality in this site is clear and obvious, protest is nonexistent and the social-political structure has remained stable. Partly, this is due to the safety valve of outmigration for frustrated blacks, but it is largely the result of stability built into the system. Unlike the Indians described above, the blacks here are accommodated within the overall structure and have no alternative institutions. As long as blacks acquiesce in subordinate status, they are usually able to obtain jobs and services from the local white-dominated institutions. Without alternative organizations, any protest against inequality would have to be by an unsupported individual, who would thereby be alienating the only sources of jobs and services.

Housing is supplied almost entirely by the private market, with some federal loan subsidies or guarantees. The current stagnation in the market reflects national economic trends, rather than any specifically local phenomena. This case thus illustrates the ways in which a private market supplies housing differentially by race, and how this pattern has continued unchallenged to the present day.

It is worth stressing that in the operations of the private housing market, this case is entirely typical of the four southern sites. The black protest and political activity observed on other sites concerned specific public interventions—redevelopment projects—and neither affected nor attempted to affect the "business-as-usual" patterns of market segmentation. Similarly, the pattern here of total racial segregation applies to the other sites as well, with the highly visible exceptions of only five families in all sites combined who have ever attempted to cross neighborhood barriers.

The Setting

County G is a small rural county located on the coastal plain of southeast Georgia. Its only urban place is the county seat which, with 9,091 persons, contains about half the population of the county.[1] The land in this area of Georgia is low and flat. While field crops and pastureland can be seen, especially north and west of the town, much of the southern half of the county is swampland unsuitable for agriculture. The wet uninhabited land with its extensive stands

121

of timber reminds the visitor that the beginning of the Okefenokee Swamp is nearby and gives the area an appearance of remoteness which is somewhat misleading. Town G is in fact easily accessible by highway and rail; until the recent construction of an interstate which bypasses the town by 25 miles, the north-south highway passing through the town was the major route to Florida.

The Economy

While distinctly rural in character, County G has never been predominantly agricultural. It is, rather, one of the major timber-producing counties in the South. The swampland to the south of the town is almost exclusively devoted to timber production, while the farms to the north are often cleared patches surrounded by timber.

Since World War II, the county has undergone the consolidation of land holdings characteristic of rural areas. In this case, however, the purchasers have been not agribusinesses but pulp and paper companies. Four such companies were named by respondents as the present major landholders in the county; one of these was estimated by the tax commissioner to own about one-quarter of the county's land.

None of the local respondents reported controversy or social dislocation resulting from this land acquisition. Much of the timber is in swampland which was sparsely inhabited; in the better drained land which was partially in farming, the purchaser would often lease the cleared land back to the farmer. In addition, and increasingly after about 1955, agricultural holdings were somewhat consolidated, resulting in a movement of farmers off the land and into metropolitan areas in Georgia and elsewhere up the East Coast. Between 1960 and 1970, the rural farm population of the county decreased by 35 percent (to 1800 in 1970), while the number of farms and the total acreage in farming both decreased by 8 percent between 1964 and 1969.[2] Holdings are still not completely concentrated, however: of the 593 farms remaining in 1970, 13 were over 1,000 acres while the average size was 179 acres.[3]

Distinguishing County G from the surrounding counties is its industrial base, which began to develop unusually early for the region. A division of ITT producing chemical cellulose located in Town G in the early 1950s and has since become the county's largest employer. Smaller but still substantial industries, mainly textile and garment factories employing 3-800, have in-located since. The result is that manufacturing is by far the largest sector of the economy in terms of employment, accounting for one-third of the jobs in the county. Agriculture and forestry combined provide about 7 percent.

Population Trends

Most of the 17,858 people in County G live in Town G or in one of the very small (under 1,000) other towns. Fifty percent of the people live in Town G and another 40 percent in the towns, leaving a farm population of 1800 (10 percent). Blacks comprise about one-fifth of the county's population, and virtually none of its farmers. Over 80 percent of the county's blacks live in Town G (giving the town a population 29 percent black), and practically all the rest live in the small towns. Only 17 black persons (0.1 percent) live on farms.

The current population distribution resulted from gradual changes over the years, without any dramatic shift within the memory of local respondents. Blacks have never been land-holding farmers—"except maybe a hundred years ago," ventured one respondent. After World War II, farm and timber land was owned almost entirely by whites, with some black sharecropping. With the increasing consolidation of these holdings, a gradual migration out of the county began.

This trend reversed with the beginnings of industrialization in the 1950s: in that decade, the county showed a 26 percent population increase, while the surrounding nonindustrialized counties showed population changes ranging from +5% to -17%. During that time there was also some movement from the county into the town to take advantage of manufacturing employment, but this was not a large factor in population change. All of the county falls within a twenty-mile radius of Town G, a feasible commuting distance for those who retained part-time farms or other rural residences. According to local observers, most of the people who moved off the land, both black and white, moved to metropolitan areas rather than to Town G.

Since the leveling off of industrial growth, outmigration has resumed. During the 1960s, the county population was virtually unchanged, with a 15 percent outmigration offsetting natural increase. (The 25 percent increase in Town G's population over the 1960s was due not to inmigration but to an annexation which tripled the land area of the town.) The white population changed 0 percent (one person), while the black population changed -1% (77 persons). Local respondents confirmed that the outmigration has conformed to the usual rural pattern, with the younger and better educated people the most likely to leave and unlikely to return. The reason for leaving is lack of employment opportunities, particularly those attractive to high school and college graduates.

Among those remaining, there is considerable poverty, but County G is by no means a depressed area. Median family income almost doubled over the 1960s, from $3,581 to $6,909, and 10 percent of the families earned over $15,000 in 1970. High-income people tend to be the local professionals and the managers of industries. Middle incomes result from well-paying blue-collar jobs in manufacturing, as well as from increasingly common two-income families. (Female labor force participation in 1970 was 38 percent and most working women (62 percent) were married with husbands present.)

Blacks on the whole fare considerably worse than whites, however. Black median family income is about half the white level, $3,826 as compared with $7,741, and the incidence of poverty much more extensive: 52 percent of black

families vs. 16 percent of white. These figures reflect the striking difference in
the occupational structures of the two groups. Aside from teachers and one
undertaker, there are no black professionals (doctors, lawyers, realtors, etc.) in
the town. Three out of four blacks work in low-skill, low-paying jobs—men as
operatives and laborers and women as service and domestic workers. However,
there are several moderate-income and a few high-income blacks who are teachers, merchants, and skilled factory workers. Thirty-seven percent of black families earn between $4,000 and $8,000, and 11 percent between $8,000 and
$25,000.

Poverty is not confined to one part of the county; rather, it is equally visible in both the towns and the outlying rural areas. One of the most visually
striking features of the towns is the close proximity of prosperous well-kept
homes and stores and, within a few blocks, dilapidated structures, some best
described as shacks. In the rural areas as well, the contrast exists between shabby houses, sound and well-maintained farm houses, and every now and then, a
strikingly new and expensive house on a landscaped one- to-five-acre lot.

The Social-Political Structure

The social and political institutions in Town G are dominated by an elite
of white-collar and professional people, and within this group, by a few families
with long-established wealth and land holdings. Of the names mentioned of
"leading families," none appeared among public office-holders, but most were
prominent on civic and public boards. Although no detailed inquiry into the
white power structure was made, there were no obvious divisions within the
group.[a] Since agriculture has never been a large factor on the local scene,
social and political organizations are generally business-oriented and receptive
to new industries. Town-county conflict is not frequent: they have many joint
functions, including a joint planning board, recreational facilities, etc. While
only the town has water and sewerage, there have been no conflicts with the
county on this account since the town, without much opposition, annexed the
undeveloped land surrounding it in 1966. Hence, all properties now receiving
municipal services pay town property taxes, and with the large amount of
available vacant land, this will continue to be the case for the foreseeable future.

The business, political, and social institutions have one thing in common:
they are all white. In Town G one can easily understand what blacks mean when

---

[a]Several respondents mentioned that a previous town manager had resigned under
pressure because his Housing Code enforcement policies conflicted with the interests of the
land-holding families. This could not be directly confirmed (the man is since deceased), but
is not implausible.

they refer to their colonial status in American society. Blacks have no institutions of their own other than the churches, and the ministers commute in from outside the county. The Community Action Agency is headed by a white, and has not become a focus for organizing the poor, either white or black. Aside from small family retail and service establishments, there are no black-owned businesses, and none relevant to the housing market: no black real estate agents, lenders or builders. At one time there was a black school system, but schools were integrated in the 1960s, and black teachers and students were absorbed into a group where they reportedly feel subject status. The black principal was not offered a comparable position in the new system, although he was senior in experience to the white principal. He refused the offer of an assistant principalship and left the area.

The result of this situation is a black population entirely lacking in organization or distinctive political goals, dependent on white-dominated institutions. Without pressure for change, this appears to be a fairly stable, and certainly long-standing, condition. It could be described as a "pre-civil rights movement" structure—several respondents, black and white, described County G as "about 15 years behind the rest of the South" in terms of race relations—characterized by passive, dependent blacks and dominant but usually paternalistic whites.

The pivotal figure between blacks and whites is the black undertaker who is also in his second term as a town councilman, having won a seat in an at-large election. (He is also by appointment a member of the town-county planning and zoning commission.) It is to this person that blacks go when they need to approach a white institution they are unfamiliar with, and to him that whites turn when they wish to know the views or needs of the "black community." This man obviously enjoys the role of community spokesman and ombudsman, which he has successfully performed for the last twenty years, and could hardly be expected to become an active, much less militant, proponent of change.

"Troublemakers," or active proponents of change, are in fact rare in the county. This may be due in part to the absence of a highly visible issue: when schools were integrated in the 1960s, considerable progress was also made in the integration of public accommodations and employment. The major employers are branches of large, outside-owned corporations who are sensitive to equal opportunity pressures from home offices, and who employ large numbers of blacks, including some in supervisory positions. No one complained of blatant discrimination in employment, and it is therefore possible that the lower income and occupational status of blacks could be largely attributable to the fact that blacks wishing better employment tend to leave the area, and those remaining have less education (median school years completed is 7.0 for blacks, compared with 10.1 for the county as a whole).

A more important reason for black inactivity, however, is a lack of community organization, which in turn reflects what a sympathetic observer called "rampant apathy" on the part of the area's blacks. Local respondents attributed this very apparent inactivity to a variety of causes: discouragement that anything could ever be changed and fear of economic reprisals (mainly job loss) if one should "make waves" were most often mentioned, as well as "complacency" on the part of those who had achieved moderate income and acceptable housing.

Whatever the reasons, there has in fact been very little civil rights activity and none in the area of housing. The only national organization which has ever been active in the county is the NAACP, which became involved in some issues of school and employment integration, but has since become inactive. Its leaders are self-described as tired—discouraged as much by lack of support among blacks as by resistance from whites. An occasional black is appointed to civic and public boards, but these appointments were invariably described as "token" and those blacks appointed as people who won't "speak up" or "make waves." Significantly, it was pointed out almost as often that "even if they did, no one would back them up."

In sum, the black population is powerless. Without institutions of their own, they are dependent on white institutions, most immediately for jobs, and for social goods and public services as well. Without leadership or organization, the black population must accept and has largely internalized a subordinate status. Many are poor as well, lacking economic leverage; the educated tend to migrate out, leaving behind a small middle class hesitant to jeopardize its hard-won security. Should an individual black protest the status quo, he or she risks exclusion from the benefits conferred by white-controlled institutions,[b] which are, in the absense of black institutions, "the only game in town." The result is a passivity, either frustrated or resigned, which permits white dominance without many instances of overt repression.

The Housing Market

Housing in Town G is a need, but not an issue. Residential segregation is complete, and substandard conditions much in evidence, especially in the poor black areas of town. Yet no one, black or white, public official or private citizen, has in any way made (or been able to make) housing a political goal or a visible issue demanding attention. The housing market therefore continues to operate as it has for some time—tight money has decreased the *volume* of construction and transactions, but the *manner* in which housing is supplied and acquired is unchanged. This section surveys briefly the current housing stock

---

[b]A group of black high school students recently organized a sit-in to protest some aspect of school conditions, and were quickly suspended. Those whose parents brought them back to school with promises of good behavior in the future were readmitted. Black respondents viewed this as a case of "pushing out" those who would not keep "their place" as defined and required in relations between the races.

in Town G, and then analyzes the interactions comprising the housing market as an institution. The following section focuses more specifically on access to housing, with emphasis on the ways in which race becomes a factor in the market.

The Housing Stock

Town G is for the most part a pleasant-looking, uncongested town. Practically all buildings are one or two stories high, and except for those in the small central business district, most are detached structures with yards between. Homes mix with churches, small professional offices, and in the less restrictively zoned areas, stores. The mixture and close proximity of different land uses attests to the relatively recent arrival of zoning and planning (1960s). The town is bisected in both directions by railroad tracks, but recently constructed bypasses divert highway traffic around the town. Industries are located within the town limits, but outside of the developed areas.

Despite the compact size of the town, distinct neighborhoods reflecting differences in income range and race are clearly visible. In the northern section and closest to the center of town is the moderate-income black section, containing mostly old and a few deteriorated houses, and dotted with occasional retail stores and mobile homes. Newer and more expensive single-family homes occupied by blacks have been built beyond this section, toward the outskirts of town.

Separated from the business district by a railroad spur and accessible by dirt road is "Pepper Hill," the low-income black enclave with its unpaved roads and large proportion of dilapidated houses. This section contains the worst housing in town, much of it described by one resident as "not fit for chickens." This section abuts a new development of moderate-income black homes recently constructed on the site of condemned and reportedly severely dilapidated housing.

Behind the black development is a slightly more prosperous-looking new white development. Middle-income white housing, both old and new, comprises the neighborhoods to the south and west of the town proper. Slightly detached but still within town limits to the west is a high-income new white development, with $40,000--$100,000 homes and a new shopping center under construction nearby. Slightly detached to the south is the poor white section known by the colorful name of "Bloody Bucket."

Racial boundaries have remained unchanged and unchallenged for years. Some whites have been moving to more expensive homes in the county, or into the newer subdivisions. As they move, their homes are bought by other whites, either newly-formed families or families newly arrived in connection with one of the industries. As black incomes have increased, families have moved to newer housing built on the perimeter of the black quarter of town, or on the site of

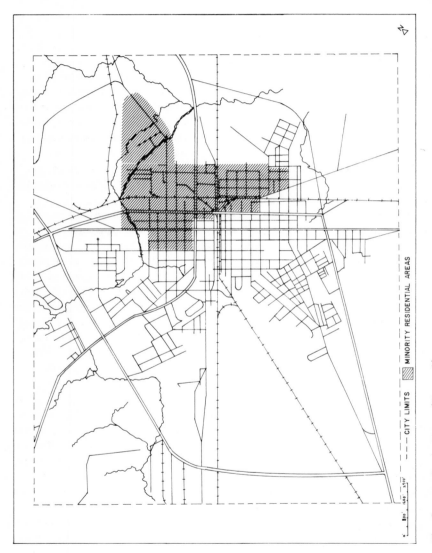

Figure 7-1. The Georgia Study Town (Town G)

demolished black housing. While the boundary between neighborhoods may be only a street or a small strip of vacant land, it is acknowledged as a boundary and unbreached by either side. Blacks and whites live in close proximity, but there are no "transitional neighborhoods."

In Town G, most blacks live in rental housing, while most whites live in owner-occupied housing. Of the 2,060 white households in 1970, 1,392 were owner-occupied housing, vs. 668 in rental. For the 661 black households, the corresponding figures are 280 vs. 381. Of the black-occupied housing units, almost half (305) lacked some or all plumbing, and 97 were overcrowded (more than one person per room). Some of the rental housing, especially in the moderate-income northwest part of town, is black-owned. A common situation there is for a black to own three or four units, live in one and rent the rest. However, much of the black housing in the badly rundown section is white-owned and in the hands of a smaller number of individuals. Groups of houses (numbering perhaps 20 to 40) have been in the hands of families long enough that the family name is used as an address; e.g., one lives in the "Murphy's quarters" or the "Dean's quarters," etc.

On the basis of 1970 Census cross-tabs prepared for the county as a whole,[4] the housing stock could be described as somewhat inadequate in terms of number of units, and more seriously inadequate in terms of condition. In 1970, 10 percent of the county's units were overcrowded (down from 21 percent in 1960), and the vacancy rate of 5 percent was higher than the surrounding counties and higher than the 3.8 percent for Georgia as a whole. As for condition, the 1970 Census provides only the number lacking some or all plumbing, which must then serve as an indication of substandard: 19 percent of the count's housing units were in this category (compared with 13 percent for Georgia as a whole). The total substandard, including units either overcrowded or lacking plumbing, but without double-counting, was 28 percent.

Not surprisingly, the proportion lacking plumbing among poverty-level households was much higher than overall—39 percent. However, blacks as a group fared worst of all—51 percent of black-occupied units lacked complete plumbing, and 30 percent were overcrowded, for a total of 64 percent substandard conditions.

Conditions have changed somewhat since 1970, mainly through a spurt of new HUD Section 235 housing developments that were built in 1971 and 1972. Various officials and builders estimated that about 100-140 single-family homes were built and sold under this program, some on vacant land and some on the site of demolished housing. Overall, 199 building permits for single-family homes have been issued since (and including) 1970, plus another four for about 20 units of multi-family housing. At the same time, an estimated 220 residential structures have been condemned and demolished, practically all of which were single-family. (Since building permits are not required beyond town limits, there is no estimate of new housing in the open country.)

The most dramatic increase recently seen in housing has been in mobile homes. In 1970, there were only 282 mobile homes in the county, but the county tax commissioner estimates that about 1,000 permits have been issued since then. Many of these homes are visible in the town, which has five licensed trailer parks (with perhaps 10 more out of the county) and parking mobile homes on private lots is permitted in the least restrictive residential zoning category.

Local respondents often suggested, however, that neither of these developments—the building of 235's or the increase in mobile homes—has made a great difference in housing supply in relation to need. A large proportion (various estimates ranged from one-fourth to one-half) of the 235 houses built were foreclosed, and many still stand vacant. Mobile homes are typically second-hand or very inexpensive models, and are seen as last-resort housing for those not in a position to buy (or unable to find) conventional homes. When asked about housing need, one respondent said "everywhere you see a mobile home, there's a need for a house."

At the same time, officials and certain housing market participants, when asked about "housing problems," tended almost invariably to speak of a housing *surplus*—referring in most cases to the vacant 235's—and to define the town's housing-related problems as the severe decline in the construction industry which has accompanied tight money, rising interest rates and the freezing of HUD programs in 1973. Instead of better housing for the currently ill-housed, hopes were expressed for increased new demand from the expansion of a nearby army base, which would stimulate business and employment in construction. The problem is that those who need housing are not able to exert effective demand, as well as that the housing supply system does not meet the demand.

Housing Market Participants

Housing-related activities in Town G consist of acquiring housing or obtaining improvements in existing housing and services. Retaining title or tenancy is not a large problem in or around the town, with the exception of the 235 experience where retention is part of the same story as the recent acquisition. In other owner-occupied housing, foreclosures are rare, and tax foreclosures unheard of— the county tax commissioner reports that there has not been even one in the last ten years. Evictions from rental housing are almost equally rare. Acquisitions and housing improvements on the part of private individuals comprise practically all market activities.

Private Suppliers. The key figures in the housing market are the private builders. These include three comparatively large developers, who build mostly on speculation, and a number of smaller contractors who usually build on contract, but may speculate on one or two houses at a time. A large majority of the new houses produced have been built on speculation by the local developers. Hence, the economics of the building industry, as well as the builders' perception of effective demand in the market, goes far to account for the number, the type and price range, and the location of new housing.

Before analyzing the role of the builders and the effects on the housing market of this role, it would be useful to identify the other participants. The only local sources of home financing are a small savings & loan (assets $6 million), which entered the long-term mortgage market only recently after merging with a much larger Savannah S&L in 1972. In addition, the Farmers Home Administration office serving Town G, but located some forty miles away in the next county, has provided financing under the Section 502 home ownership program with and without interest credit. There are two commercial banks in Town G, neither of which makes long-term mortgage loans. The vast majority of mortgage loans are provided by out-of-town private mortgage credit companies, with whom the local builder acts as the intermediary.

There are four major real estate agencies in the town, who act almost entirely as brokers on behalf of homeowners wishing to sell. They deal, therefore, in transfers of existing owner-occupied housing; only rarely would they handle rentals, and more rarely still would they handle new housing. The latter case would occur when occasionally a builder is unable to sell a new house immediately and a real estate agent happens to find a buyer. More commonly, builders act as their own brokers and avoid the 6 percent agent's fee.

Public Suppliers. Public intervention in the housing market has involved the provision and the financing of housing, as well as provision of services and application of building and housing regulations. Town G's housing authority provides 110 units of low-rent public housing in two projects. One project of 54 duplex units is located on the north side of town in the traditionally black section, and is occupied entirely by blacks. The other, 56 units on the south side, is entirely white. These units were constructed in three stages between 1951 and 1960, and many are still occupied by the original tenants. Applications for additional units filed in 1966 and 1970 were rejected on the grounds of inadequate funding as there were other communities with greater need, and the Authority has made no further efforts since. Since vacancies are extremely rare, and no new units are likely to be built, the public housing is more a feature of the existing stock than a factor in the housing market.

The government's role in insured financing has been considerable over the last few years. While FmHA operations have been limited, HUD's 235 program has been used for more than half of the new housing constructed since 1970. Currently, the FHA and VA tandem plan (with below-market interest rates) is most often used.

Local government services are provided by the town, which in 1966 extended its then-current limits by 4-9,000 feet in all directions. The immediate reason for this action was to bring the site of a proposed industrial park within the range of town taxes[c] and services, as well as to provide services to the "Bloody Bucket" area, whose lack of sewerage was becoming something of a health hazard. The effect has been to bring in a great deal of vacant and developable land as well, some of which has since sprouted subdivisions. Since the county does not provide water and sewerage, homes located outside the town must be provided with a well and septic tank. Since the annexation, however, the entire urbanized area of the town, as well as many sites available for new development, are well within the town limits.

While the county has no housing-related codes in effect other than health codes, the town has adopted the Southern Standard Building and Housing Codes, zoning regulations and a subdivision code. The latter two, at least, are regularly enforced and variances are prohibited by town ordinance. Enforcement of the housing code has been more selective (see below).

Housing Market Interactions

The demand, or potential demand, for new or improved housing is locally generated. Few people are moving into Town G, except occasionally a manager transferred in by one of the industries or a new teacher in the school system. These families would normally seek out real estate agents for direction to available units, and tend to buy existing housing. Locally generated demand arises from new family formation, as well as from families seeking improved housing. It is this demand which the local developers attempt to gauge, and within the perceived constraints of profitable business, provide for.

Impact of National Trends. The trends in the national economy have had strongly adverse effects in the Town G housing market for the last year or so. The almost complete reliance on outside capital markets has afflicted the town with the high interest rates and tight money characteristic of the national market, with the result that building and sales have almost stopped. Mortgage money is running about 9 percent plus points, when there is money to be had. The builders and real estate agents generally shop around the state's metropolitan areas for the best mortgage terms.

The market has also been affected by the national recession, since the major employers in the area—outside-owned manufacturers dependent on national or regional markets—have been cutting back. There have been a number of layoffs and a general cutback of overtime. The actual loss of income for some, plus the

---

[c]Real estate is taxed by the county at 25 mills, with the first $2,000 of assessed value untaxed under a Homestead provision. Town taxes are 13.5 mills. Both assess at 40 percent of market value.

uncertainty of those still employed as to their future job security, has made families put aside thoughts of home purchase at present. Finally, many of the high-income professional families, the potential market for $50,000+ homes, have been hurt in the stock market and are putting off or giving up the idea of buying.

The result of these three national trends has been that the housing market is barely operating in Town G at present. Building has almost stopped, and purchases of existing housing are down substantially from former years. However, it is still possible to gain insight into the operations of the market by asking respondents to describe their experience over the last several years, before the current slump was felt.

Builders. In this perspective, the builders emerge as the key figures in the supply of housing. Until about 1970, most housing was built on contract and located on scattered sites out in the county. Several subdivisions were built on speculation on the periphery of the developed part of the town, but this was less common than the building of single homes on contract. By 1970, almost half the county's housing (45 percent) was old, having been built prior to 1950. About one quarter of the 1970 stock was built during the 1960's.

HUD 235 Program. During the period 1971-72, practically all new housing was built under HUD's 235 program. Several new builders entered the market at this time, and all specualted on comparatively small subdivisions (8-10 houses per site). These were moderately priced single-family houses, selling for about $17,000 with a $200 down payment. It was the builders who, without urging from public or community groups, perceived the potential market for this housing, and who arranged financing (almost entirely with outside mortgage companies). The amount of housing produced was that within the capabilities of the local builders. No outside builders entered the market at this time, since developments of fifty or more houses at a time were considerably more profitable, and large outside builders tended to concentrate on urban and metropolitan areas of the state.

The location of the housing depended on the sites available: some houses were built within the town on sites of demolished housing, and some on newly developed sites on the perimeters of town. The interest in newly vacated sites arose because of the town's tight enforcement of the subdivision code, which requires expensive site improvements such as curb and gutter, underground utilities, etc. However, if a builder could acquire land which was already subdivided, the code did not apply and his costs were thereby substantially reduced.

The builders' natural preference for previously subdivided sites resulted in the development of numerous small subdivisions within the town, served by town water and sewerage, but often poorly drained, lacking both curb and gutter (many still with unpaved streets) and with utility poles. In fact, the only subdivision which appeared to be in full conformity with subdivision regulations is the high-income development on the west side of town.

The sale of these houses proceeded largely by word of mouth, although there was some advertising of specific units not yet sold. Town G is small enough that most potential home-buyers were aware of new developments, and those unfamiliar with the program, largely blacks, were channeled to the builders by the black "liaison man." Blacks and whites in about equal numbers bought the homes—whether a unit is "for whites" or "for blacks" depends entirely on its location in relation to the traditional black-white neighborhood boundaries.

Nearly all respondents, with the notable exception of the builders themselves, reported that the houses were of extremely shoddy construction and not worth the $17,000 price tag. Visits to some of the homes revealed kitchen fixtures which needed to be replaced after two years, a single heating outlet for a five-to-six-room house, a few buckling floors, etc. There is also a built-in fire hazard in the design most commonly used, which has caused most of the fires in Town G. The local building inspector pointed this out, but the design was not corrected. The government inspector assigned to the area works out of Savannah and covers a large area; inspection during construction was apparently no more than cursory.

At the same time, marketing was vigorous and often described as "high-pressure." The low down payment made the houses attractive to families who had never before considered buying, and who were often unfamiliar with the financial details of the 235 program and with the criteria by which to assess a property. After the sale was made, the buyer would be responsible for payments to a nonlocal mortgage company, and would not have a local person from whom to seek advice on maintenance and money management.

The result of a number of factors—mainly the poor screening of buyers and the dissatisfaction of some buyers with the quality of the home—was that an estimated 50 percent of the 235's were foreclosed, most from black buyers. Most of the single-family houses currently for sale in the town are in this category. When asked if the 235 program was "a good thing for the town," one public official replied, "It sure was a good thing for the builders." While the housing was considerably better than the old rental housing from which many of the purchasers had been drawn, its high turnover rate indicates that it was not a satisfactory solution to the need for moderate-income housing.

When the federal government froze the 235 program in January 1973, the builders moved to high-income housing. Significantly, the speculative 235's which had not been sold before the freeze were extremely hard for the builders to dispose of. This was largely because the homes were not attractive to families who could afford the private market down payment (10-20 percent).

Farmers Home Administration (FmHA). The only other source of moderate income home financing is the Farmers Home Administration. The county supervisor is responsible for four counties and has had limited operations in County G (about fifteen Section 502 loans in the last two to three years, nearly two-thirds of which were with interest credit). Again, the role of the builders accounts for this low level of involvement. The location of the FmHA office, some forty miles from Town G, makes it generally unfamiliar to consumers in the county (the black leader, for instance, had never heard of it). Walk-in applications are therefore rare, and most potential borrowers must be referred by builders or real estate agents who are familiar with the FmHA programs. The FmHA has generated news articles and arranged meetings with builders, real estate brokers, building suppliers, Chamber of Commerce, etc., but failed to generate interest. In other counties, the FmHA has also met with community groups to inform potential consumers of the programs, but in County G there is no such group to contact.

In the absence of such channels, the FmHA must rely on builders to generate use of the programs. However, the relations between FmHA and local builders are not good. The county supervisor is closer at hand than the FHA and VA fee inspectors operating out of Savannah and Atlanta respectively, and reports that builders frequently cut corners, use materials not up to the specifications, etc. The builders in turn complain of "red tape" and low appraisals on the part of FmHA (often $2,000 lower than VA and FHA appraisals). After some clashes on these issues, the builders lost interest in dealing with FmHA, and the few instances where its programs have been used in the county have generally resulted from direct contact by a householder who was having a house custom built.

Modular and Mobile Homes. With the builders concentrating on high-income housing, both on speculation and contract, the only sources of new housing for low- to moderate-income families are mobile homes and the one builder of modular housing in town. Modular homes, costing between $10,000 and $22,000 for a three-bedroom unit, have met no resistance from local builders, since they serve a clientele (families with income of, say, $8,000 per year) which the builders are not trying to attract. As with most homes in Town G, the modular homes are financed by outside lenders, and arrangements are made by the builder. Modular homes have not (at least as yet) become a major factor in the housing market, however, since the single supplier began operation about a year ago, just as the housing market began to freeze.

Mobile homes are the only other source of new housing, and have accounted for most of the new units since 1970. At one point, the local market supported four or five dealers, only one of which was a local resident. When sales took a sharp decline in 1973, all dealers except the local resident closed up and moved out. The former dealers had operated largely through outside service companies, who took applications and placed the loan with lenders. In contrast, the one remaining dealer works directly with lenders and continues to service the loan after purchase. In addition, local commercial banks (but not the S&L) make mobile home loans as consumer loans with a 25 percent down payment and a five- to six-year term at 10.9 percent interest.

The banks report that delinquency and repossession rates on mobile homes are high. This is partly because such homes are bought by families of low and moderate income who have been hurt by the recession, and more often because families do not correctly assess the costs of the home. Most are placed on private lots, where the cost of connecting water, utilities, etc. is about $350. This plus the high cost of utilities, interest, and taxes has often pushed the monthly payments above what the family could afford.[d]

Existing Housing. The sales and rental of existing housing comprise a different market in which the builders play no part. Like the market for new housing, the market for existing housing has been hurt by the economic slump and is currently largely frozen. With fewer families buying new housing, and outmigration concentrated among young people who have not yet established households, not many houses other than the 235's are on the market, and rentals are also experiencing very low turnover.

This market has in common with the new housing market the features that practically all financing is nonlocal and that communication is mostly by word of mouth and direct observation by the potential consumer. Except for families new in town, most potential consumers do not use real estate brokers to locate housing for sale, but rather ask around or drive around until seeing a suitable unit, and then contact the agent handling the sale. Rentals are handled entirely by word of mouth, and the system appears to function effectively in a town this size. Residents appeared to know where units are available, who the landlord is, how the landlord generally deals with tenants on maintenance, rent collection, etc.

Housing Improvements. Rehabilitation of substandard housing is not particularly common in Town G. The study team found no evidence that families would prefer to rehabilitate their present housing rather than find new housing, and in fact, much of the substandard housing was described as beyond repair. Housing improvements tend to be mostly on standard housing—adding a room or a carport, for instance—rather than the extensive repairs that would be required for the town's numerous substandard units.

Enforcement of the housing code is limited, as attested by the high visibility of dilapidated units. Many of the rental units, especially in the black sections, are substandard, but a limited code enforcement begun six or seven years ago met strong resistance. At most, the owner would install a toilet on the back porch surrounded by a plywood enclosure for a cost of about $250, including sewer tap. The reason given for resistance was that the tenants could not afford the additional

---

[d]Mobile homes are taxed as personal property unless permanently affixed to the ground. The rates are the same as real estate rates, though personal property does not benefit from the Homestead deduction.

rent that repair would necessitate—many are very low-income families paying $25-40 per month in rent.

In owner-occupied housing, the owner tended to be without the resources in cash or credit to rehabilitate the house, and the code was not enforced unless the family left the house; it would then be condemned and removed from the market. In both cases, it was generally reported by both blacks and whites that the cost of code enforcement would have been more than residents of substandard housing could pay, and they had nowhere else to go.

Access to Housing

Equal access to housing by blacks and whites is clearly not the case in Town G, where the boundaries of segregated neighborhoods have never been breached. Nor is the housing "separate but equal," since the housing supply is tighter in the black submarket, and the units available for poor blacks are in substantially worse condition than the poor white housing. Unequal access to housing arises from long and unchallenged tradition which makes overt discrimination on the part of housing suppliers unnecessary.

That there is direct discrimination in County G when blacks "get out of line" is undisputed. One such case became a court suit recently. A black woman invested her savings in a bar catering to black clientele and was then refused a license by the county commission. Unable to find assistance locally—there are no black lawyers or lawyers willing to handle civil rights litigation—she hired a Savannah lawyer. She reported that had it not been that her entire savings had been invested, she would never have taken such a step, but would have let the matter pass. The federal judge, finding that the commissioners could offer no reason for denying the woman a license, ordered them to grant it.

No comparable cases of local blacks attempting to gain equal access to housing have occurred. Builders and real estate brokers all have Equal Opportunity signs prominently displayed, and all serve black clients as well as whites. As long as blacks confine their interest to the traditionally black areas, they report being fairly served by these institutions. Lenders, the majority of which are nonlocal, are not directly discriminatory, but since contact is made through the builder or real estate agent, the separation of black and white submarkets occurs before the lender becomes an actor in the sale.

The discrimination which underlies segregation is deeply internalized. Since blacks rarely challenged the tradition, overt and illegal discrimination on the part of housing suppliers is not common. When asked what would happen if a black tried to move into a white area, a typical black respondent replied, "I couldn't say—there's no one as ever tried it." On the other hand, another black respondent's reply to the same question was, "They'd be killed."

Interviews with black householders revealed that this tradition is supported by a combination of fatalism and fear. In the low-income decrepit Pepper Hill section, respondents took segregation entirely for granted as part of the natural order of things and had never even thought of living outside of the black section. The same fatalism also described much of the relationship between tenants and landlords—one or two complaints might be made by the tenant over severe maintenance problems, but if the problem was not corrected, the tenant would just live with it. In this case, fear of eviction was also a factor, since the public projects rarely had vacancies and there was nowhere else to go but to another comparable rental unit.

Interviews with middle-income households revealed that fear of economic reprisals was paramount; that is, fear of job-loss and general harassment from white-dominated institutions was sufficient to maintain segregation. In addition, the expectation that one's white neighbors would not be receptive even if a black should manage to secure housing outside the black areas made the prospect of undertaking such a purchase unattractive. As long as there was housing of the type desired available in the black areas, no one wanted to become a "test case" and risk the considerable investment that home purchase entails. Middle-class blacks were quite conscious of the insult implied in segregation, but were much more concerned that sufficient housing be available in black areas than with "scoring a point" by integrating a white area.

Some direct discrimination was visible in the provision of town services. While unpaved streets could be seen in some of the poor and moderate-income white areas, lack of paving was much more common in black areas. Residents of Pepper Hill had tried several times to get the town to pave its mud streets, but when they met with no response they gave up. Garbage collection is usually not discriminatory, except when a holiday or other factor interferes with the normal schedule. Then, report black residents, garbage will be collected in white areas but not in the black areas.

The most visible problem is the preservation of housing values through zoning. The town was zoned in the 1960s by the regional planning agency working with local public officials, and zones follow black/white boundaries fairly closely. Practically all the black areas, including the middle-income areas, are zoned R-3, the least restrictive category which permits parking mobile homes on private lots. Most white areas are zoned R-1, the most restrictive category, and some of the moderate-income areas are classified R-2. Only the very poor white section and one or two other very small sections are zoned R-3.

The director of the Town G housing authority realizes that the complete segregation of public housing units is against federal policy, but claims that this expresses the preferences of the tenants. When given a choice, a tenant prefers to move into the project of his or her own color, and when only one unit is vacant, only an applicant of the "appropriate color" will move in. Other respondents could not recall an instance where a black family had attempted to claim a unit in the white project, but suspected that names are selected from the waiting list according to which project has a vacancy. No local blacks expressed opposition to this situation, however—it appeared to be another case of segregation accepted as the natural order to things. However, it is more nearly a case of "separate but equal" with public housing than private housing. There are equal numbers of units in the two projects, and both consist of extremely well-maintained duplexes of the same design.

Much of the inequitable treatment of blacks in regard to housing results as a by-product of actions which are not intentionally discriminatory, but when combined with the tradition of segregation and the condition of the current stock in black sections as compared with white sections, such actions may have this effect.

The most obvious factor in this regard is the economic motivations of the builders. Since the black population is on the average less affluent than whites, and since much of the black occupied housing is substandard, the major need of the black population is for decent low- and moderate-income housing. It is housing in this price range that the builders have traditionally avoided as being much less profitable than upper-income housing. Confined by tradition to areas which have tighter supply, blacks are therefore confined in general to lesser quality housing than whites of comparable income. This situation is most visible in comparing the poor black and poor white neighborhoods: while most poor black housing is deteriorated or worse and much lacks complete plumbing, the poor white area contains no occupied dilapidated units and the general condition of homes is far better.

There is no foreseeable likelihood that the supply of low-income housing will be increased or the current supply up-graded. Code enforcement is limited for reasons discussed earlier, and the financial position of low-income home-owners often prohibits repairs that would bring the houses up to standard. The supply of public housing is not likely to be increased, since after two refusals the director stopped applying for additional units. In any case, public housing is not perceived by its administrators to be a primarily low-income supply; practically all tenants pay the maximum rent of $119, and the Authority takes pride that rents cover operating costs. In fact, when asked about the housing needs of the very low-income population, the director pointed out that federal regulations prohibit building a "welfare ghetto," and took this as evidence that public housing was not meant as a low-income program.

With the advent of the Section 235 program, the builders became involved in the moderate-income market for the first (and so far for the last) time. It was immaterial to the builders whether the buyers were black or white, and they served both populations according to the location of sites acquired. Perhaps because there was more pent-up demand in the black population, and/or because, given past supply restrictions, blacks were less familiar with the procedures and perils of homeownership and less able to critically evaluate sales pitches, many more blacks than whites were "burned" in the 235 market. Sales to blacks and whites were about equal, while foreclosures of black homes were much more frequent.

At present, the only moderate-income program available is the FmHA Section 502 program, but this is being avoided by the builders. Without channeling from the builders—who are practically the only people on the local scene who understand the complexities of government housing programs—FmHA programs are very rarely utilized.

High-income housing, either speculative or custom built, is the range most frequently produced since the end of the 235 program. Builders and real estate agents claim there is no discrimination here, but attribute the lack of black buyers to the lesser incomes of black people. There are, in fact, a few high-income black families in Town G, but they have avoided trouble by building in the traditionally black areas.

The current situation of complete segregation and tighter supply for blacks is likely to continue for the foreseeable future, as it has gone unchallenged by any organized group. As mentioned earlier, there are no organizations of blacks except a currently inactive NAACP chapter. Churches have not served as socially or politically active groups since their ministers do not reside locally. The community action agency has no housing-related programs, and most black respondents were unaware of its activities in any area. There is a nonprofit housing development corporation serving an eight-county area which includes County G, but without a local group with whom to work, this corporation has been generally unsuccessful in starting operations in County G. For each county in the corporation's territory, an advisory group is appointed by town and county officials, and it is this group that is charged with setting the priorities for that county. County G's group ignored the visible housing problems of the county, and instead set as its priority a home for retarded children (most of whom, given the population distribution, are white).

The current housing situation is largely stable since there is no pressure, public or private, for change. Blacks are unorganized, lack political power, and are like most consumers generally uninformed about such housing programs as are on the books. FmHA does not advertise, and is therefore generally unknown to local residents. Those who have heard of it tend to confuse it with the 235 program, and believe either that its programs are frozen or that it is a "gyp." Misconceptions about the 235 program abound, which prevent many from buying the foreclosed units.

Interest in housing on the part of public officials, both town and county, is minimal. Top priority is given to somehow revitalizing the commercial strip along the highway that had served heavy tourist traffic before being by-passed by a new interstate. Housing does not appear at all among public priorities, except for the hope that new demand from expansion of a nearby army base might generate additional demand and put the construction sector back in business. This is an overly optimistic hope, which is not shared by the local builders. The base is too far away for it to make much impact on the local housing market, and the major part of the demand it will generate is for low- to moderate-income housing (e.g.,

$110 to $125 per month of off-base housing allotments), exactly the sector of the market which is not served by private institutions now.

Perhaps the greatest constraint to improving the housing conditions of the town's blacks is the misconception among them that there is no problem. Poor blacks seem to take their shabby housing and lack of alternatives with a kind of fatalism that does not even imagine alternatives. Middle-class blacks are powerless themselves and not apt to push for the interests of poor blacks. Most of those interviewed felt that poor blacks had about the kind of housing they wanted or deserved—presumably if they wanted better housing, they would be able to obtain it. Some even attributed the structural deterioration of rental housing to lack of upkeep by tenants. For their own part, the black middle class, fearful of reprisals against their hard-won security and without hope of overcoming the long history of segregation, confine their aspirations to buying or building in the black areas.

Notes

1. Unless otherwise specified, all population, employment, and housing figures in this section are drawn from the United States Census, 1960 and 1970.
2. *County and City Data Book*, U.S. Department of Commerce, 1972.
3. Ibid.
4. *Regional Housing Aggregate Market Analysis*, Altamaha Georgia Southern Area Planning and Development Commission, Baxley, Georgia, 1973.

8 Conclusions

In five of the six areas covered by this study, there is clear evidence of institutionalized discrimination — not simply scattered instances of illegal behavior, but discrimination built into the operations of the housing market as a system. All six areas showed measures of inequality in the housing conditions of minorities and female-headed households, although in the New Mexico site, inequality appears to reflect income differences rather than ethnic background. The Spanish-surnamed there have a history of employment in mining and agriculture which has left many unprepared for the new directions the economy has taken. This group is thus disproportionately low-income, and suffers worse housing conditions than other whites. There is no residential segregation, however, and Spanish-surnamed appear to participate in the housing market equally with other whites of comparable income. The New Mexico site is thus an exception to the general finding of institutionalized discrimination.

In the other five sites — South Dakota and the four southern areas — several forms of systematic inequality have been demonstrated. First, minorities and women are less likely to own their homes in lieu of renting than white male-headed households, thus lacking the equity base and tax savings which home ownership affords. This form of inequality is related directly to race and sex, and cannot be attributed to income or any other socioeconomic variable.

In addition, blacks are systematically and almost totally segregated in both private and public housing in the four southern sites. Segregation cannot be attributed to income differences, even though blacks are disproportionately low-income, since grouping the households of similar income without regard to race would lead to much less than the virtually total segregation observed. Two of the southern sites have no residential integration whatever; the others have only two black families living in white neighborhoods, and no whites in black neighborhoods. One of these towns has recently established, under outside pressure and with considerable difficulty, the only integrated public housing project observed in the four southern sites.

This finding of virtually complete residential segregation is based on data obtained on site: interviews and observation of neighborhood boundaries, and plotting of minority addresses where these were available. Segregation cannot be determined from Census data since the smallest geographic unit available for most rural areas, the enumeration district, is still large enough to introduce a significant aggregation bias. Unless the enumeration district boundaries should happen to coincide with clear neighborhood boundaries — and most of those

not — analysis of Census data presents a severely distorted picture
it of segregation and other neighborhood characteristics.
our sites exhibiting racial segregation were analyzed to determine
here is a segmented or dual housing market, with price differentials
comparable houses in comparable neighborhoods, the latter differing
racial composition. In Tennessee, the test was inconclusive because the
price and other data needed were inadequate and inconsistent. In the other three
sites, tests showed clear price differentials between comparable housing in black
vs. white neighborhoods. Surprisingly, the differential was in most cases a premium for black housing, as high as 29 percent for low-income blacks in Georgia.
The fact of a price differential alone demonstrates the existence of a segmented
market, with separate supply and demand forces operating in the submarkets.
However, the "ghetto premiums" observed in the urban literature have usually
been attributed to demand pressures from inmigrating blacks. This study uncovered not only differentials, but in some cases black premiums in areas of
black outmigration, where the black population is in absolute and relative
decline.

The fact of inequality, including segregation, is not in itself *prima facie*
evidence of discrimination, although it is suggestive. A possible alternative explanation is that separate institutions serve the separate submarkets, responding
to unrelated supply and demand forces and thus reaching unrelated equilibrium
prices. Such a situation would, however, lead to a strong presumption that discrimination does exist, for it is difficult to see, in the absence of some barrier,
why the prices would not equilibrate. The argument is not cogent, in any case;
this study demonstrates that the separate submarkets in the southern sites are
served by a *single* set of institutions. There are no black lenders or real estate
agencies, and only one black builder was found. In addition, there are no white
institutions which concentrate exclusively on the black submarket. Instead, a
single set of white-dominated institutions serves both white and black consumers,
but serves them separately and unequally.

It might be further argued that inequality reflects not discrimination but
consumer preferences, i.e., a desire to live with neighbors of one's own color.
This self-segregation hypothesis was often suggested by white interview respondents (though never by black respondents). However, the actual cause of segregation appears to be internalized discrimination—actions predicated on the
expectation that discrimination will be practiced—rather than voluntary self-
segregation. The fact that blacks almost never ask for listings or financing for
housing in white areas was explained by black respondents as resulting from the
expectation that they would be refused and subject to reprisals. These expectations were borne out in the few cases where black families did attempt to secure
housing in white neighborhoods. Perhaps most significant in relation to the
question of self-segregation is the experience of the mobile home parks recently
established. According to numerous reports, blacks made many attempts to
integrate white parks but met with not a single instance of success.

However, the single most important factor in accounting for segregation and other forms of inequality is not overt acts on the part of suppliers, but general acquiescence in the communities to a long tradition of discrimination. Inequality results, that is, more from lack of pressure by minorities and women than from direct refusals by the white males who dominate the markets. This does not imply, of course, that minority and female pressure would result in equal treatment—evidence suggests the contrary. It does mean, however, that behavior by housing market actors which would be actionable under Fair Housing legislation is comparatively rare. The tradition of inequality is so visible and deeply engrained that minorities and women often dare not insist on equal treatment, and tend not to institute complaints when incidents do occur. Internalized discrimination makes overt supplier discrimination unnecessary, and Federal Fair Housing legislation—which relies on complaints of overt discrimination—has therefore not affected inequality in housing.

Inequality is maintained as well by the general social stability of the areas. In relation to segregation specifically, there is less pressure forcing blacks toward integration than one would normally encounter in an urban area. The sites studied all lack the "noose effect," where a surrounded black neighborhood has no possibility of expansion except onto a currently white-occupied area. Rather, the black areas can expand without resistance onto abutting undeveloped land. In addition, the "expanding circles" phenomenon, where jobs and necessary services are retreating to great distances from central cities, was not encountered in these small, single-jurisdiction towns. It is not necessary for families to challenge the segregation tradition to reach jobs and services, since these are easily accessible from black neighborhoods as currently designated.

Minority acquiescence results from the lack of such pressures toward integration, as well as from the perceived costs to individuals of breaking the unwritten rules of inequality. It would not be correct to conclude that acquiescence means agreement, however. Minorities expressed considerable resentment against enforced segregation and other forms of inequality, particularly against perceived discrimination in financing. Yet there is little possibility of organized challenge to the housing status quo. Minorities are generally powerless and women invisible as a political force. No women's political groups were encountered on the sites, and only two active black organizations were found. The black organizations have so far focused on the issue of employment discrimination, with housing inequality having lower priority in the allocation of scarce political resources. The level of protest has not been sufficient to impair the social-political stability of the southern areas, and has not in any way affected the operations of the private housing market. In contrast, the political structure of the South Dakota site has been severely strained by the refusal of Indians to accept subordinate status. This group has the resource of strong community organization (including the tribe), and a level of benefits from local white institutions which is so low that they have comparatively little to lose through reprisals.

Another factor contributing to observed patterns of inequality is the very limited new construction and low turnover of existing units observed on every site. As a result, consumers have little opportunity to change their housing (even apart from the obstacles posed by direct discrimination), and are therefore frozen into the current unequal occupancy patterns. Housing shortages cannot be attributed to lack of developable land, building capacity or capital, but rather to supply conditions while make new housing prohibitively expensive to all but the very affluent. Since the moratorium on HUD homeowner subsidy programs in 1973, practically all new housing is in the $35,000+ range; and with the recent dramatic increase in mortgage interest rates, even the affluent are often unable or unwilling to build or purchase. All areas visited exhibited extremely low vacancy rates and other indicators of shortage in the face of, in most cases, the existence of clear-title developable land, underutilized builders, and capital exporting.

Local governments were found to play a limited role in the housing market, apart from setting codes and regulations. Zoning ordinances and building codes exist in every area, but are not used specifically to contain minority neighborhoods. The tradition of segregation, plus the safety valve of open land available for black expansion, has maintained neighborhood boundaries without the active intervention of local governments. Housing codes exist but are typically not enforced on substandard housing because of lack of public funds for redevelopment and the professed inability of owners to afford rehabilitation.

Where code enforcement and redevelopment have occurred, the effects have been racially selective in that the blighted areas designated for renewal are minority neighborhoods. The two towns which attempted redevelopment found the programs resisted (and in one case, halted) by ad hoc organizations of the minority residents affected. Resentment did not stem from removal of minority households, since displaced families were relocated in the same neighborhood. Rather, the residents—especially homeowners—resisted plans which had been developed exclusively by white decisionmakers, which did not reflect residents' perceived needs and priorities, and which seemed in fact threatening to their interests. The perceived threat was sufficient to bring out organized protest even among persons who had never before dared challenge the status quo on any issue.

Federal action has served some of the housing needs of women and minorities, but has not generally affected segregation where it exists. The most-used federal subsidy programs—FmHA 502, HUD 235, and HUD Public Housing—tend to serve women and minorities at least equally, and in some cases in greater numbers than their proportion of the population. These programs are, however, administered locally by housing suppliers engrained in local traditions of segregation, and serve a clientele for whom the expectation of discrimination is produced by long experience. In the four southern sites, all 502 and 235 units in the towns are segregated (segregation in open country is not a meaningful concept); and all public housing projects, with one exception, are segregated.

The role of the federal government in these markets is likely to be considerably reduced in the future. Only one of the six areas surveyed had participated in HUD categorical grant programs which would entitle it to CDBG monies under the 1974 Housing and Community Development Act. Given the competition for nonmetropolitan discretionary funds, the other five are unlikely to benefit from the program. Section 8 Leased Housing—the only categorical HUD program currently in operation—is still new and poorly understood by local officials. However, it is tentatively perceived by them as much less suitable for the needs of rural housing markets than the conventional public housing which it supplants.

Appendix A: General Housing Characteristics, 1970

Table A-1
General Housing Characteristics, 1970

	AR		GA		NM		NC		SD		TN	
	County	Town	County	Town	County	Town	County	Town	County	Town	County	Town
TOTAL HOUSEHOLDS	7,535	1,979	5,273	2,722	3,794	2,259	7,019	1,975	3,455	948	8,238	3,642
% Minority	26	27	18	24	39	43	38	41	8	15	12	17
% Female Headed Families	10	7	13	18	12	14	13	11	9	17	10	15
YEAR-ROUND UNITS	8,240	2,091	5,928	2,982	4,785	2,515	7,585	2,121	3,868	994	9,062	3,810
% In One-Unit Structures	90		86		87		89		89		85	
% Structures Built in 1960 or Later	33		26		18		20		8		27	
VACANCY RATE												
% Homeowner	1		1		2		1		1		2	
% Rental	10		11		10		7		5		5	
OCCUPIED UNITS	7,535	1,979	5,273	2,722	3,794	2,259	7,019	1,975	3,455	948	8,238	3,642
% Owner-Occupied	71	72	67	61	70	72	57	53	72	55	73	64
% Lack Plumbing	21	5	21	18	17	8	35	25	30	16	21	12
% Overcrowded	12	9	12	12	16	14	13	12	13	14	9	6
WHITE-OCCUPIED UNITS	5,589	1,471	4,348	2,060	2,077	1,277	4,366	1,161	3,188	802	7,274	3,035
% Owner-Occupied	76	76	72	68	74	75	67	53	76	64	76	67
% Lack Plumbing	12	2	15	8	22	11	19	6	NA	NA	17	6
% Overcrowded	8	5	8	7	3	2	5	5	NA	NA	7	5
MINORITY-OCCUPIED UNITS	1,946	508	925	661	1,717	982	2,653	814	267	146	964	602
% Owner-Occupied	56	61	43	42	66	69	39	39	39	10	54	47
% Lack Plumbing	49	13	53	46	11	5	62	53	NA	NA	49	40
% Overcrowded	25	20	30	30	31	33	27	23	NA	NA	24	16

Appendix B: Glossary of Federal Housing-Related Programs and Agencies

Department of Housing and Urban Development (HUD)

The federal department which administers, through regional and area offices, many of the housing subsidy and assistance programs listed here, and is responsible for the enforcement of Federal Fair Housing legislation where applicable. Most HUD programs were put under moratorium in January 1973, while the administration reconsidered housing policy and priorities. These programs, along with conventional public housing, have been allowed to remain inactive, since the HCDA of 1974 shifted the emphasis of federal housing assistance to CDBG's and Section 8 leased housing.

Farmer's Home Administration (FmHA)

An agency of the Department of Agriculture which administers housing assistance programs specifically aimed at rural areas, including Sections 502, 504, 515 and 524. Its programs were frozen along with HUD's in January 1973, but were reactivated nine months later, following litigation. Areas eligible for FmHA programs included open country and towns up to 10,000 until 1974, when the population limit was raised to 20,000 by the HCDA.

Community Development Block Grants (CDBG) – Title I of the Housing and Community Development Act of 1974 (P.L. 93-383)

A new community development funding program under which HUD provides fiscal assistance to communities for a wide range of housing and community development activities. The program replaces eight former categorical grant and loan programs by a unified system of "block grants." Grant recipients are free to use their funds within the constraints of broad federal objectives. Communities must apply for federal funds; maximum amounts for CDBG are established for individual communities through an entitlement formula which generally excludes small towns and rural areas without previous activities under the programs replaced by CDBG.

Federal Housing Administration (FHA) Insurance

Under the Housing Production and Mortgage Credit/FHA Agency, HUD insures lenders against loss on mortgage loans. The types of assistance may be guaranteed/insured loans and/or direct payment for specified use. The FHA makes no loans but functions as an insuring agency on loans made by other agencies under prescribed conditions.

Housing Improvement Program (HIP)

A housing program administered by the Bureau of Indian Affairs (BIA) which provides grants to very low-income families under BIA jurisdiction to repair, rehabilitate or construct homes.

Public Housing

A housing program established by the Housing Act of 1937 as a federally financed but locally operated program. The 1937 law, (amended several times, most notably in the Housing Act of 1949 and in the Housing and Community Development Act of 1974), authorized federal financial aid through HUD for low-income housing built and managed by local housing authorities (LHA). LHA's were created by state or local governments under state law and have primary responsibility for public housing units. The primary production programs under public housing have been conventional, turnkey and leased housing. The Administration's FY '76 budget continues the moratorium on this program, providing only for the funding of commitments made prior to January 5, 1973 or amendments to existing projects. However, housing for Indians is continued under the conventional public housing program.

Section 8–Leased Housing (formerly Section 23)

Administered by HUD, Section 8 of the Housing Act of 1937, as revised by the HCD Act of 1974, is currently the only operative HUD housing subsidy program. Its purpose is to provide existing, new and substantially rehabilitated housing for low and moderate income families. Families with incomes below 80 percent of the median income for the area may qualify. HUD contracts directly with the owner of the housing for the payment of the difference between the fair market rent for the unit and the tenant's payment, which is based on gross income (tenant share varies between 15 percent and 25 percent of the gross income). LHA's may also participate in the program.

Section 235—Homeownership Assistance Program

A housing program, administered by HUD, which was established by the Housing and Urban Development Act of 1968 to provide home-buying assistance to lower-income families. Under the program, the mortgagee receives periodic payments which serve to reduce interest costs on a market rate home mortgage. The reduction in the interest cost effectively lowers monthly mortgage payment requirements. The amount of the assistance payment cannot exceed the difference between the required monthly payment and that amount which would be required for interest and principal if the mortgage bore interest at 1 percent. In addition, the mortgage cannot exceed a specified amount. Contract authority can be allocated under Section 235 (j) to nonprofit sponsors who purchased or rehabilitated housing suitable for resale to lower income families. The Section 235 program expires on August 22, 1975, although legislation is pending to extend it.

Section 236—Rental and Cooperative Housing for Lower Income Families

A housing program administered by HUD which was established by the Housing and Urban Development Act of 1968 and amended in 1974 to incorporate rent supplements. The legislation authorized interest reduction subsidy payments by the federal government which reduce the rental charge to the tenant of rental or cooperative housing. The payments are made to the mortgagee on behalf of the tenant. Mortgagors must be nonprofit entities or cooperatives, or a limited-dividend corporation. Residents of the dwelling must not exceed income levels specified for their geographic area. The Administration's FY '76 budget continues the moratorium on Section 236, providing only for the funding commitments made prior to January 5, 1973 or amendments to existing projects.

Section 502—Homeownership Loan and Interest Credit Loan Program

Administered by the Farmers Home Administration (FmHA), this housing program was established under Title V of the Housing Act of 1949 to assist rural families to obtain decent, safe, and sanitary dwellings and related facilities. FmHA makes and insures loans for purchase, construction, or improvement of homes for rural residents unable to secure credit from other sources at reasonable rates and terms. Interest rates are from 8.125 percent to 1 percent with up to thirty-three years to repay. The amount of the interest credit depends on income and family size. The Administration's FY '76 budget reduces the amount and number of units to be subsidized under Section 502. The amount of unsubsidized housing assistance under Section 502 remains the same.

Section 504—Loans and Grants for Home Repair

A housing program administered by FmHA which makes loans or combinations of loans and grants for making minor repairs and improvements to dwellings or farm buildings and facilities that are unsafe or hazardous to health. Those who may qualify are rural homeowners or lessees of housing sites who lack sufficient income to qualify for a Section 502 loan and have questionable repayment ability. The loans carry an interest rate of 1 percent for ten years with the maximum amount of assistance being $5,000. Loans exceeding $2,500 are secured. Maximum time is twenty years. The Administration's FY '76 budget provides $20 million for loans under Section 504. Grants authorized by Section 504 have not been implemented because of riders in the appropriations acts.

Section 515—Rural Rental Program

Under this program, FmHA makes direct loans to finance rental or cooperative housing and related facilities for occupancy by low- to moderate-income rural families and senior citizens sixty-two years and older. Loans are made to construct, purchase or rehabilitate rental housing; projects may be leased to local housing authorities. Sponsors can be nonprofit, profit-oriented, or limited-profit organizations or corporations, individuals, and public bodies. Interest rates are from 8.125 percent to 1 percent, repayable over fifty years. The Administration's FY '76 budget retains the 1975 level of funding for Section 515, although the number of units to be provided is smaller because of rising costs. A rent supplement program provided in the HCD act of 1974 has not been implemented because HUD Section 8 is the preferred mechanism to assist rural families who would be eligible for rent supplements.

Section 524—Rural Housing Site Loans

Under this program, short-term loans are available through FmHA to public bodies or private nonprofit organizations to finance the purchase and development of building sites. Loans may include the cost of construction of streets and the installation of water and sewer facilities. Sites financed with Section 524 loans must be sold for use in connection with a federally-assisted housing program. Interest rates are determined by the secretary of agriculture, taking into account the cost to the government of borrowing money. The FY '76 budget continues allocations to rural housing site loans at the 1975 level of $3 million.

Veterans Administration (VA) Home Loan Programs

VA home loans can be guaranteed, insured or direct. Under the guarantee program, VA agrees to pay a lender up to 60 percent of the mortgage in the case of default by a borrower. The VA insured loan program creates insurance accounts in the names of qualified lenders. The direct loan program is designed to provide housing finance in areas of the country where mortgage credit is unavailable to returned veterans.

Appendix C: Federal Fair Housing
Legislation and Regulations

Five major pieces of federal legislation and regulations affecting equal access to housing are discussed below. They are:

1. Executive Order 11063, issued November 20, 1962 entitled Equal Opportunity in Housing, 27 Fed. Reg. 11527;
2. Title VI of the Civil Rights Act of 1964, 42 USC 2000 which concerns nondiscrimination in federally assisted programs;
3. Title VIII of the Civil Rights Act of 1968, 18 USC 245, referred to as the Fair Housing title;
4. Section 808 of the Housing and Community Development Act of 1974, 88 Stat. 633, which amends the Fair Housing title of the Civil Rights Act of 1968 by adding the word "sex" to those regulations prohibiting discrimination on the basis of race, color, religion or national origin; and
5. Amendments to the rules and regulations of the Federal Home Loan Bank System, 12 CFR 528 and 531 (Nondiscrimination Requirements and Guidelines Relating to Nondiscrimination in Lending), which add the word "sex" to the regulations prohibiting discrimination on the basis of race, color, religion, or national origin.

In addition, Part VI briefly discusses the channels through which complaints of discrimination directed against the Farmers Home Administration are made.

Executive Order 11063, Equal Opportunity
in Housing

This order was signed by President Kennedy on November 20, 1962. Section 101 of E.O. 11063 directed "all departments and agencies in the executive branch of the federal government, insofar as their functions relate to the provision, rehabilitation, or operation of housing and related facilities, to take all action necessary and appropriate to prevent discrimination because of race, color, creed, or national origin. . . " Part II orders federal agencies to issue regulations implementing the order, and section 302 of part III recommends that federal agencies cancel contracts, and refrain from extending further aid to parties that are guilty of discrimination. Parts IV and V of the Executive Order establish the President's Committee on Equal Opportunity in Housing to set further federal policies. E.O. 11063 has been superceded (see Title VI of the Civil Rights Act of 1964 and Title VIII of the Civil Rights Act of 1968 below).

Civil Rights Act of 1964: Nondiscrimination in Federally Assisted Programs

Title VI of the Civil Rights of 1964, 42 USC 2000a, states that "no person in the United States shall, on the grounds of race, color, or national origin, be excluded from participation in, be denied the benefits of, or be subjected to discrimination under any program or activity receiving federal financial assistance." Section 602 of the law directs federal agencies to issue rules, regulations, and orders to implement the policies of Title VI. It further indicates that compliance with Title VI can be accomplished "by the termination of or refusal to grant or to continue assistance under such program or activity to any recipient as to whom there has been an express finding on the record, after opportunity for hearing, of a failure to comply with such requirement . . ."

Civil Rights Act of 1968

Title VIII of this act provides for the following:

A. Discrimination in the "sale or rental of housing" is prohibited except for single family residences sold or rented by the owner without either advertising or brokerage services, if such owner does not own more than three such residences at any one time. The "sale or rental of housing" means:

1. To refuse to sell or rent after the making of a bona fide offer, or to refuse to negotiate for the sale or rental of, or otherwise make unavailable or deny, a dwelling to any person because of race, color, religion, or national origin.

2. To discriminate against any person in the terms, conditions, or privileges of sale or rental of a dwelling, or in the provision of services or facilities in connection therewith, because of race, color, religion, or national origin.

3. To make, print, or publish, or cause to be made, printed or published any notice, statement, or advertisement, with respect to the sale or rental of a dwelling that indicates any preference, limitation, or discrimination based on race, color, religion, or national origin, or an intention to make any such preference, limitation, or discrimination.

4. To represent to any person because of race, color, religion, or national origin that any dwelling is not available for inspection, sale, or rental when such dwelling is in fact so available.

5. For profit, to induce or attempt to induce any person to sell or rent any dwelling by representations regarding the entry or prospective entry into the neighborhood of a person or persons or a particular race, color, religion, or national origin.

B. Discrimination in the financing of housing is prohibited. This applies to any bank, building and loan association, insurance company, etc., whose business it is to make loans for the purpose of purchasing, construction, improving, repairing or maintaining a dwelling. It applies to all terms and conditions of loan—amount, interest, rate, duration, etc.

C. Discrimination in the provision of brokerage services is prohibited. See (3), (4), and (5) above. Also, it is unlawful to deny access to, membership or participation in any multiple-listing service, real estate brokerage service, etc.

D. Compliance and Enforcement:

1. Any person who claims to have been injured or who believes that he/she will be irrevocably injured by a discriminatory housing practice may file a complaint with the Department of Housing and Urban Development (HUD) and such will be processed through the Department's Regional Administrator under regulations prescribed by the Assistant Secretary for Equal Opportunity.

2. The assistant secretary shall investigate the complaint within thirty days and, if it has merit, shall attempt to resolve it through voluntary compliance or shall transfer it to an appropriate state agency (see Section F below). If voluntary compliance has not been obtained, the assistant secretary may:

a. Recommend to the U.S. Attorney General that he institute civil proceedings under section 813 of Title VIII, or other appropriate action;

b. Institute enforcement proceedings under E.O. 11063 or Title VI of the Civil Rights Act of 1964; and/or

c. Inform any other concerned federal agency.

3. If voluntary compliance has not been obtained by the assistant secretary, the aggrieved person may commence a civil action in the U.S. District Court to secure the rights established by Title VIII. Also, a party who claims to have been injured in regard to rights granted under sections 803, 804, 805 or 806 (a, b, and c above) may commence a civil action *ab initio.*

E. Affirmative Marketing:

1. In addition to its compliance work, HUD has developed affirmative policies to promote equal opportunity in housing. All subdivisions, multi-family projects, and mobile home parks of five or more lots, units or spaces, as well as single family home mortgage requests for five or more units, must submit an affirmative fair housing marketing plan to HUD before feasibility or fund reservations will be granted. The procedures for affirmative marketing are outlined in HUD circular 8000.4, "Implementation of Fair Housing Marketing Regulations" and 24 CFR 200.600 to 200.640. According to Section 200.600 of the regulations, such a plan should include at a minimum: (1) an affirmative program to attract buyers or tenants of all minority groups for initial sale or rental; (2) a nondiscriminatory hiring policy for rental and sales staff; (3) oral and written instruction to all sales and rental personnel on fair marketing; (4) specific solicitation of eligible buyers or tenants referred to the project by HUD;

(5) prominent display in the project of HUD's fair housing poster; and (6) prominent display at the project site of HUD's housing logo or statement on equal opportunity.

2. In addition to its fair marketing regulations, HUD has published advertising guidelines for fair housing. These specifically prohibit (a) the use of words, phrases, sentences, and visual aids which have a discriminatory effect, and (b) selective use of advertising media or content with discriminatory effect. The guidelines also set out policies for the use of HUD equal opportunity material, the use of human models for display and advertising, and notification of clients and employees about fair housing policy.

3. HUD also requires that its fair housing poster be prominently displayed in sales and rental offices, as well as project sites for all units covered under Title VIII. The guidelines for the display of the poster, which is available from all HUD area and regional offices, are set out in 24 CFR 110.1 to 110.25.

F. Referrals and Recognition of Substantially Equivalent Laws:

1. Whenever the assistant secretary determines that a state or local fair housing law provides rights and remedies substantially equivalent to those provided by Title VIII for a person aggrieved by a discriminatory housing practice, the complaint shall be referred to such state or local fair housing agency.

2. Such referred complaint may be reactivated whenever the assistant secretary certifies that such reactivism is required to protect the rights of the parties. This is routinely certified if the local agency has not commenced proceedings within thirty days of the referral.

3. The procedure for the recognition of state laws is set forth in 24 CFR 115.1 to 115.12.

Section 808 of the Housing and Community Development Act of 1974

The Housing and Community Development Act of 1974, 88 Stat. 633, effective August 22, 1974, amends the Fair Housing Title of the Civil Rights Act of 1968 by adding the word "sex" after the word "religion" in those sections of the title which prohibit discrimination on the basis of race, color, religion, or national origin in the sale, rental, or financing of housing or provision of brokerage services.

In addition, Title V of the National Housing Act is amended to prohibit discrimination on the basis of sex in connection with "federally related mortgage loans, insurance guaranty, or related assistance."

Section 527 of the National Housing Act as enacted by the Housing and Community Development Act requires every lender making federally related mortgage loans to "consider without prejudice the combined income of both husband and wife for the purpose of extending mortgage credit."

*Amendments to Rules and Regulations of
the Federal Home Loan Bank System*

The Federal Home Loan Bank Systems rules and regulations, 12 CFR 528 and 521, have been amended to conform with Section 808 of the Housing and Community Development Act of 1974 (see above). The Sections amended are: § 528.1, 528.3, 528.5, 528.8, and 531.8. Four of the revised sections are presented below.

1. § 528.2, Nondiscrimination in lending and other services is revised to read:

(a) No member institution shall deny a loan or other service rendered by the member institution for the purpose of purchasing, constructing, improving, repairing, or maintaining a dwelling, or discriminate in the fixing of the amount, interest rate, duration, application procedures, collection or enforcement procedures, or other terms or conditions of such loan or other service because of the race, color, religion, sex, or national origin of

   (1) An applicant for any such loan or any other service rendered by the member institution;
   (2) Any person associated with such applicant in connection with such loan or other service or the purposes of such loan or other service;
   (3) The present or prospective owners, lessees, tenants, or occupants of the dwelling or dwellings in relation to which such loan or other service is to be made or given; or
   (4) The present or prospective owners, lessees, tenants, or occupants of other dwellings in the vicinity of the dwelling or dwellings in relation to which such loan or other service is to be made or given.
(b) A member institution shall consider without prejudice the combined income of both husband and wife for the purpose of extending mortgage credit to a married couple or either member thereof.

2. § 528.3, Nondiscrimination in Application, is revised to read:
   No member institution shall refuse or decline to allow, receive, or consider any application, request, or inquiry with respect to a loan or other service rendered by the member for the purpose of purchasing, constructing, improving, repairing, or maintaining a dwelling, or discriminate in the imposition of conditions upon, or in the processing of, any such application, request, or inquiry, or make statements which discourage any such application, request, or inquiry because of the race, color, religion, sex, or national origin of any prospective borrower or other person who

(a) Makes application for any such loan or other service;

(b) Requests forms or papers to be used to make application for any such loan or other service; or

(c) Inquiries about the availability of such loan or other service.

3. § 528.5, Equal Housing Lending Poster, paragraph (b) is revised to read as follows:

(b) The text of the Equal Housing Lender Poster shall be as follows (except that the legend "Equal Opportunity Lender" may be substituted for the legend "Equal Housing Lender"):

It is illegal, because of race, color, religion, sex, or national origin to:

Deny a loan for the purpose of purchasing, constructing, improving, repairing, or maintaining a dwelling or

Discriminate in fixing of the amount, interest rate, duration, application procedures or other terms or conditions of such a loan.

If you believe you have been discriminated against, you may discuss the matter with the management of this institution or send a complaint to:

Assistant Secretary for Equal Opportunity, Department of Housing and Urban Development, Washington, D.C. 20410, or call your local HUD or FHA office.

You may also send a copy of the complaint to the Office of Housing and Urban Affairs, Federal Home Loan Bank Board, Washington, D.C. 20552.

4. § 528.8, Complaints, is revised to read:

Complaints regarding discrimination in lending by a member institution should be referred to the Office of Housing and Urban Affairs, Federal Home Loan Bank Board, Washington, D.C. 20552, or to the Assistant Secretary for Equal Opportunity, U.S. Department of Housing and Urban Development, Washington, D.C. 20410. Complaints regarding discrimination in employment by a member institution should be referred to the Equal Employment Opportunity Commission, Washington, D.C. 20506.

Farmers Home Administration (FmHA)

FmHA administers housing programs for low- to moderate-income families in rural areas. FmHA must comply with all applicable fair housing legislation and federal regualtions (see above).

A. Complaints of discrimination directed against the Farmers Home Administration or FmHA borrowers that are directly received by the County Office staff are sent to a State Director. All such complaints will be forwarded to the Civil Rights Coordinator.

B. Discrimination complaints against packagers, contractors, or others with whom FmHA deals are filed with the Department of Housing and Urban Development. However, these complaints may be accepted by FmHA personnel and routed through the State Director to the Civil Rights Coordinator.

Appendix D: Detailed Results of the "Dual" Housing Market Analysis

Detailed regression results are presented in tables D-1 - D-6 with brief comments on each state given below.

Arkansas (Tables D-1 and D-2). The Arkansas equations are fairly powerful owing in part to the larger sample size. Significant variables have correct signs and reasonable magnitudes. In table D-2 the low value subsample is further stratified to test whether the race effect between the two towns for which data was obtained. It appears to be somewhat more pronounced in town B.

Georgia (Table D-3). The Georgia equation is not as strong in overall explanatory power as are equations for other states, but significant coefficients still have correct signs and reasonable magnitudes. The race effect in Georgia is the most powerful detected.

North Carolina (Table D-4). Again, significant coefficients have correct signs and reasonable magnitudes. The overall fit is quite good. The most interesting result is that the race effect is positive for low value homes and negative for high value homes (see text of Chapter 2 for a discussion).

Tennessee (Table D-5). The results in Tennessee are inconclusive due primarily to the small number of observations on black homes and the observed inconsistency of property records for low value properties. Although the equation estimated with the entire sample is fairly powerful, the race effect is ambiguous; it is negative in the LOG/LOG specification and positive in the linear. Estimates using the low value sample only are very weak.

New Mexico (Table D-6). The explanatory power of both equations is quite good with ten significant independent variables in each. The "Spanish variable" is insignificantly different from zero in both equations. There were not enough observations to permit stratification into low and high value subsamples.

Table D-1
Regression Results of Dual Housing Market Study (Arkansas) (Figures in parentheses are *t*-statistics)

	LOG/LOG Specification*		Linear Specification	
	Lows	Highs	Lows	Highs
Year Built	.38 (1.9)[2]	.59 (3.6)[1]	35.7 (1.7)[3]	278 (3.4)[1]
Quality (1-99)	.12 (2.6)[1]	.44 (4.2)[1]	56.4 (6.4)[1]	160 (3.5)[1]
Condition (1-3)	-.03 (0.6)	.18 (1.7)[3]	-7.9 (0.1)	1294 (0.6)
Bathrooms (#)	.06 (3.0)[1]	.12 (2.4)[1]	669 (1.8)[3]	226 (2.3)[2]
Fireplaces	.003 (0.3)	.02 (3.3)[1]	332 (.14)[4]	1092 (2.2)[2]
Basement (00-10)	—	.02 (0.9)	—	543 (1.4)[4]
Int. Space (sq ft)	.55 (8.3)[1]	.75 (10.6)[1]	3.54 (9.2)[1]	10.29 (7.9)[1]
Lot SAE (sq ft)	.11 (3.4)[1]	.03 (0.7)	0.01 (1.3)[4]	-.03 (2.7)[1]
Rooms (#)	.13 (2.0)[2]	.18 (2.6)[1]	73 (.09)	1077 (2.7)[1]
Access (miles)	.07 (1.4)[4]	.07 (2.3)[2]	400 (2.8)[1]	696 (1.3)[4]
Neighborhood Condition (1-10)	.07 (2.0)[2]	.18 (5.1)[1]	104 (2.1)[2]	1255 (5.8)[1]
Central Heat (D)*	.12 (3.0)[1]	.04 (1.2)	547 (2.7)[1]	-286 (0.3)
Flush Toilet (D)*	-.01 (0.1)	—	589 (1.4)[4]	—
Garage (D)*	.03 (0.8)	.07 (2.8)[1]	-30 (0.2)	1070 (1.5)[4]
Sewer (D)*	-.10 (1.7)[3]	-.27 (3.4)[1]	-354 (1.2)	-9249 (3.5)[1]
Air Conditioned (D)*	—	-.01 (0.2)	—	-1171 (1.1)
Brick/Stone (D)*	—	.14 (3.9)[1]	—	1334 (1.3)[4]
Paved Road (D)*	-.02 (0.4)	.48 (6.1)[1]	-81 (0.2)	8993 (5.2)[1]
Piers (D)*	-.17 (4.8)[1]	-.11 (1.9)[2]	-831 (4.0)[1]	-2290 (1.3)[4]
Mod. Kitchen (D)*	—	.02 (0.6)[1]	—	1070 (1.1)[1]

Table D-1 (cont.)

	LOG/LOG Specifications*		Linear Specification	
	Lows	Highs	Lows	Highs
Pool (D)*	--	.34 (3.3)[1]	--	13140 (4.5)[1]
Subtown A (D)*	-.18 (4.7)[1]	0.04 (1.2)	-812 (3.8)[1]	-1147 (1.1)
Race (D)*	.11 (1.7)[3]	.09 (1.3)[4]	443 (1.4)[4]	3726 (2.1)[2]
Constant*	6.7 (2.0)[2]	.25 (1.4)[3]	-3179 (2.4)[1]	-46810 (7.5)[1]
R^2	79	94	80	90
N	194	116	194	116
RSS	7.036	1.158	$.1902 \times 10^9$	$.1072 \times 10^{10}$

*Coefficients of log variables are elasticities. Coefficients of dummies (D) Log/Log Specification are converted to fractions, i.e., if $\hat{B}i^* = 0.25$, presence of attribute i raises value 25%. If $\hat{B}i^* = -0.25$, presence of the attribute lowers value by 25%. Constant term is converted to analog.

1. Significant at 1% level.
2. Significant at 5% level.
3. Significant at 10% level.
4. Significant at 20% level.

Table D-2
Regression Results of Dual Housing Market Study Results in Arkansas—Low Value (Figures in parentheses are *t*-statistics)

	LOG/LOG Specification*		Linear Specification	
	Town A	Town B	Town A	Town B
Year Built (00–74)	.18 (0.9)	.22 (0.4)	34.2 (1.4)[4]	-5.9 (0.1)
Quality (1–99)	.06 (1.7)[3]	.48 (1.8)[3]	52.6 (4.9)[1]	72.1 (3.5)[1]
Condition (1–3)	-.08 (1.8)[3]	.13 (0.8)	-257 (1.4)[4]	378 (1.0)
Bathrooms (#)	-.02 (0.9)	.08 (2.2)[2]	14.4 (0.3)	155 (2.1)[2]
Fireplaces (#)	.02 (1.6)[3]	.02 (0.3)	643 (2.4)[1]	368 (0.8)
Basement (00–10)	—	—	—	—
Int. Space (sq ft)	.50 (8.8)[1]	.62 (3.0)[1]	3.71 (9.1)[1]	2.94 (3.2)[1]
Lot Size (sq ft)	.05 (1.4)[4]	.11 (1.8)[3]	.002 (0.2)	.03 (2.4)[1]
Rooms (#)	.11 (2.0)[2]	.08 (0.3)	100 (1.3)[4]	-63 (.03)
Access (miles)	.23 (4.3)[1]	-.03 (0.2)	197 (4.3)[1]	-188 (0.7)
Neighborhood Condition (1–10)	.007 (0.2)	.04 (0.5)	12.0 (0.2)	125 (1.2)
Central Heat (D)*	.06 (1.9)[2]	.25 (1.8)[3]	302 (1.4)[4]	1283 (2.5)[1]
Flush Toilet (D)*	.33 (1.9)[2]	-.13 (0.6)	864 (1.3)[4]	-29.9 (0.0)
Garage (D)*	.02 (0.4)	-.03 (0.4)	101 (0.4)	-77.1 (0.2)
Sewer (D)*	.07 (0.6)	-.10 (0.7)	-144 (0.2)	-729 (1.3)[4]
Air Conditioned (D)*	—	—	—	—
Brick/Stone (D)*	—	—	—	—
Paved Road (D)*	-.002 (9.0)	- 0.4 (0.2)	280 (0.5)	211 (0.3)
Piers (D)*	-.09 (2.5)[1]	-.19 (2.3)[2]	-526 (2.1)[2]	-921 (2.4)[1]
Mod. Kitchen (D)*	—	—	—	—

Table D-2 (cont.)

	LOG/LOG Specification*		Linear Specification	
	Town A	Town B	Town A	Town B
Race (D)*	.09 (1.2)	.22 (1.3)[4]	850 (1.7)[3]	1109.8 (1.9)[2]
Constant*	33.11 (3.8)[1]	1.78 (0.2)	-3475 (2.2)[2]	-2062 (0.7)
R^2	82	80	82	84
N	132	62	132	62
RSS	2.290	3.389	$.1029 \times 10^9$	$.5362 \times 10^8$

*Coefficients of log variables are elasticities. Coefficients of dummies (D) in Log/Log Specification are converted to fractions, i.e., if $\hat{B}i* = 0.25$, presence of attribute i raises value 25%. If $\hat{B}i* = -0.25$, the presence of attribute i lowers value by 25%. Constant term is converted to analog.

1. Significant at 1% level.
2. Significant at 5% level.
3. Significant at 10% level.
4. Significant at 20% level.

Table D-3
Regression Results of Dual Housing Market Study (Georgia) (Figures in parentheses are t-statistics)

	LOG/LOG Specification*		Linear Specification	
	Lows	Highs	Lows	Highs
Year Built	.01 (0.17)	.14 (1.3)[4]	16.7 (1.1)	44.9 (0.9)
Quality (1–5)	-.61 (1.5)[4]	-.26 (1.6)[3]	-617 (1.2)	-1007 (0.8)
Condition (1–3)	.20 (1.7)[3]	.04 (0.3)	904 (2.3)[2]	-122 (0.1)
Baths (#)	-.08 (0.3)	-.12 (1.8)[3]	-15.0 (0.1)	-94.3 (0.6)
Space (sq ft)	.48 (2.6)[1]	.31 (2.8)[1]	2.45 (2.1)[2]	4.20 (2.5)[1]
Lot Size (sq ft)	.18 (3.2)[1]	.16 (3.2)[1]	3.35 (1.7)[3]	2.08 (3.4)[1]
Rooms (#)	.05 (0.2)	.29 (1.7)	190.1 (0.7)	754.4 (1.0)
Neighborhood Condition	.21 (2.6)[1]	.12 (1.4)[4]	585.1 (4.2)[1]	943.8 (1.8)[3]
Access (Miles)	.02 (2.6)[1]	.02 (0.4)	-8.66 (0.0)	-620.5 (0.7)
Central Heat (D)*	-.11 (0.7)	.18 (2.2)[2]	-614.0 (0.8)	2792 (1.6)[3]
Hot Water (D)*	.64 (0.7)	——	1002 (0.8)	——
Brick/Stone (D)*	.09 (0.6)	.04 (0.6)	1320 (1.6)[3]	542.9 (0.3)
Subtown A (D)*	-.16 (0.4)	-.09 (0.4)	-922 (0.9)	-2365 (0.6)
Subtown B (D)*	.09 (0.2)	.05 (0.2)	281 (0.3)	2198 (0.5)
Pool (D)*	——	-.04 (0.2)	——	-4059 (0.9)
Air Conditioned (D)*	——	.15 (2.6)[1]	——	3225 (2.6)[1]
Mod. Kitchen (D)*	——	.07 (1.0)	——	2300 (1.4)[4]
Race (D)*	.29 (2.4)[1]	.19 (2.9)[1]	1127 (2.4)[1]	2836 (2.2)[2]
R^2	.71	.70	.74	.70
N	87	75	87	75
RSS	6.76	1.55	.1866 x 10⁹	.8019 x 10⁹

*Coefficients of log variables are elasticities. Coefficients of dummies (D) in Log/Log Specification are converted to fractions, i.e., if $\hat{B}i^* = 0.25$, presence of attribute i raises value by 25%. If $\hat{B}i^* = -0.25$ the presence of attribute i lowers value by 25%. Constant term is converted to analog.

1. Significant at 1% level.
2. Significant at 5% level.
3. Significant at 10% level.
4. Significant at 20% level.

Table D-4
Regression Results of Dual Housing Market Study (North Carolina) (Figures in parentheses are t-statistics)

	LOG/LOG Specification*				Linear Specification			
	Lows		Highs		Lows		Highs	
Quality (1-99)	.35	(6.2)[1]	.45	(3.0)[1]	90.0	(4.5)[1]	183	(2.8)[1]
Condition (10-30)	.09	(1.1)	.09	(0.6)	19.4	(0.5)	14.7	(9.1)
Year Built	.17	(3.6)[1]	.14	(1.7)[3]	49.7	(4.1)[1]	135	(2.4)[2]
Baths (#)	.02	(0.3)	.14	(1.5)[4]	-7.6	(0.15)	244	(1.7)[3]
Lot Size (sq ft)	.07	(1.2)	.01	(0.3)	.10	(1.4)[4]	-1.25	(0.1)
Int. Space (sq ft)	.13	(1.4)[4]	.45	(3.7)[1]	1.12	(1.8)[3]	6.23	(3.7)[1]
Rooms (#)	.59	(4.4)[1]	.42	(2.7)[1]	614	(2.7)[1]	2413	(4.0)[1]
Neighborhood Condition (1-10)	.01	(0.2)	.01	(0.1)	352	(2.1)[2]	331	(0.7)
Insulation (D)*	.10	(1.2)	.11	(1.1)	11.1	(9.0)	3219	(1.1)
Hot Water (D)*	.17	(2.2)[2]	—	—	1182	(2.3)[2]	—	—
Brick-Stone (D)*	.08	(.09)	.02	(0.3)	694	(1.1)	37.1	(0.0)
Subtown A (D)*	-.06	(0.8)	.02	(0.5)	-559	(1.0)	1380	(1.0)
Subtown B	-.17	(1.7)[3]	-.21	(1.8)[3]	-1241	(1.4)[4]	-3056	(0.9)
Race (D)*	.057	(0.8)	-.086	(1.6)[3]	772	(1.3)[4]	-2446	(1.5)[4]
Constant	459	(6.1)[1]	14.1	(3.9)[1]	-3779	(3.1)[1]	-30590	(5.8)[1]
R^2	84		85		83		87	
N	85		70		85		70	
RSS	2.525		1.152		.1729 x 10⁹		.9069 x 10⁹	

*Coefficients of continuous variables in Log/Log Specification are elasticities. Coefficients of dummies (D) in Log/Log Specification are converted to fractions, i.e., if $\hat{B}i^* = 0.25$, presence of attribute i raises value by 25%. If $\hat{B}i^* = -0.25$ the presence of attribute i lowers value by 25%. Constant term is converted to analog.

1. Significant at 1% level.
2. Significant at 5% level.
3. Significant at 10% level.
4. Significant at 20% level.

Table D-5

Regression Results of Dual Housing Market Study (Tennessee) (Figures in parentheses are *t*-statistics)

	LOG/LOG Specification*		Linear Specification	
	Entire Sample	Lows Only	Entire Sample	Lows Only
Year Built	.06 (1.4)[4]	.03 (0.4)	59.3 (2.3)[2]	30.3 (1.5)[4]
Quality (1-99)	.31 (5.8)[1]	.49 (0.6)	250 (7.7)[1]	32.1 (0.9)
Condition (1-3)	-.38 (5.7)[1]	-.71 (4.5)[1]	-2161 (2.8)[1]	-2238 (4.3)
Baths (#)	.01 (0.3)	.02 (0.5)	136 (2.3)[2]	964 (1.5)[4]
Basement (00-10)	.06 (2.8)[1]	.10 (1.8)[3]	258 (1.6)[3]	280 (1.7)[3]
Int. Space (sq ft)	.19 (3.6)[1]	.35 (2.3)[1]	.00 (0.2)	2.03 (1.5)[4]
Lot Size (sq ft)	.04 (1.1)	-.06 (1.1)	.03 (2.1)[2]	.00 (0.4)
Access (miles)	-.02 (0.4)	.06 (0.6)	146 (0.7)	35.5 (0.2)
Neighborhood Condition (1-9)	.04 (0.5)	-.16 (1.4)[4]	208 (1.0)	-96.6 (0.4)
Hot Water (D)*	.45 (3.0)[1]	.34 (1.8)[3]	2138 (1.4)[4]	1328 (1.5)[4]
Central Heat (D)*	.12 (1.5)[4]	-.05 (0.3)	-264 (0.3)	-418 (0.6)
Flush Toilet (D)*	.19 (1.2)	-.26 (0.9)	-3313 (1.7)[3]	-1044 (0.6)
Fireplace (D)*	.11 (1.1)	—	3150 (2.6)[1]	—
Garage (D)*	.21 (3.0)[1]	-.09 (0.6)	2342 (2.9)[1]	-621 (0.7)
Sewer	-.17 (3.0)[1]	.04 (0.3)	330 (0.3)	87 (0.1)
Air Conditioned (D)*	.26 (3.0)[1]	—	3948 (4.0)[1]	—
Brick/Stone (D)*	.13 (1.8)[3]	-.14 (1.3)[4]	1363 (1.6)[3]	-871 (1.2)
Paved Road (D)*	.12 (1.3)[4]	.28 (1.0)	1320 (1.2)	1523 (1.1)
Piers (D)*	.29 (1.8)[3]	-.03 (0.2)	3120 (2.1)[2]	-45.8 (0.0)
Race (D) *	-.09 (0.8)	-.11 (0.9)	1754 (1.4)[4]	306 (0.3)

Table D-5 (cont.)

	LOG/LOG Specification*		Linear Specification	
	Entire Sample	Lows Only	Entire Sample	Lows Only
Constant*	507 (10.7)[1]	7.39 (6.3)[1]	-723 (0.2)	5627 (2.0)[2]
R^2	83	64	85	65
N	172	65	172	65
RSS	15.44	5.09	$.2368 \times 10^{10}$	$.1770 \times 10^{9}$

*Coefficients of log variables are elasticities. Coefficients of dummies (D) in Log/Log Specification are converted to Fractions, i.e., if $\hat{B}i^* = 0.25$, presence of attribute i raises value 25%. If $\hat{B}i^* = -0.25$, the presence of attribute i lowers value by 25%. Constant term is converted to analog.

1. Significant at 1% level.
2. Significant at 5% level.
3. Significant at 10% level.
4. Significant at 20% level.

Table D-6

Regression Results of Dual Housing Market Study (New Mexico)

(Figures in parentheses are *t*-statistics)

	LOG/LOG Specification* Entire Sample		Linear Specification Entire Sample	
Quality (1–99)	.37	$(1.6)^3$	56.5	(0.4)
Condition (10–30)	.39	$(2.1)^2$	368	$(3.1)^1$
Baths (#)	.15	$(1.9)^2$	438	$(4.0)^1$
Basement (00–10)	.02	(0.7)	−57.5	(0.5)
Access	.05	(0.3)	592	(0.7)
Neighborhood Condition (1–10)	.29	$(2.2)^2$	35.8	(0.9)
Int. Space (sq ft)	.44	$(1.8)^3$	8.01	$(3.7)^1$
Lot Size (sq ft)	.24	$(2.9)^1$	0.19	$(2.5)^1$
Rooms (#)	−.16	(0.6)	−1102	$(2.1)^2$
Year (00–74)	−.05	(0.6)	91.7	$(2.4)^2$
Hot Water (D)*	.06	(0.2)	−4392	$(1.6)^3$
Heat (D)*	.38	$(1.8)^3$	−581	(0.2)
Mod. Kitchen (D)*	.28	$(2.4)^2$	2967	$(2.4)^2$
Fireplace (D)*	.14	$(1.3)^4$	2418	$(1.9)^3$
Garage (D)*	.29	$(3.3)^1$	1285	$(1.4)^3$
Brick/Stone (D)*	−.04	(0.9)	44.5	(0.1)
Spanish (D)*	−.04	(0.1)	793	(0.6)
Constant	.031	(0.0)	−.1340 x 10^5	$(2.9)^1$
R^2	.83		.83	
N	81		81	
RSS	8.207		.1273 x 10^{10}	

*Coefficients of log variables are elasticities. Coefficients of dummies (D) in Log/Log Specification are converted to fractions, i.e., if $\hat{B}i^* = 0.25$, presence of attribute i raises value 25%. If $\hat{B}i^* = -0.25$, the presence of attribute i lowers value by 25%. Constant term is converted to analog.

1. Significant at 1% level.
2. Significant at 5% level.
3. Significant at 10% level.
4. Significant at 20% level.

Appendix E: Technical Description
of Tenure Choice Analysis

The purpose of this appendix is to detail more formally our LOGIT statistical model, its estimation, and its results. The discussion below presents much the same material as that contained in the chapter text, with the addition of a section on the computation of the estimates, but covers these issues in a more technical and less intuitive way than did the body of the chapter.

The Statistical Methodology

The LOGIT Model

As was discussed in the final section of Chapter 2, the central problem with linear least-squares (OLS) probability models is that their central assumption, that the true probabilities lie along a line, *must* be false, unless the independent variables are bounded in a fairly small range. The practical manifestation of this problem is that the OLS model predicts probabilities outside the unit interval for some values of the independent variables. The most straightforward solution to this problem is to estimate something other than the probability. Typically, one chooses some invertible transform of the probability that maps the interval (0,1) into the whole real line, and then estimates a model that predicts the value of the transformed variable. This can then be converted through the inverted transform into an estimate of the corresponding probability, which will, by construction, lie in the unit interval. Theoretically, any strictly monotonically increasing cumulative distribution function will suffice for the transform, but in practice it appears to make little difference which is selected, and the choice is usually made on grounds of computational convenience. The binomial LOGIT model estimated here corresponds to the LOGIT transform

$$\text{LOGIT}(p) = \ln (p/1 - p)$$

which is particularly simple to evaluate. Since $p/1 - p$ is the odds of ownership, $\text{LOGIT}(p)$ is simply the natural logarithm of the odds of owning. Thus, we choose a model that estimates

$$\text{LOGIT}(p) = a + \sum_{i=1}^{n} b_i z_i$$

where p = the probability of ownership for the household in question,
   z = the vector of characteristics associated with the household, and
   b = the vector of model parameters to be estimated.

The probability corresponding to a particular estimate of LOGIT(p) is readily evaluated. Inverting the transform, we have

$$p = \frac{1}{1 + e^{-(a + \sum_i b_i z_i)}} \, .$$

Clearly, no matter what values b or z may assume, the estimate for p is always in the interval (0,1).

Figure E-1 illustrates in two dimensions the relationship between the LOGIT model discussed here and the ordinary least-squares "linear probability model." The latter estimates probability as a linear function of the characteristics,

$$p = c + \sum_{i=1}^{n} d_i z_i \, .$$

In the area where the predicted probabilities are not close either to zero or to one, the models usually agree fairly closely. It is only when the probabilities are above 0.75 or less than 0.25 that the models tend to give substantively different results in interpreting most sets of data. In these regions, the LOGIT model "smooths" the estimates, causing them to asymptote to the estimates of 0 or 1, rather than to cross those boundaries as the OLS estimates do.

Given that the estimates of the two models are close in the midrange of probabilities, it might seem that there is no reason to try to differentiate between them. In fact, there are at least two important reasons. First, the theory of estimation and of statistical significance in any statistical procedure is predicated on the assumption that the underlying model is correct. If we know that it is not, then we cannot make *any* theoretically correct statements about the nature of the resulting estimates other than the trivial statement that they are not trustworthy. Practically speaking, of course, the estimates may be fairly good, but we can offer no formal statistical justification for their use. This alone is a powerful argument for rejection of the OLS model.

There is, however, an additional reason why the LOGIT model is preferable. It relates to the fact that the slope of the OLS relation is, by assumption, constant over the entire range of the independent variables, while that for the LOGIT relation is small when the probability is close to 0 or to 1, and larger when the probability is in the midrange. Since the slope of the relation (in both cases) denotes the *rate of change* of the predicted probability as the independent variable

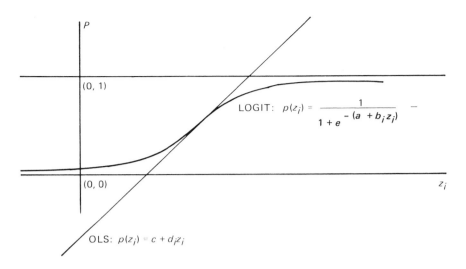

Figure E-1. LOGIT Choice Model

is changed, the OLS model embodies the unlikely assumption that a $1000
change in income has the same effect on the probability of homeownership for
a family with $500,000 of income per year as for a family with $7,000 of
income per year. By contrast, the LOGIT model permits the rate of change to be
influenced by the current value of the probability. (This relation is derived
explicitly in the discussion of the presentation of results below.) If the probability is close either to 0 or to 1, a change in an independent variable has less
effect than if the probability is close to 1/2. Clearly, this is a more reasonable
assumption than that embodied in the OLS model.

It is evident that these two considerations that differentiate the OLS and
LOGIT models are interrelated, but are distinct in their emphasis. Both argue
strongly for the use of the LOGIT framework.

Estimation. Because of the nonlinear nature of the LOGIT model, there
is no clearly dominant method for estimating its parameters from a particular
data base. Frequently chosen is the "maximum-likelihood" technique, which
chooses those values for the parameters that maximize the probability of having
observed the data set in question. This technique has the advantage that it has
an unambiguous claim to "optimality," at least in a purely statistical sense.
However, in reasonably large data sets of the kind we are examining, what
appear on common sense grounds to be rather significant changes in the parameters around the maximum likelihood point frequently leave the value of the
likelihood practically unchanged. In effect, choosing the maximum likelihood

point can resemble choosing a point in the Bonneville Salt Flats as an observation platform because it is one-quarter of an inch higher than any other point. As an alternative, we have chosen here to exploit the relation between the OLS and LOGIT models, which has been developed formally in the statistical literature on LOGIT analysis.[1]

The method is based upon the "discriminant" analysis approach, whereby the investigator examines the statistical differences between the characteristics of two or more subclasses of a population. In our case, for example, the discriminant problem would be to estimate the distribution function for the characteristics of owners and for those of renters. With these distributions in hand, one can then evaluate the conditional probability that an individual with a particular set of characteristics belongs to the group of owners. In the case where there are two subclasses, this conditional probability analysis can readily be related to the parameters of the LOGIT model. Moreover, the parameters of the conditional probability, or discriminant function, can be obtained from least squares estimation. This gives a formal link between the OLS and LOGIT models. The transformation from the OLS to the LOGIT model depends upon the sample size, the percentage of the sample in each population subclass, the sum of squared residuals from the OLS regression, and the regression parameter estimates, as follows:

$$a = \ln(n_1/n_2) + w(c - \frac{1}{2}) + n(\frac{1}{n_1} - \frac{1}{n_2})/2$$

$$b = wd$$

where a, b, c, d = are as in the definitions of the OLS and LOGIT probability models above

n = sample size

n_i = the number in subclass i

w = n/SSE

SSE = the sum of squared errors from the OLS regression.

These estimates have the appropriate asymptotic properties, and tend to approximate the maximum likelihood estimates in sufficiently large data sets.

Because the OLS estimates are consistent in the discriminant model, the regression statistics that emerge from the least-squares procedure are statistically interpretable as the usual significance tests. Thus, for example, the t-statistics from the regression test the statistical significance of the difference between the estimated value of the coefficient in question and 0. Accordingly, we report these statistics as approximate significance tests in the presentation of results below.

The Results

Method of Presentation

As was mentioned in the discussion of the LOGIT model, the interpretation of the estimated parameters is not completely straightforward. Accordingly, before examining the results themselves, we must first develop a framework within which to view them. For movers and nonmovers in each state considered, we will present three interrelated parameterizations of the results. First, we will examine the coefficients of the LOGIT model itself, with their associated t-statistics. Second, we will examine the corresponding "maximum effect" of each variable. Finally, using the LOGIT model with parameters as estimated, we will present predicted probabilities of ownership for a selected set of family types differing by the value of only one socioeconomic characteristic at a time, so as to be able to examine directly the predicted effects of, for example, changing the head of household from male to female on the likelihood of homeownership. The correct interpretation of each of these is more fully described below.

1. *The LOGIT Coefficients.* We can readily derive from the model itself what the coefficients of the model represent. From the basic equation

$$p = \frac{1}{1 + e^{-(a + \sum_{i=1}^{n} b_i z_i)}} = \left[1 + e^{-(a + \sum_{i=1}^{n} b_i z_i)} \right]^{-1}$$

we see that the rate of change of the probability with respect to the value of a particular characteristic, z_i, is given by

$$\frac{\partial p}{\partial z_i} = -[1 + e^{-(a + \sum_{i=1}^{n} b_i z_i)}]^{-2} (-b_i) e^{-(a + \sum_{i=1}^{n} b_i z_i)}$$

$$= b_i \frac{1}{1 + e^{-[a + \sum_{i=1}^{n} b_i z_i]}} \frac{e^{-[a + \sum_{i=1}^{n} b_i z_i]}}{1 + e^{-[a + \sum_{i=1}^{n} b_i z_i]}}$$

$$\frac{\partial p}{\partial z_i} = b_i p(1 - p)..$$

Thus, the estimated coefficient b_i is related to the rate of change of the probability of ownership, but its effect is moderated by the factor $p(1 - p)$.

2. *The "Maximum Effect."* The presence of the factor $p(1 - p)$ in the equation for $\partial p/\partial z_i$ embodies the fact mentioned in our discussion of the LOGIT model that the rate of change of the probability of ownership with respect to the value of a particular characteristic is smaller when the probability itself is close either to 0 or to 1 than when it is in the midrange of the interval. The factor has the value of 0 when p is either 0 or 1, and is maximized when p is 1/2, where it takes on a value of 1/4. Thus, the maximum effect that a change in the value of a characteristic can have on the likelihood of ownership occurs when that probability is 1/2. It is this maximum value that is reported as the "maximum effect," and it is equal to the LOGIT coefficient b_i times 1/4.

3. *The Predicted Probabilities.* Given the parameter estimates for the LOGIT model as applied to a particular sample, it is a trivial task to calculate predicted probabilities for a range of family types, so as to observe the estimated practical effect of changing socioeconomic status, as contrasted with the maximum possible effects as outlined above. Accordingly, for movers and nonmovers separately within each state, the predicted probability of home ownership was calculated for

1. The "average" family in the sample, defined as the family having as its vector of characteristics the mean value for each characteristic in the sub-sample.
2. The "black" family, whose head is black, but which is otherwise "average."
3. The "white" family, whose head is white, but which is otherwise "average."
4. The "female-headed" household, which is otherwise "average."
5. The "male-headed" household, which is otherwise "average."
6. The "high-income" family, which hypothetically receives $20,000 in income, but is "average" in every other way.
7. The "low-income" family, with $2,000 in income, and otherwise average characteristics.
8. The "old person-headed" family, whose head is 60 years of age.
9. The "young person-headed" family, whose head is 30 years of age.
10. The "on welfare" family.
11. The "off welfare" family.

The estimates

The results have been discussed substantially in the main text, but a few technical notes are more appropriate in the context of this appendix. Tables E-1 through E-6 present the estimated LOGIT coefficients, t-statistics, and "maximum effects" for movers and nonmovers in the six states studied, and table 2-6 in the main text of Chapter 2 presents the predicted probabilities.

In each case, the model fitted is the same, with the exception that in South Dakota Race=1 identifies American Indians, and in New Mexico Race=1 identifies persons with a Spanish surname. Several results emerge as particularly outstanding. The evidence of both race and sex differentials is overwhelming. In the four southern states, there is but one case of a positive sign on a race or sex coefficient (sex, in the nonmovers equation in Tennessee). Table E-7 summarizes this result. In many cases, the t values are not strongly significant, but taken together, the evidence is overpowering.

Table E-7 further reveals that it is consistently the case that the maximum effect of race is both larger and generally more significant statistically than that of sex. Estimates for the maximum effect of sex lie generally within the range of –0.05 to –0.20, while the range for the maximum effect of race is both higher and larger, from about –0.05 to –0.50.

It should also be noted that the maximum effects are generally larger for nonmovers than for movers. As mentioned earlier, this evidence is not easy to interpret. It is generally consistent with, though not strongly supportive of, the hypothesis that the effects of race and sex are smaller now than they were historically. A more likely explanation would appear to be that they are smaller because the characteristic of being a mover is itself such a powerful explanatory variable, as can be seen from a comparison of the predicted probabilities for any mover sample with those for any nonmover sample.

Moreover, as we saw above, the maximum effects are attained only if the probability of ownership is approximately 0.5. If, for example, the probability is instead around 0.8, the effect actually attained is only 64% of the maximum possible. When we examine the predicted probabilities, this fact turns out to be quite important. For example, the effect of sex in North Carolina is about the same for movers as for nonmovers (-0.12 as against -0.13) even though the maximum possible effect is substantially smaller for movers than for nonmovers (-0.13 as against -0.27). The difference, obviously, is that the maximum effect is attained by perturbations around the average family for movers but not for nonmovers.

Notes

1. See, for example, Max Halpern, William C. Blackwelder, and Joel I. Verter, "Estimation of the Multivariate Logistic Risk Function: A Comparison of the Discriminant Function and Maximum Likelihood Approaches," *Journal of Chronic Diseases* 24 (1971): 125-158.

Table E-1
LOGIT Coefficients for Movers/Nonmovers in North Carolina

	Coefficient	Movers t (350)	Maximum Effect
Constant	−1.2607	−1.233	−−
Income	.0077	3.557	.0019
Education	.0086	.214	.0021
Family Size	−.0159	−.234	−.0040
Age	.0261	2.566	.0065
Welfare	−1.2479	−1.883	−.3120
Unemployed	.0016	.005	.0004
Veteran	.0983	.358	.0246
Sex	−.5016	−1.519	−.1254
Race	−.4734	−1.420	−.1183
	Coefficient	Nonmovers t (485)	Maximum Effect
Constant	.8201	7.411	−−
Income	.0005	.165	.0001
Education	.0362	.828	.0089
Family Size	−.0754	−.757	−.0185
Age	.0163	1.104	.0040
Welfare	−1.9730	−1.849	−.4833
Unemployed	.0547	.129	.0134
Veteran	−.0208	−.058	−.0051
Sex	−1.1149	−2.741	−.2731
Race	−1.7473	−4.333	−.4280

Table E-2
LOGIT Coefficients for Movers/Nonmovers in Georgia

	Coefficient	Movers t (291)	Maximum Effect
Constant	-1.1294	-1.453	--
Income	.0035	1.739	.0009
Education	.0385	1.048	.0096
Family Size	.0351	.525	.0088
Age	.0220	2.392	.0055
Welfare	-.2105	-.378	-.0526
Unemployed	-.3353	-.858	-.0838
Veteran	-.0106	-.037	-.0027
Sex	-.2205	-.600	-.0551
Race	-1.0773	-3.165	-.2693
	Coefficient	Nonmovers t (311)	Maximum Effect
Constant	1.5012	5.288	--
Income	-.0002	-.064	--
Education	.0359	.676	.0090
Family Size	-.0875	-.823	-.0219
Age	.0226	1.492	.0057
Welfare	-1.8987	-2.597	-.4747
Unemployed	.1282	.294	.0320
Veteran	-.2497	-.602	-.0624
Sex	-1.4094	-3.035	-.3524
Race	-1.7984	-3.684	-.4496

Table E-3
LOGIT Coefficients for Movers/Nonmovers in Tennessee

	Coefficient	Movers t (281)	Maximum Effect
Constant	-2.1407	-.223	--
Income	.0084	2.459	.0022
Education	.0777	1.688	.0194
Family Size	.1043	1.201	.0261
Age	.0218	2.143	.0054
Welfare	-.6744	-.912	-.1686
Unemployed	-.7964	-1.937	-.1991
Veteran	-.1351	-.445	-.0338
Sex	-.3083	-.766	-.0771
Race	-.2570	-.506	-.0643
	Coefficient	Nonmovers t (285)	Maximum Effect
Constant	.9602	7.195	--
Income	.0030	.719	.0008
Education	.0718	.973	.0180
Family Size	-.1402	-.756	-.0351
Age	.0324	1.418	.0081
Welfare	-1.5223	-1.092	-.3806
Unemployed	-.3078	-.045	-.0770
Veteran	.7765	1.344	.1941
Sex	.1493	.211	.0373
Race	-3.7192	-3.641	-.9298

Table E-4
LOGIT Coefficients for Movers/Nonmovers in Arkansas

		Movers	
	Coefficient	t (197)	Maximum Effect
Constant	−.8628	−1.555	−−
Income	−.0010	−.373	−.0002
Education	.0450	1.009	.0113
Family Size	.0221	.257	.0055
Age	.0297	2.584	.0074
Welfare	−.1862	−.234	−.0465
Unemployed	−1.0901	−2.488	−.2725
Veteran	−.5441	−1.563	−.1360
Sex	−.8433	−1.752	−.2108
Race	−.8306	−1.574	−.2077
		Nonmovers	
	Coefficient	t (219)	Maximum Effect
Constant	2.5934	6.503	−−
Income	.0041	.692	.0010
Education	.0572	.669	.0143
Family Size	.0803	.423	.0201
Age	−.0163	−.649	−.0041
Welfare	.6975	.641	.1744
Unemployed	.9199	1.266	.2300
Veteran	−.8388	−1.356	−.2097
Sex	−.6341	−.870	−.1585
Race	−1.0269	−1.258	−.2567

Table E-5
LOGIT Coefficients for Movers/Nonmovers in South Dakota

	Coefficient	Movers t (77)	Maximum Effect
Constant	-2.1541	-.248	--
Income	.0064	1.249	.0016
Education	-.0188	-.171	-.0047
Family Size	.1898	1.102	.0474
Age	.0293	1.429	.0073
Welfare	-2.4693	-1.331	-.6173
Unemployed	.4427	.556	.1107
Veteran	1.0868	1.742	.2717
Sex	-1.3976	-1.730	-.3494
Race	-1.7295	-.848	-.4324

	Coefficient	Nonmovers t (92)	Maximum Effect
Constant	.8874	3.190	--
Income	-.0053	-.438	-.0013
Education	.2489	1.207	.0622
Family Size	-.3313	-1.065	-.0828
Age	.0771	1.280	.0193
Welfare	-19.5917	-5.556	-1.0000
Unemployed	-1.7491	-1.125	-.4373
Veteran	2.2958	1.889	.5739
Sex	-.3399	-.218	-.0850
Race	3.1688	.598	.7922

Table E-6
LOGIT Coefficients for Movers/Nonmovers in New Mexico

	Coefficient	Movers t (93)	Maximum Effect
Constant	−.8561	−.975	−−
Income	.0184	3.254	.0046
Education	−.0676	−.920	−.0169
Family Size	.1443	1.035	.0361
Age	.0023	.128	.0006
Welfare	−1.0279	−.738	−.2570
Unemployed	.9309	1.433	.2327
Veteran	−.5490	−1.056	−.1373
Sex	−.5336	−.733	−.1334
Race	.8266	1.441	.2066

	Coefficient	Nonmovers t (75)	Maximum Effect
Constant	.2835	2.826	−−
Income	.0056	.708	.0014
Education	.0857	.683	.0214
Family Size	−.1134	−.525	−.0283
Age	.0225	.627	.0056
Welfare	1.7956	.766	.4489
Unemployed	−.0875	−.079	−.0219
Veteran	.8230	.809	.2057
Sex	.0634	.049	.0159
Race	−.4257	−.407	−.1064

Table E-7
Maximum Effect of Race and Sex for Movers and Nonmovers in Six States
(Figures in parentheses are *t*-statistics)

		Movers		Nonmovers	
NC	Sex	−.1254	(−1.519)	−.2731	(−2.741)
	Race	−.1183	(−1.420)	−.4280	(−4.333)
GA	Sex	−.0551	(−.600)	−.3524	(−3.035)
	Race	−.2693	(−3.165)	−.4496	(−3.684)
TN	Sex	−.0771	(−.766)	.0373	(.211)
	Race	−.0643	(−.506)	−.9298	(−3.641)
AR	Sex	−.2108	(−1.752)	−.1585	(−.870)
	Race	−.2077	(−1.574)	−.2567	(−1.258)
SD	Sex	−.3494	(−1.730)	−.0850	(−.218)
	Race	−.4324	(−.848)	−.7922	(−.598)
NM	Sex	−.1334	(−.733)	.0159	(.049)
	Race	.2066	(1.441)	−.1064	(−.407)

Appendix F: Occupants of Substandard Housing

The following four tables present detailed cross-tabulations of families in the four southern states by socioeconomic characteristics and dwelling unit attributes. A discussion of the major results is contained in the section "Occupancy of Substandard Housing." The tables present for each subcategory of families the percentage of dwelling units which possess the indicated characteristic. Dwelling unit characteristics are based on the following Census Public Use Sample 5 percent questionnaire responses:

Characteristic	*Variable*
Lack of Toilet	H23
Lack of Bath or Shower	H24
Lack of Some Major Piece of Plumbing	H25
Lack of Installed Heating System	H51
Overcrowded	H84

Table F-1
Southern States White Male-Headed Households

	Lacks Toilet	Lacks Bath or Shower	Lacks Some Major Plumbing	Inadequate Heat	Over-crowded	Sub-standard	Standard
INCOME:							
< 5,000	22.4	23.1	25.5	40.4	6.3	50.1	49.9
10,000	6.7	6.4	8.0	24.9	11.4	35.2	64.8
>10,000	3.8	3.1	4.2	11.9	6.7	18.2	81.8
FAMILY SIZE:							
<5	9.5	9.6	11.0	24.9	1.3	30.0	70.0
5 or more	16.3	15.5	18.3	31.6	38.5	56.8	43.2
AGE OF HEAD:							
under 30	7.1	7.3	8.3	23.4	8.3	31.4	68.6
30-60	9.6	9.1	10.8	23.6	11.1	33.6	66.4
over 60	18.1	18.9	21.4	26.0	1.5	43.4	56.6
WELFARE:							
on welfare	42.9	45.2	52.4	64.3	9.5	76.2	23.8
not on welfare	10.1	9.9	11.5	25.3	8.5	34.2	65.8
EMPLOYMENT:							
not employed	19.4	20.2	22.7	37.9	5.3	47.5	52.5
employed	8.5	8.2	9.7	23.0	9.3	31.9	68.1

Total Number of Observations: 1,874.

Table F-2
Southern States White Female-Headed Households

	Lacks Toilet	Lacks Bath or Shower	Lacks Some Major Plumbing	Inadequate Heat	Over-crowded	Sub-standard	Standard
INCOME:							
<5,000	17.6	18.9	22.6	32.2	1.3	42.2	57.8
10,000	6.6	7.7	9.9	22.0	8.8	30.8	69.2
>10,000	0.0	5.0	5.0	10.0	5.0	20.0	80.0
FAMILY SIZE:							
<5	14.0	15.5	18.7	28.2	1.0	37.3	62.7
5 or more	19.2	19.2	23.1	38.5	34.6	57.7	42.3
AGE OF HEAD:							
under 30	14.3	14.3	17.9	35.7	3.6	35.7	64.3
30-60	13.6	16.2	19.5	29.9	5.2	40.9	59.1
over 60	14.8	15.7	18.7	27.4	1.7	37.4	62.6
WELFARE:							
on welfare	27.3	34.1	43.2	50.0	4.5	65.9	34.1
not on welfare	12.8	13.6	16.0	26.4	3.0	35.3	64.7
EMPLOYMENT:							
not employed	20.0	21.2	25.2	33.2	3.2	44.8	55.2
employed	5.6	7.4	9.3	22.2	3.1	29.0	71.0

Total Number of Observations: 298

Table F-3
Southern States Black Male-Headed Households

	Lacks Toilet	Lacks Bath or Shower	Lacks Some Major Plumbing	Inadequate Heat	Over-crowded	Sub-standard	Standard
INCOME:							
<5,000	50.8	54.5	61.4	68.3	26.5	83.1	16.9
10,000	26.1	36.4	44.3	47.7	40.9	69.3	30.7
>10,000	14.3	14.3	14.3	28.6	28.6	33.3	66.7
FAMILY SIZE:							
<5	35.3	41.2	46.0	57.2	4.3	69.0	31.0
5 or more	50.5	55.0	64.9	63.1	75.7	86.5	13.5
AGE OF HEAD:							
under 30	26.0	30.0	40.0	50.0	28.0	68.0	32.0
30-60	45.9	49.4	55.2	58.0	41.3	75.6	24.4
over 60	39.5	50.0	56.6	68.4	9.2	80.3	19.7
WELFARE:							
on welfare	57.7	69.2	73.1	84.6	34.6	92.3	7.7
not on welfare	39.3	44.1	51.1	57.0	30.6	73.9	26.1
EMPLOYMENT:							
not employed	47.4	53.8	60.3	73.1	23.1	84.6	15.4
employed	38.6	43.6	50.5	54.5	33.6	72.3	27.7

Total Number of Observations: 298.

Table F-4
Southern States Black Female-Headed Households

	Lacks Toilet	Lacks Bath or Shower	Lacks Some Major Plumbing	Inadequate Heat	Over-crowded	Sub-standard	Standard
INCOME:							
<5,000	39.3	49.5	56.1	50.5	17.8	73.8	26.2
10,000	44.4	50.0	55.6	61.1	44.4	77.8	22.2
>10,000	25.0	25.0	25.0	0.0	75.0	75.0	25.0
FAMILY SIZE:							
<5	34.4	45.2	51.6	50.5	4.3	68.8	31.2
5 or more	52.8	58.3	63.9	50.0	72.2	88.9	11.1
AGE OF HEAD:							
under 30	25.0	25.0	25.0	15.0	35.0	50.0	50.0
30-60	38.6	50.9	59.6	50.9	29.8	75.4	24.6
over 60	46.2	55.8	61.5	63.5	11.5	82.7	17.3
WELFARE:							
on welfare	46.4	60.7	67.9	57.1	28.6	82.1	17.9
not on welfare	37.6	45.5	51.5	48.5	21.8	72.3	27.7
EMPLOYMENT:							
not employed	50.6	58.2	64.6	57.0	29.1	81.0	19.0
employed	22.0	34.0	40.0	40.0	14.0	64.0	36.0

Total Number of Observations: 129.

Bibliography

Bibliography

Concepts, Conditions, and Trends in Access to Housing: Background and General Readings

Abrams, Charles. *The Future of Housing*. New York: Harper and Brothers, 1946.

Avins, Alfred, ed., *Open Occupancy vs. Forced Housing Under the 14th Amendment*. New York: Bookmailer, 1963.

"Background: Rural Housing Problems." Washington, D.C.: Rural Housing Alliance, November 1972.

Bahr, Howard M., Bruce A. Chadwick, and Robert C. Day, eds. *Native Americans Today: Sociological Perspectives*. New York: Harper and Rowe, 1972.

Barron, Milton Leon, ed. *Minorities in a Changing World*. New York: Alfred A. Knopf, 1968.

Bennett, Fay. *Condition of Farm Workers and Small Farmers in 1969: A Report*. New York: National Board of National Sharecroppers' Fund, 1969.

Beyer, Glenn H. *Housing and Society*. New York: MacMillan, 1965.

Brink, William and Louis Harris. *Black and White*. New York: Simon and Schuster, 1967.

Butler, Stephen and Susan Peck. *Alternative Low-Income Housing Delivery Systems for Rural America*. Washington, D.C.: Washington Housing Assistance Council, 1944.

Calvert, Robert A., Renato Rosaldo, and Gustav L. Seligman, *Chicano: The Beginnings of Bronze Power*. New York, N.Y.: William Morrow & Co., Inc., 1974.

"Can We Ever Build Cheaper Houses?" *Changing Times: The Kiplinger Magazine* (October 1970). Rural Housing Alliance Reprint No. 5, December 1970.

Castro, Tony. *Chicano Power, The Emergence of Mexican America*. New York, N.Y.: E.P. Dutton & Co., Inc., 1974.

Caudill, Harry M. *Night Comes to the Cumberlands*. Boston: Little, Brown and Company, 1962.

Coles, Robert. *Children of Crisis*. New York, N.Y.: Dell Publishing Company, Inc., 1967.

Commission on the Rights, Liberties and Responsibilities of the American Indian. *The Indian, America's Unfinished Business*. Report. Norman: University of Oklahoma Press, 1966.

197

A Decent Home. Report of the President's Committee on Urban Housing, 1968.

Deloria, Vine, Jr. *We Talk, You Listen.* New York, N.Y.: Dell Publishing Company, 1970.

Denton, John H. *Apartheid American Style.* Berkeley: Diablo Press, 1967.

Doams, Gerrit. *Summary of Segregation, Discrimination and Open Housing.* Kent, Ohio, 1965

Dolbeare, Cushing. "The Housing Stalemate: A Failure of Will and Understanding." *Dissent,* September 1974.

Freeman, Robert E. *Rural Housing: Trends and Prospects.* AER Report #193. Washington, D.C.: U.S. Department of Agriculture, Economic Research Service, 1970.

Glazer, Nathan and Davis McEntire, eds. *Studies in Housing and Minority Groups.* Berkeley: University of California Press, 1960.

Government and Housing: Citizen's Rights and Federal Responsibilities. Washington, D.C.: Rural Housing Alliance, May 1973.

Grier, George W. *Equality and Beyond.* Chicago: Quadrangle Books, 1966.

Griggs, Anthony. "How Blacks Lost 9,000,000 Acres of Land." *Ebony* (October 1974): 29, 12 96-104.

Johnson, Helen W. "Rural Indian Americans in Poverty." AER Report #167. Washington, D.C.: U.S. Department of Agriculture, Economic Research Service, 1969.

Kain, John F., ed. *Race and Poverty: The Economics of Discrimination.* Englewood Cliffs, N.J.: Prentice-Hall, 1969.

Margolis, Richard J. *All Their Days, All Their Nights: Notes on Rural America.* Washington, D.C.: Rural Housing Alliance, 1969.

McEntire, Davis. *Residence and Race: Final and Comprehensive Report to the Commission on Race and Housing.* Berkeley: University of California Press, 1960.

Mittlebach, Frank G. and Grace Marshall. *The Burden of Poverty.* Los Angeles: Division of Research, Graduate School of Business Administration, University of California, 1966.

Pavlick, Anthony L. and Robert I. Coltrane. *Quality of Rural and Urban Housing in the Appalachian Region.* AER Report #52. Washington, D.C.: U.S. Department of Agriculture, Economic Research Service, 1964.

The People Left Behind. A Report by the President's National Advisory Commission on Rural Poverty, September 1967.

Pierce, James M. "The Condition of Farmworkers and Small Farmers", *Report to the National Board.* National Sharecroppers Fund and Rural Advancement Fund (n.d.).

Reno, Lee P. *Pieces and Scraps: Farm Labor Housing in the United States.* Washington, D.C.: Rural Housing Alliance, September 1970.

Rose, Arnold M., and Caroline B. Rose. *Minority Problems.* New York: Harper and Row, 1965.

Rural Poverty in the United States. A Report by the President's National Advisory Commission on Rural Poverty, Washington, D.C., May 1968.

Salamon, Lester M. *Black-Owned Land: Profile of a Disappearing Equity Base: State-Level Analysis.* Report to the Office of Minority Business Enterprise, U.S. Department of Commerce, April 1974.

Sherrill, Robert. "The Black Humor of Housing." *The Nation* (March 29, 1971), Rural Housing Alliance Reprint No. 7, April 1971.

Taeuber, Karl E. and Alma F. "The Negroes as an Immigrant Group." *American Journal of Sociology*, 64, 4 (January 1964).

Waddell, Jack O. and O. Michael Watson, eds. *The American Indian in Urban Society.* Boston: Little, Brown and Company, 1971.

Wilner, Daniel et al. *The Housing Environment and Family Life.* Baltimore, Maryland: The Johns Hopkins University Press, 1962.

Rural Housing Needs and Markets

Alford, Terry. *Rural Housing Rehabilitation Demonstration, Princeville, N.C.* Raleigh, N.C.: North Carolina State University, School of Design, 1972.

Bird, Ronald and Lucia Beverly. *Status of Rural Housing in the U.S. AER Report* #144. Washington, D.C.: U.S. Department of Agriculture, Economic Research Service, 1968.

Cochran, Clay L. *Rural Housing and Rural America: 1973 Report of the Rural Housing Alliance.* September 1973.

———. "The Scandal of Rural Housing." *Architectural Form* (March 1971). Summary of his statement before the Senate Select Committee on Nutrition and Human Needs, October 7, 1970.

———. "The Single-Family Slum." *Planning* (August 1973). Reprinted by the Rural Housing Alliance with the permission of the American Society of Planning Officials.

———. *Statement before the Committee on Agriculture and Industry.* U.S. Senate, February 5, 1973.

Dolbeare, Cushing N. *Statement before the U.S. Senate Subcommittee on Housing of the Committee on Banking, Housing and Urban Affairs.* October 4, 1973.

Johnson, Robert E. *Statement before the U.S. House of Representatives Subcommittee on Housing.* October 19, 1973.

Jones, Lawrence. *Rural Home Financing Through the Voluntary Home Mortgage Credit Program.* Economic Research Service, Department of Agriculture, 1966.

"A Legal Right to a Home . . . ." Resolutions of the Second National Rural Housing Conference. Washington, D.C., November 30, 1972.

MacFall, Emily A., and E. Quinton Gordon. *Mobile Homes and Low-Income Rural Families.* Washington, D.C.: Office of Economic Opportunity, 1973.

Margolis, Richard J. "Metropollyana and Rural Housing." *New Leader* (February 5, 1973).

_____ *Mobile Homes and the Rural Poor; An Alternative Solution.* Washington, D.C.: Rural Housing Alliance, November 1972.

_____ "Welfare and Metropollyana." *Low-Income Housing Bulletin* (April 1973): 3.

The National Academy of Sciences. *The Quality of Rural Living: Proceedings of a Workshop.* Washington, D.C., 1971.

North Dakota Basin Electric Power Cooperative. *People's Housing Program: A Rural Delivery Demonstration Project 1970-1972.* Bismarck, North Dakota, 1973.

Penney, P.L. "Low-Cost Housing for Indians," *Christian Science Monitor* (May 22, 1970).

Popular Government. "Costs of Poor Housing in Rural North Carolina." (November 1967).

Self-Determination: A Program of Accomplishments. Published by the Arizona Affiliated Tribes, Inc., Indian Community Action Project, May 1971.

Solberg, Erling D. *The Why and How of Rural Zoning.* AER Report #196. Washington, D.C.: U.S. Department of Agriculture, Economic Research Service, Revised 1967.

Williams, Dorwin and Frank Miller. *A Profile of Rural Home Buyers and Builders and Their Use of Housing Credit.* Agriculture Experiment Station, University of Missouri, 1968.

Factors Affecting Housing Market Discrimination and/or Segregation

Abrams, Charles. *Forbidden Neighbors: A Study of Prejudice in Housing.* New York: Harper and Bros., 1955.

_____ "The Housing Problem and the Negro." *Daedalus* 95 (Winter 1966): 64-76.

Apgar, William C. and John F. Kain. "Neighborhood Attributes and the Residential Price Geography of Urban Areas." Paper presented at the Econometric Society Meetings, December 1972.

Bachmura, F.T. and J.H. Southern. *Economic Bases and Potential of Rural Communities.* Washington, D.C.: National Committee for Children and Youth (n.d.).

Bailey, Martin. "Effects of Race and Other Demographic Factors on Values of Single-Family Homes." *Land Economics* 42 (May 1966): 215-220.

Becker, G.S. *The Economics of Discrimination.* Chicago: University of Chicago Press, 1947. Chapters 1, 2 and 5.

Briggs, Vernon M., Jr. *Chicanos and Poverty*. Baltimore: The Johns Hopkins University Press, 1973.

Carlson, J.E. "Can the Housing Census Measure Quality?" *Architectural Record* 151 (April 1972): 74.

Collard, D. "Price and Prejudice in the Housing Market." *Economic Journal* 83 (June 1973): 510–515.

David, Martin. *Family Composition and Consumption*. Amsterdam: North-Holland Publishing Company, 1962.

Dietsch, R.W. "Why So Few Black Homeowners?" *New Republic* 167 (July 8, 1972): 12-13.

Downs, Anthony. "An Economic Analysis of Property Values and Race." *Land Economics* 36 (May 1960).

Gelfand, Jack E. "The Credit Elasticity of Lower-Middle Income Housing Demand." *Land Economics* 42 (1966): 464-72.

Helper, Rose. *Racial Policies and Practices of Real Estate Brokers*. University of Minnesota Press, 1969.

Kain, John F. and John M. Quigley. "Housing Market Discrimination, Homeownership and Savings Behavior." *American Economic Review* 63 (June 1973): 263-277.

King, A.T. and P. Mieszkowski. "Racial Discrimination, Segregation, and the Price of Housing." *Journal of Political Economy* 81 (May 1973): 590-606.

Ladd, W.M. "Effect of Integration on Property Values." *American Economic Review* 52, 4 (September 1962).

Lapham, Victoria. "Do Blacks Pay More for Housing?" *Journal of Political Economy* 79 (November/December 1971): 1244-1257.

Little, James T., Hugh O. Nourse, and Donald Phares. "The Neighborhood Succession Process, A Summary." In *The Neighborhood Succession Process*. St. Louis, Missouri: Washington University, The Institute for Urban and Regional Studies, August 1974.

Moore, Joan W. and Frank G. Mittlebach. *Mexican-American Study Project: Residential Segregation in the Urban Southwest—A Comparative Study*. Advance Report No. 4. Los Angeles: Division of Research, Graduate School of Business Administration, University of California, 1966.

National Association of Real Estate Brokers. *Survey on Racial Discrimination in Mortgage Financing of Minority Real Estate Brokers in the United States*. May 1971.

Northwood, Lawrence K. and Ernest T. Barth. *Urban Desegregation*. Seattle: University of Washington Press, 1965.

Pascal, Anthony H. *The Economics of Housing Segregation*. Santa Monica, California: The RAND Corporation, March 1965.

——— "The Economics of Housing Segregation." Memorandum RM-5510-RC. Santa Monica: The RAND Corporation, November 1967.

——— ed. *Racial Discrimination in Economic Life*. Lexington: Lexington Books, D.C. Heath and Co., 1972.

Peterson, George E. "The Effects of Zoning Regulations on Suburban Property Values." Working Paper 1204-24. The Urban Institute, March 1973.

Phares, Donald. "Racial Change and Housing Values: Transition in an Inner Suburb." *Social Science Quarterly* (December 1971).

Reid, Margaret. *Housing and Income*. Chicago: University of Chicago Press, 1962.

Rucker, George W. *The Geography of Leased Public Housing Under Section 23: More Discrimination Against Rural and Small Town People*. Washington, D.C.: Rural Housing Alliance, February 1974.

———— *Indian Housing: A Background Paper*. Washington, D.C.: Rural Housing Alliance, October 1973.

Rural Housing Alliance. "Three Studies of Rural Rental Housing." Washington, D.C.: Rural Housing Alliance, November 1971.

Smith, Clarence G. *Containment of Minority Groups through Housing*. Toledo, Ohio: NAACP, 1968.

Stegman, Michael A., ed. *Housing and Economics: The American Dilemma*. Cambridge, Mass.: The MIT Press, 1971. Chapters 1, 3, 4, and 9.

Steiner, Stan. "The American Indian: Ghettos in the Desert." *The Nation* 198 (June 22, 1964): 624-627.

Taeuber, Karl E. and Alma F. Taeuber. "The Negro as an Immigrant Group." *American Journal of Sociology* 64, 4 (January 1964).

Government Policies and Programs

Overviews and Evaluations

Dolbeare, Cushing. *Federal Tax Rip-Offs: Housing Subsidies for the Rich*. Washington, D.C.: Rural Housing Alliance, November 1972.

Eley, Lynn W. and Thomas W. Casstevens, eds. *The Politics of Fair-Housing Legislation: State and Local Case Studies*. San Francisco: Chandler Press, 1968.

Federal Deposit Insurance Corporation. *Assets and Liabilities—Commercial and Mutual Savings Banks*. June 30, 1973.

Grigsby, William G. *Housing Markets and Public Policy*. Philadelphia: University of Pennsylvania Press, 1963.

Housing Assistance Council. "The Administration's FY 75 Budget and Rural Housing." *HAC Information* (May 30, 1974).

National Community Relations Division, American Friends Service Committee. *Memorandum*, in Response to Request for Comments and Information for Use in Review and Evaluation of HUD Programs. April 30, 1973.

Peake, G. Ronald. *Housing Program for Indians*. Washington, D.C.: Bureau of Indian Affairs, Division of Housing Assistance, July 1970.

——— "Indian Housing Program Options." A Memorandum to the Commissioner of Indian Affairs, July 8, 1974.

The RHA Reporter. July 1974.

Rural Housing Alliance. *Low-Income Housing Programs for Rural America.* Washington, D.C.: Rural Housing Alliance, January 1973.

——— *OEO and Rural Housing.* Washington, D.C.: Rural Housing Alliance, 1972.

Schafer, Robert. "Section 235 of the National Housing Act." In G. Lefcoe, *Land Finance Law: Materials and Cases* (1969), p. 250.

——— "Section 235 of the National Housing Act: Homeownership for Low-Income Families?" *Journal of Urban Law* 46 (1969): 667-685. (with C. Field)

Sorkin Alan L. *American Indians and Federal Aid.* Washington, D.C.: Brookings Institute, 1971.

Taggart, Robert, III. *Low-Income Housing: A Critique of Federal Aid.* Baltimore: The Johns Hopkins Press, 1970.

U.S. Commission on Civil Rights. *Mortgage Money: Who Gets It?* Clearinghouse Publication No. 48. June 1974.

U.S. Commission on Civil Rights. *Understanding Fair Housing.* Washington, D.C.: U.S. Government Printing Office, 1973.

United States Department of Housing and Urban Development. *A Report on the Transitional Housing Experiment, Rosebud Indian Reservation.* Washington, D.C.: U.S. Government Printing Office, 1969.

Public Housing

Freedman, Leonard. *Public Housing: The Politics of Poverty.* New York: Holt, Rinehart & Winston, 1969.

Housing Assistance Administration. *Housing for Low-Income Families.* Washington, D.C.: U.S. Department of Housing and Urban Development, 1967.

National Association of Housing and Redevelopment Officials. "63 Indian Tribes Set Up Authorities, Plan Public Housing" *Journal of Housing*, No. 3 (April 1964): 124-128.

Rural Housing Alliance. "Public Housing." Washington, D.C.: Rural Housing Alliance, March 1972.

——— "Public Housing: Where It Is and Isn't—A Summary." Washington, D.C.: Rural Housing Alliance and Housing Assistance Council.

Smolensky, Eugene. "Public Housing or Income Supplements—The Economics of Housing for the Poor." *AIP* 34, 2 (March 1968): 94-101.

Self-Help Housing

Margolis, Richard J. *Something to Build On–The Future of Self-Help Housing in the Struggle Against Poverty.* Washington, D.C.: International Self-Help Housing Associates and the American Friends Service Committee, 1967.

Rural Housing Alliance. "Common Questions and Answers on Self-Help Housing." Washington, D.C.: Rural Housing Alliance, June 1974.

_____ *Self-Help Housing Handbook–Organizing a Self-Help Housing Program.* Vol. I. Washington, D.C.: Rural Housing Alliance, February 1971.

Sprague, Chester L. *A Self-Help Housing Process for American Indians and Alaskan Natives.* 1970.

Farmers Home Administration

Abuse of Power–Studies in Bad Housing in America. A Case Study of the Rural Housing Program of the FHA as Administered by a County Supervisor in Two Florida Counties. Rural Housing Alliance, October 1971.

Farmers Home Administration Home Ownership Loans (Section 502), Vol 1. Rural Housing Alliance and Housing Assistance Council, April 1972.

Farmers Home Administration Home Repair Loans (Section 504), Vol. 2., Rural Housing Alliance and Housing Assistance Council, (January 1973).

Farmers Home Administration Farm Labor Housing Loans and Grants (Sections 514-516), Vol. 3. (April 1972).

Farmers Home Administration Rental Housing Loans (Section 515), Vol. 4. (December 1972).

Farmers Home Administration Self-Help Technical Assistance Grants (Section 523), Vol. 6. (April 1972).

Farmers Home Administration Rural Housing Site Loans (Sections 523-524), Vol. 7. (April 1972).

Farmers Home Administration Water and Sewer Loans and Grants, Vol. 8. (September 1972).

Farmers Home Administration Water and Sewer Planning Grants, Vol. 9. (April 1972).

"FmHA and Minorities." *Low-Income Housing Bulletin* (January 1973), pp. 6-8.

Guide to Farmers Home Administration Regulations. Rural Housing Alliance, August 1972.

Hightower, Jim. "Farmers Home Administration and Farm-Labor Housing: Missing the Mark." Background Paper No. 10, National Rural Housing Conference. Airlie House, Warrenton, Virginia, June 9-12, 1969.

Statement in the FY 75 Budget–*Rural Housing.*

Winn, William. "Red Tape: FmHA Is More Sensitive to Congress Than to Poor." *South Today* (May 1971).

Zimmerman, Stanley. "Legal Control of Government Benefit Programs: A Study of the Farmers Home Administration." NYU Law Library, New York University, 1968.

Relevant Methodologies

Berkson, Joseph. "Maximum Likelihood, Minimum χ^2 Estimates of the Logistic Function." *Journal of the American Statistical Association* 50 (1955): 130-162.

Berry, Brian. *Strategies, Models and Economic Theories of Development in Rural Regions.* AER Report #127. Washington, D.C.: U.S. Department of Agriculture, Economic Research Service, 1967.

Center for National Policy Review. *Affirmative Fair Housing Marketing Plans: Instructions for Completing Reporting Forms.* (n.d.)

Griliches, Zvi. "Hedonic Price Indexes Revisited: Some Notes on the State of the Art." *American Statistical Association Proceedings of the Business Economics and Statistics Section,* 1967.

———. ed. *Price Indices and Quality Change.* Cambridge, Mass.: Harvard University Press, 1971.

Haggstrom, Gus W. *Logistic Regression, Discriminant Analysis.* The RAND Corporation Memorandum. April 3, 1974.

Haugen, Robert A., and A. Jones Heins. "A Market Separation Theory of Rent Differentials in Metropolitan Areas." *Quarterly Journal of Economics* 83 (November 1969): 660-672.

Henning, John A. and Donald G. Ridker. "The Determinants of Residential Property Values with Special Reference to Air Pollution." *Review of Economics and Statistics* 44, 2 (May 1967).

Hoffman, Stanley R. and William Diemar. *The Los Angeles Housing Policy Evaluation Model.* Los Angeles Community Analysis Bureau, April 1974.

Ingram, Gregory K. "A Simulation Model of a Metropolitan Housing Market." Ph.D. dissertation, Harvard University, 1971.

Kain, John F. and John M. Quigley. *Discrimination and a Heterogeneneous Housing Stock: An Economic Analysis.* National Bureau of Economic Research, 1972 (Processed). Chapters 3, 5 and 6.

———. "Measuring the Value of Housing Quality." *Journal of the American Statistical Association* 65 (June 1970): 532-548.

Karlen, David H. "Racial Integration and Property Values in Chicago." Urban Economics Report #7. University of Chicago, April 1968.

King, Thomas and Peter Mieszkowski. "An Estimate of Racial Discrimination in Rental Housing." Cowles Foundation Discussion Paper 307. Yale University, February 1971.

Kish, Leslie and John B. Lansing. "Response Errors in Estimating the Values of Homes." *Journal of the American Statistical Association* 49 (September 1954): 520-538.

Laurenti, Luigi. *Property Values and Race: Studies in Seven Cities.* Berkeley: University of California Press, 1960.

Lee, Tony Hun. "Demand for Housing: A Cross-Section Analysis." *Review of Economics and Statistics* 45, 2 (May 1963): 190-196.

Mausel, Sherman J. "Rates of Ownership, Mobility and Purchase." *Essays in Urban Land Economics.* Los Angeles: Real Estate Research Programs, University of California, 1966, pp. 76-108.

McKenna, Joseph P. and Herbert D. Werner. "The Housing Market in Integrating Areas." *The Annals of Regional Science* 4, 2 (December 1970).

Ohta, M. and Z. Griliches. "Automobile Prices Revisited: Extensions of the Hedonic Hypothesis." Presented at the National Bureau of Economic Research Conference on Research in Income and Wealth. 1973.

Orcutt, Guy H. et al. *Micro-analysis of Socio-economic Systems.* New York: Harper and Brothers, 1961.

Quigley, John M. "Residential Location: Multiple Work Places and a Heterogeneous Housing Stock." Ph.D. dissertation, Harvard University, 1972.

Rosen, Sherwin. "Hedonic Prices and Implicit Markets." *Journal of Political Economy* 82, 1 (January/February 1974).

Schelling, Thomas C. "On the Ecology of Micromotives." *The Public Interest*, No. 25 (Fall 1971): 59-98.

Schnare, Ann. *An Empirical Analysis of the Dimensions of Neighborhood Quality.* The Urban Institute, 1975.

Schnare, Ann B. and Raymond J. Struyk. *Segmentation in Urban Housing Markets.* Paper presented at the Committee on Urban Economics Conference on Housing Research. Washington University, St. Louis, Missouri, October 4-5, 1974.

_____ *The Price of Rental Housing Services in Nonmetropolitan Cities.* North Carolina Housing Market Study, Working Paper No. 12. September 3, 1974.

_____ *Racial Segregation and Price Discrimination in Nonmetropolitan Rental Housing Markets.* North Carolina Housing Market Study, Working Paper No. 14. October 22, 1974.

Stegman, Michael A. and Howard J. Sumka. *Market Organization and Landlord Behavior in Nonmetropolitan Rental Housing Markets.* North Carolina Housing Market Study, Working Paper No. 13. September 9, 1974.

Straszheim, Mahlon. *An Econometric Analysis of the Urban Housing Market.* National Bureau of Economic Research, 1974.

Taeuber, Karl E. and Alma I. *Negroes in Cities: Residential Segregation and Neighborhood Change.* Chicago: Aldine Publishing Co., 1965.

Congressional Acts, Reports, and Hearings

The Housing and Community Development Act of 1974. Public Law 93-383.

93rd Congress, S. 3066. August 22, 1974.

The Rural Development Act of 1972. Public Law 92-419. 92nd Congress, H.R. 12931. August 30, 1972.

The State and Local Fiscal Assistance Act (Revenue Sharing). Public Law 92-512. October, 1972.

U.S. Congress, House of Representatives, Committee on the Judiciary, Committee Print, *The Civil Rights Acts of 1957, 1960, 1964, 1968; The Voting Rights Act of 1965 and the Voting Rights Act Amendments of 1970*. Washington, D.C.: U.S. Government Printing Office, 1971.

—— "Congress Pledges Commitment to Meet Needs of Heartland", *Congressional Record*, Vol. 120, No. 10 (February 4, 1974).

—— *Eleventh Report by the Committee on Government Operations: Farmers Home Administration Rural Housing Program Operations*. December 7, 1973.

—— Committee on the Judiciary, Subcommittee No. 4, "The Role of the Farmers Home Administration in the Achievement of Equal Opportunity in Housing".

—— *Hearings before a Subcommittee of the Committee on Government Operations*. June 5, 6, and 7, 1973.

—— Senate Committee on Interior and Insular Affairs, *A Staff Report on the Indian Housing Effort in the United States with Selected Appendices*. Washington, D.C.: U.S. Government Printing Office, February 1975.

—— Senate Subcommittee on Housing and Urban Affairs of the Committee on Banking, Housing and Urban Affairs, *Hearings: Oversight on Rural Housing Programs*. November 19, 20, and 21, 1974. Washington, D.C.: U.S. Government Printing Office, 1974.

—— Senate, "The Need for a Comprehensive Rural Housing Delivery System." *Congressional Record* 112, 122 (July 30, 1973).

—— Senate Select Committee on Nutrition and Human Needs. "Promises to Keep: Housing Need and Federal Failure in Rural America." (April 1972—Revised).

Periodicals and Specialized Sources

The Bureau of National Affairs, Inc., *Housing and Development Report*.

Department of Housing and Urban Development, *HUD News*.

Rural Housing Alliance, *RHA Reporter*.

The Rural Housing Information Service.

Selected "701" Planning Documents.

Census Data Sources

U.S. Bureau of the Census. *Census of Housing: 1970. Vol. I, Housing*

Characteristics for States, Cities, and Counties. Washington, D.C.: U.S. Government Printing Office, 1972.

———— *Census of Housing: 1960. Vol. I, States and Small Areas.* Washington, D.C.: U.S. Government Printing Office, 1962.

———— *Census of Population: 1970. Vol. I, Characteristics of the Population.* Washington, D.C.: U.S. Government Printing Office, 1973.

———— *Census of Population: 1960. Vol. I, Characteristics of the Population.* Washington, D.C.: U.S. Government Printing Office, 1963.

———— *Census of Population: 1970, First Count Summary Tapes, File A (Microfilm).* Arkansas, Georgia, New Mexico, North Carolina, South Dakota, Tennessee.

———— *Census of Population and Housing: 1970. One-in-a-Hundred Public Use Sample.* Arkansas, Georgia, New Mexico, North Carolina, South Dakota, Tennessee.

———— *County and City Data Book, 1972 (A Statistical Abstract Supplement).* Washington, D.C.: U.S. Government Printing Office, 1973.

———— *Census of Housing: 1970. Block Statistics.* Final Report HC(3)-44. Selected areas in Tennessee. Washington, D.C.: U.S. Government Printing Office, 1971.

Index

Index

Section I

American Indians, 5, 6t, 57, 63-64,
77, 85, 96, 99-120, 145; American
Indian Movement, 85-86, 107-109;
and Segregation, 21; In substandard
housing, 36; Tribal administration,
4, 8, 107-108
Assessors' records, 6, 16, 27-31

Brink, William, 49n
Builders, 2, 7, 10, 52, 57-58, 73-74,
75, 78, 96, 130-131, 133-135,
137, 139-140
Building costs, 12, 78-80, 114
Bureau of Indian Affairs, 8, 85, 102,
110, 115

Census, U.S. Bureau of the: Black
statistics, 15, 19-21; Enumeration
district data, 15-21, 143; Public Use
Sample data, 6, 26, 34-36, 38, 41-
42. *See also* Migration; Poverty
Churches, 82-83, 87-88, 124
Communication. *See* Information exchange; Real estate agents
Community action agencies, 57, 64,
82-83, 87-88, 125
Community organizations, 3f, 4, 7,
56-57, 61-62, 81-88, 91, 109, 125-
126, 140, 145-146
Custom. *See* Regulations

David, Martin, 50n
DeCoteau vs. District County Court,
21
Discounts. *See* Price differentials
Dual housing market. *See* Segmenta-
tion in housing markets
Duncan, Beverly, 19
Duncan, Otis Dudley, 19

Economic analysis, 1, 2, 5-7, 12, 15-
50. *See also* Segmentation in housing markets; Segregation; Substandard housing; Tenure choice analysis

Fair Housing. *See* Federal Fair
Housing legislation
Farmers Home Administration. *See*
Federal housing subsidy programs
Federal Fair Housing legislation, 51,
54, 59, 93, 96-97, 145
Federal housing subsidy programs, 2,
4, 7, 13n, 56-59, 73, 82, 89, 92-
96, 115-119, 129, 131, 133-135,
139-140, 146
Female-headed households, 5, 6t, 60,
143; in substandard housing, 34-36;
tenure choice of, 44-49
Financing, 2, 3f, 12, 56-58, 78-80. *See*
also Federal housing subsidy programs
Foreclosures, 13n, 57, 130, 134

Griggs, Anthony, 13n
Griliches, Zvi, 25, 50

Harris, Louis, 49n
Hedonic price indices, 25-34. *See also*
Segmentation in housing markets
Henning, John A., 50n
Housing and Community Development
Act of 1974, 12, 92, 147
HUD. *See* Federal Fair Housing legisla-
tion; Federal housing subsidy pro-
grams

Income, median for Study Sites, 12
Indians. *See* American Indians
Information exchange, 3f, 4, 5, 51-58,

211

About the Authors

Janet K. Marantz, a Senior Research Analyst at Urban Systems Research & Engineering, did her graduate work in Political Science at Harvard University. The study of power—public and private—has continued to be the focus of her research since then. She has directed or contributed to studies of community power structures, successful community resistance to airport projects, and the use of power to exclude minorities and women from social benefits. Social-political analysis of rural areas has been a second focus of her work, encompassing studies of the social forces affecting the distribution of jobs, housing, investment capital and public services in rural areas.

Karl E. Case II is Head Tutor (Director of Undergraduate Studies) in Economics at Harvard. He teaches both in the Department of Economics and at Harvard Law School. His previous work has focused in the area of state and local public finance and has included research on the property tax. He was co-author of recent articles on fiscal burdens and benefits and on alternative ways of financing state and local governments.

Herman B. Leonard is a Ph.D. candidate in Economics at Harvard University concentrating in urban economics and public finance. His previous work has focused on the construction of large scale econometric and computer simulation models. He has been engaged in the construction of the National Bureau of Economic Research Urban Simulation Model for the last two years.